"Heart & Hands conveys the essence of midwifery! To supplement today's abundant scientific and technological information, it literally describes the missing dimension—a commitment to the *art* of midwifery."

> —Dorothea M. Lang, C.N.M., M.P.H.
> North American Regional
> Representative,
> International Confederation of Midwives
> (ICM)

"Provides a rich assortment of anecdotes and remedies for common problems . . . the author is to be commended for her emphasis on the fourth trimester, the important three-month period when mothers and babies are recovering from birth and becoming acquainted. It is fortunate for midwives and prospective parents that this book has been expanded and updated."

> —John Kennell, M.D.
> Professor of Pediatrics
> Rainbow Babies and Childrens Hospital,
> University Hospitals of Cleveland

"Portrays well the beauty and power of birth. It honors the central role of the midwife in prenatal care, birth, and post-natal care, precisely the role recommended repeatedly by the World Health Organization for all the countries of the world. This book should be read by all birth attendants, be they lay midwives, nurse-midwives, or doctors."

> —Marsden Wagner, M.D.
> Neonatologist, Perinatal Epidemiologist
> Regional Director for Maternal and
> Child Health
> World Health Organization (WHO)

"Much more than a textbook, *Heart & Hands* combines solid practical advice with interesting anecdotes and sensitivity to the needs of women giving birth . . . immensely valuable to students of midwifery, obstetricians, and couples planning to give birth at home, in birth centers, or in the hospital."

> —Don Creevy, M.D., FACOG
> Clinical Assistant Professor in
> Gynecology and Obstetrics
> Stanford University School of Medicine

"Emphasizes pregnancy as wellness . . . this book parallels the family-centered approach that I advocate in established medical and nursing practices."

—Celeste R. Phillips, R.N., Ed.D.

"An impressive and deeply caring book. Elizabeth Davis writes vividly, succinctly, and joyously. She explores important issues in midwifery and reveals a shrewd and compassionate sensitivity to women's needs in pregnancy and childbirth, and clear insight into both the personal and professional aspects of midwives' lives."

—Sheila Kitzinger
Author, *The Experience of Childbirth, The Complete Book of Pregnancy and Birth,* and *The Place of Birth*

"In 1981, Elizabeth Davis filled a great need by creating *Heart & Hands,* a practical and detailed instruction colored by the author's kindness and enhanced by Linda Harrison's magnificent drawings. The 1987 version provides not only a detailed technical update but the photos of birth journalist Suzanne Arms."

—Margot Edwards
Women's Health Counseling Services
Co-author, *Reclaiming Birth: History and Heroines of American Childbirth Reformed*

"The elements of *caring for* and *caring about* women are so maturely thought out and articulated that I readily recommend the book to all midwifery students of any type of educational program, for any practice setting. Parents-to-be will find informative sections written just for them."

—Mary V. Widhalm, C.N.M., M.S.
Director of Midwifery
Lincoln Medical and Mental Health
 Center
Bronx, New York

"Detailed and compassionate, *Heart & Hands* offers child-bearing women, midwives, and doctors a wealth of practical information. It provides a view of pregnancy and birth not as a purely medical, mechanical event, but as a complex physical, emotional, social, and spiritual experience. Elizabeth Davis loves and respects women, and her work places childbearing where it belongs—in the strong and capable hands of mothers and midwives."

—The Boston Women's Health Collective
Authors of *The New Our Bodies, Ourselves*

"A unique book, because despite the fact that the author does not possess the usual academic credentials to be a C.N.M., she presents an excellent articulation of the art and science of midwifery practice. Sections on professional issues are right on target, as is her insight into the emotional responses of women and their families. A significant achievement!"

—Betty Watts Carrington, C.N.M., Ed.D.
Director, Graduate Program in
Nurse-Midwifery
Columbia University School of Nursing

"A beautifully written and comprehensive guide . . . as an advocate of the newborn, I find it very comforting that this book speaks to the need to protect the baby's rights and health by insisting on competence in emergency newborn care, always in the context of respect for normal maternal-infant bonding."

—Mike Witte, M.D.
Board Certified Pediatrician
Director, Point Reyes Clinic

"Elizabeth Davis has done her profession a very valuable service by providing a textbook that is eminently readable and which gives the aspiring midwife the benefit of having a *friend and mentor* in the form of a book—and that is no small accomplishment! She delves into the area of judgement, which is the acid test for any midwife. This is the Wise Woman speaking, the Sage Femme who can cut through the morass of information, the current standards, the new theories, and take us to the heart and kernel of what this work is all about."

—Tish Demmin, L.M.
President, The Midwives Alliance
of North America (MANA)

Heart&Hands

Elizabeth Davis

Heart&Hands

A Midwife's Guide to Pregnancy & Birth

Photographs by Suzanne Arms Wimberley
Illustrations by Linda Harrison

2nd Edition

"Revised and Updated"

CELESTIAL ARTS BERKELEY, CALIFORNIA

CELESTIAL ARTS
P.O Box 7327
Berkeley, California 94707

Cover photograph by Suzanne Arms-Wimberley
Cover design by Ken Scott
Text design by Paul Reed
Composition by QuadraType, San Francisco
Back cover illustration by Linda Harrison

SECOND EDITION 1987
UPDATED EDITION 1992

Library of Congress Cataloging-in-Publication Data

Davis, Elizabeth, 1950–
    Heart & hands.

        Rev. ed. of: A guide to midwifery. 1st ed. c 1981.
        1. Midwives   2. Obstetrics.   I. Davis, Elizabeth,
1950–   . A Guide to midwifery.   II. Title: Heart
and hands.   III. Title. [DNLM: 1. Midwifery.
2. Obstetrics.   WQ 160 D255h]
RG950.D38   1987   618.4   87-13256
ISBN 0-89087-495-6
ISBN 0-89087-494-8 (pbk.)

Manufactured in the United States of America
1 2 3 4 5 6 7 8 9 0 — 96 95 94 93 92

ACKNOWLEDGEMENTS

I wish to thank Judy Lane for reviewing the original edition of this book and making excellent suggestions for this revision. I am also deeply grateful to midwives Betty Carrington, Tish Demmin, and Mary Widhalm, who carefully read the manuscript and offered invaluable criticism and technical expertise.

A special thanks to Jean Jones Burke for her insights on the psychology of pregnant women.

And for all the beautiful new photos in this edition I wish to thank Suzanne Arms Wimberley, who has been most generous with her time and energy. Thanks also to Yeshi Newmann for the photos of Nicaragua.

To Linda Harrison, midwife and artist who once again has created masterpiece illustrations, a deep acknowledgement of her commitment and friendship.

Thank you to Lynn Meinhardt for work on the layout above and beyond the call of duty, to Leroi for her excellent word processing job and to Raissa Postman for top-notch photo printing.

And for the use of photos from the first edition, I wish to thank and credit the following individuals:

Ed Buryn, pages 70, 73, 89, 116, 145, and 147, photographs copyright © 1981.

Gary Yost (Rupo), pages 103, 105 and 150, photographs copyright © 1981.

Katy Raddatz, pages 61, 75 and 84, photographs copyright © 1980.

A very special thanks and tribute to all the midwives who appear in the book, or who have assisted the families pictured. The intimate portrayal of your care is a precious edition to this work.

And finally, I must thank my editor David Hinds, for being such a pleasure to work with and for his thoroughness and commitment to every aspect of this project.

—*Elizabeth Davis*

CONTENTS

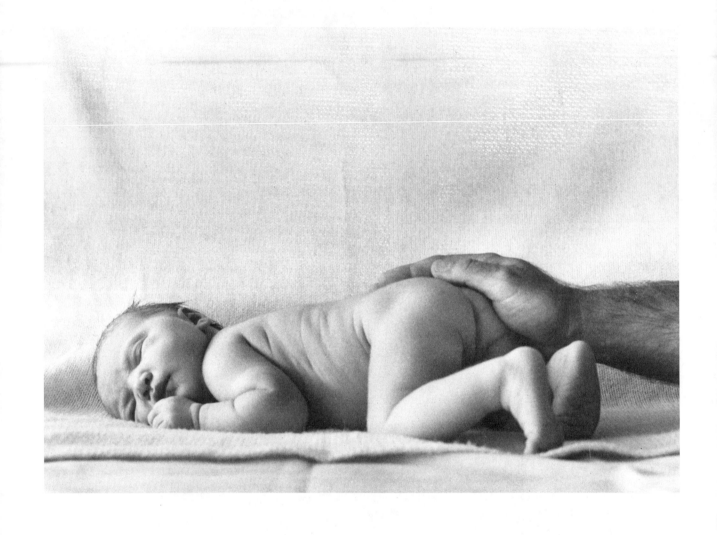

Preface to the Second Edition

When I wrote the first edition of *Heart and Hands,* I never dreamed it would be so success-ful! For me, it was a chance to deliver myself of knowledge accumulated through the years, and to provide a much needed focus on *midwifery* management. But I never imag-ined it would appeal so greatly to parents! The volume of sales—over 80,000 copies to date—and mass-market printing have shown the appeal of highly technical information to many others than the midwives for whom it was originally intended.

In fact, I considered changing the voice of the book altogether, addressing it to the general readership instead of the midwife, but realized that the intimate tone of a midwife speaking to her colleagues would be lost. Besides, I think parents appreciate insight into the midwife's assessment and decision-making processes as much as they do tech-nical information.

The decision to expand the content of the book as much as I have came about gradually. One subject led to another, and before I knew it I had nearly 30% new material. And to better meet the needs of prospective parents, I have included new sections especially for them, highlighted in the Table of Contents.

The challenge of doing a revision is to save what is timeless, while discarding any dated or outmoded material. I have tried to do my best to this end. To all who have encouraged me, or who have found my book interesting and inspiring, I am deeply grateful.

Tremendous advances have been made in humanizing childbirth. As long as parents insist on their right to choose both place of birth and provider, and as long as midwives step forward to meet these needs, advances will continue. I look forward to the day when every woman can give birth exactly as she desires, with full support and appro-priate assistance.

Preface To The Original Edition

The purpose of this book is to offer a practical guide to midwifery—to instruct those women interested in becoming midwives, and to convey the realities of practice. Midwifery is a lost and found art, finding its place in our time via its links to feminism and expanding consciousness. It also appeals to a growing do-it-yourself resourcefulness. Women who want to be midwives have usually experienced birth firsthand and want to share and facilitate a new awareness of the power of being female. Most are seeking to extend their relationships with other mothers and babies. Many women who think that midwifery is their calling will read this and realize that there are many other related areas that need expanding, such as birth education, postpartum support and family counseling.

This book is intended to demystify the medical elitism surrounding a very basic, natural body process. There are other books which give more detailed information on obstetrics, but none explains how to adapt this information to individual women and how to bend the rules to fit each situation. This is a book on *practical midwifery*, with a special focus on creative management of complications. Thus it provides some answers for parents who want more than just good quality care and are seeking to understand the various alternative solutions to problems which may arise in pregnancy and birthing. This information is also intended for midwives practicing in remote areas with little or no medical consultation.

However, this manual is only a partial guide to midwifery practice, as nothing can substitute for experience—the educated intuition which comes from attending many birthings. But at least the suggested practices and procedures may stimulate the aspiring midwife to question and study, and may also inspire dedicated practitioners to break ground with new, responsible methods. If this book moves parents and health professionals alike to innovative thought and humanistic understanding, the heart of its purpose will be realized.

Thanks be to the midwives—a positive, loving, bright and pioneering bunch of women—for freely sharing skills and information without which this book would not have been written.

I dedicate this book to my family

**Celeste and Orion,
my husband George,
and little baby John**

Heart&Hands

CHAPTER 1

The Midwife: A Profile

Throughout the ages, midwives have been the traditional birth attendants, fully respected and honored by their communities. But today's midwife is as notorious as she is powerful. Going against the grain, she supports parents in their search for safe alternatives in childbirth.

Midwifery is indisputably the world's oldest helping profession. From the very beginning, women have helped each other give birth. One who was particularly interested and attuned emerged as the local midwife, wielding the healing skills of her time and culture. This is still the case in many third-world countries today. And in modern day Denmark, Holland and Sweden, birthing with midwives is the popular norm. In fact, the five countries in the world with the lowest perinatal mortality rates make generous use of midwives; they assist 70% of all births! In the U.S., where due to political and economic constraints midwives assist only 5% of births, perinatal mortality is alarmingly high: we rank *number 24* worldwide.

Despite the obvious efficacy of midwifery, midwives have been persecuted throughout history, particularly in the West. Those practicing in Europe in the 16th and 17th centuries were "tried" and burned at the stake as witches. And to our shame, this happened also in the United States. Those were dark days for women in general, and although midwifery of necessity survived it was severely repressed once again around the turn of the century, as medicine became a profession for profit and the newly emerging male physician became eager for the revenues of childbirth.

At this point midwifery was almost totally eradicated, such was the campaign of the male physician to discredit the midwife. She was ac-cused of slovenliness, filth, sexual promiscuity and perversity. In medieval times she was labeled consort to the devil, and later she became a symbol of the "loose woman," in contrast to the "good girl" who became a nurse and accepted a role subservient to the doctor. Nevertheless, midwives continued to function within their communities, chosen by their friends and neighbors as an alternative to the physician. Left to their own devices midwives would never have survived; they were for the most part poor, powerless and disorganized. It is *community demand* for midwifery care that has kept the profession alive to this day. Midwifery is apparently a fact of life, perpetuated by the needs and desires of birthing women and their families.

Although empirical midwives (those trained by experience) have functioned almost continuously in the United States, the development of nurse-midwifery is fairly recent. The Frontier Nursing Service began training midwives in 1939, using a model developed in England. There are now over 30 schools for training nurse-midwives, but barriers to practice are considerable. Physicians have mixed reactions to the nurse-midwife: on the one hand they find her a valuable adjunct to absorb some of the workload of a busy practice, but should she desire to practice independently with her own case load, she becomes an economic competitor and a threat. Unfortunately, nurse-midwives were forced to agree to physician supervision as a condition of legal practice. The physician expects the nurse to play a subordinate role. However, the responsibilities of the midwife require that she have the autonomy to make her own decisions in case of crisis, and to use interventions, maneuvers and procedures in the event of an emergency that cross over into the physician's scope of practice. The conflict has divided the nurse-midwives among themselves; those who feel more like nurses than midwives, and those who feel more like midwives than nurses.

Meanwhile empirical midwives continue to serve their communities, often working altogether outside the law. Non-nurse midwifery has been legalized in 10 states thus far; in 21 others it is quasi-legal (not a criminal practice, but no mechanism of regulation). Notably, several states have succeeded in passing legislation that establishes midwifery as an independent profession. Throughout the country, midwives are organizing self-regulation by creating standards and mechanisms for certification, even in states where legislative efforts appear futile. This illustrates the determination of today's midwives to establish themselves as professionals, and to assure the consumer the best quality care.

Leaders in the midwifery movement predict that midwives from diverse educational backgrounds will one day unite behind the issue of independent practice. The Midwives Alliance of North America (MANA) was founded on this vision, and does include in its ranks mid-wives "of every stripe." The fight for autonomous midwifery is, in fact, an international battle; throughout the world midwives are restricted in their function. In Germany, midwives may assist deliveries but cannot give prenatal care; in Italy midwives can give prenatal care but must call in the physician when the delivery is imminent. In order to address the struggles of midwives to meet community needs and take their rightful place in the health care system, the World Health Organization drafted the International Definition of Midwifery in 1972, which has been adopted by the International Confederation of Midwives (ICM) and the International Federation of Gynecologists and Obstetricians (FIGO):

> A midwife is a person who, having been regularly admitted to a midwifery educational program duly recognized in the jurisdiction in which it is located, has successfully completed the prescribed course of studies in midwifery and has acquired the requisite qualifications to be registered and/or legally licensed to practice midwifery.
>
> The sphere of practice: She must be able to give the necessary supervision, care and advice to women during pregnancy, labor and postpartum period, to

conduct deliveries on her own responsibility, and to care for the newborn and the infant. This care includes preventive measures, the detection of abnormal conditions in mother and child, the procurement of medical assistance, and the execution of emergency measures in the absence of medical help.

She has an important task in counseling and education—not only for patients, but also within the family and community. The work should involve antenatal education and preparation for parenthood and extends to certain areas of gynecology, family planning and child care.

She may practice in hospitals, clinics, health units, domiciliary conditions or any other service.

This definition is remarkable not only for what it says, but for what it leaves unspoken. It is a perfect expression of the midwife's role.

* * *

Considering the troubled past and challenging present of midwifery, it is clear that unrelenting consumer demand is responsible for its survival. What makes midwifery such a desired birthing option?

Midwifery is a profession based on *promoting normalcy*. Essentially it is an art of service, in that the midwife must recognize, respond to and cooperate with natural forces. In this sense the midwife's work is ecologically attuned, involving the wise utilization of resources and respect for the balance of nature. How radically different from Western Medicine's infatuation with drugs and instruments! Midwifery care is *individualized* care. The experienced midwife knows that there are many normal variations on the themes of pregnancy, birth and postpartum; it is her job to decipher the patterns and facilitate a healthy outcome. By giving thorough prenatal care, the midwife becomes so familiar with each client that she will be quickly alerted to any deviation from normal. The birth is the finishing touch to a carefully developed relationship involving care on physical, emotional and intellectual levels. Every birth has some potential for complications, but the midwife's competence is aimed precisely at handling these.

Thus the essence of midwifery is staying sensitively in the moment, or in other words, being humble and paying attention. But this seemingly simple focus is not easy to maintain; it is the antithesis of control. The most serious problem with current training for obstetrics is an overriding emphasis on pathology, so that the student learns not only to identify, but also to expect complications. This generally results in a practitioner anxious to control labor so as to prevent the unexpected, which precludes letting nature take its course. Such a standardized approach has little appeal to the laboring woman. What she really wants is sensitive perspective which takes her feelings and overall state of being into account. This is exactly what midwives offer. Midwifery has often been called an art of invisibility, because it is non-interventive except to maintain balance and restore harmony.

Let's take a closer look at today's midwife: what is she like as a person, and what role does she play in society? Well, midwives certainly come in all varieties of personality and perspective but the main thing they seem to have in common is *persistence*. No matter if the midwife is a nurse or empirically trained, she must face tremendous obstacles in establishing and maintaining a practice. If she practices illegally it is especially difficult: she must risk her personal freedom in order to maintain responsibility for her clients. This takes strong, independent character, willingness to go against society's mores. Herein lies the secret to the midwife's notoriety; she is a rebel, and a female one at that!

It is ironic that the feminist movement has not yet identified with the midwifery issue, although perinatal rights are beginning to command attention. What could be more feminist than the practice of midwifery? The most potent lesson of natural childbirth is the revelation of essential feminine force. The experience of birth calls on a woman to shed her social skin and discover her unique abilities to cooperate with and surrender to natural forces. Childbirth can be utterly empowering; it can transform a woman, renew her, strengthen her faith and deepen her identity. Her ensuing change in perspective enables her to mother in a fiercely independent fashion and with new-found inner certainty. This is notably antithical to the outwardly focused, male-oriented approach of our society. Hence the midwife, guardian and facilitator of this process, is intrinsically feminist by the very nature of her work!

Often a woman studies midwifery in hopes of becoming closer to other women; not just as friends, but with the goal of establishing support systems and creating community. The evolutionary social aspect of midwifery is that it motivates women to extend the responsibility they take in birthing to one another, breaking out of isolated nuclear families into

---

Choosing A Midwife

1. *How was she trained?* In a home or hospital setting? Did she apprentice, and if so, how long was her training?
2. *What is her experience?* How many births has she attended since completing her training? Has she worked in a variety of settings/practices?
3. *What do her services include?* Complete prenatal care? Home visits (how many)? Sibling preparation? Postpartum follow up (how much)? Lab work? Birth classes?
4. *Does she work alone or with assistants?* How many? How often will you see each before the birth? If there are several, can you choose which one you want?
5. *Does she have a ceiling on the number of births she attends per month?* Is this in keeping with the amount of assistance she has? What would happen if two births were running simultaneously? Has she ever missed a birth?
6. *Who would back her up in case of emergency?* Another midwife? Will you have a chance to meet her before the birth?
7. *What is her communications system like?* Does she have a beeper? If not, how do you reach her? Is she available 24 hours a day at all times? What if she goes on vacation at some point in the pregnancy? Who takes call, and how do you reach them?
8. *What experience has she had with complications?* Which ones? Has she ever had to resuscitate a baby? How would she handle a hemorrhage?
9. *What equipment does she bring to births?* Oxygen, IV fluids, ambu-bag for baby? Medications for hemorrhage?
10. *What is her medical backup like?* Does she have a particular physician? Particular hospital? How is she usually treated in the event of transport? What are her privileges in the hospital setting? Can you choose your own physician? What about pediatric backup?
11. *What are her fees?* What is included? What if you move or change your mind during the pregnancy? Does the fee seem fair and reasonable? How does she want it to be paid?
12. *What other costs might you incur?* Lab, birth classes? In the event of transport, how much does her backup physician charge? Does he/she charge for routine prenatal consultation and if so, how much? What are basic hospital charges? If you do not have insurance, is there any type of sliding-scale available?
13. *What is her philosophy of care?* Why is she a midwife? What are her basic beliefs about birth? Does she encourage family participation? Father participation? How? What are her expectations of you regarding self-care in pregnancy?
14. *Do you like her?* Feel comfortable in her presence? Can you be honest with her? Will she be honest with you? Can you trust her, and yet feel free to make your own decisions? *Do you want her at your birth?*

networks of interdependent mothers and children, identifying and sharing their resources. Thus midwifery can be linked to social innovations such as childcare facilities on the job, and in general, a more tolerant attitude towards women who interface family life with their career.

Certainly the midwife is an advocate of choice. She vigorously defends the right of parents to choose their place of birth, as she fights for her own right to practice in a variety of settings. Hospital privileges are frequently denied midwives, or those who work with them. And home birth is still considered controversial, although statistics have repeatedly shown home delivery to be as safe, or safer than hospital birth.

The majority of women wanting midwifery care choose to give birth at home. Typical reasons include greater comfort and less intervention. Again, research has shown that the more relaxed and at ease a woman is during labor, the more efficiently her body will function. Should she be stressed or frightened, her body will release hormones (catecholamines) which will inhibit cervical dilation.

Thus a midwife's most basic responsibility to her clients is to do her utmost to promote comfort, relaxation and peace of mind. Her skills encompass both medical techniques and less concrete abilities to intuit, evoke and channel. Her hands are probably her most precious tools, as she senses, blesses and heals with her touch. The manner in which a midwife assists a birth definitely influences both pleasure and safety. She serves as a mirror, offering appropriate, timely suggestions. She strives continually to reserve judgement and yet speak the truth.

Ultimately, responsibility for the birth belongs to the parents. It is up to them to be well informed and to choose an attendant with the personal qualities and competence to suit them. And by claiming the right to experience the intimate event of birth as they choose, they open doors to unprecedented joy and fulfillment while laying the foundation for strong and sensitive parenting.

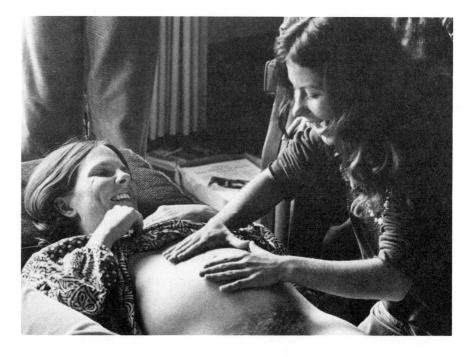

CHAPTER 2
Prenatal Care

Most midwives give complete prenatal care on a regular basis. A few limit their practice to attending births and have mothers see a physician for the prenatal, but there are serious disadvantages to this arrangement. Only by giving complete prenatal care can the midwife really get to know her client and thus *know what to anticipate during the labor.* This is the wisdom of being well informed about the unique physical and emotional state of every woman assisted.

Careful assessment during the last six weeks of pregnancy will enable the midwife to get a feel for size, position and growth rate of the baby. And on the basis of this information she may realistically prepare for a short or long labor and make suggestions to the mother concerning exercise, reading or nutrition that might make the birth easier or forestall complications. On a technical level, knowing the baby's and mother's norms will help the midwife make wise decisions regarding acceptable range during the birth itself. Prenatal care definitely proves its worth in terms of time, energy and anxiety spared at deliveries, for the family as well as the midwife.

Prenatal care really means wellness care and as such involves nutritional counseling, herbal remedy and body-mind integration techniques like yoga and relaxation. It also includes all essential procedures for screening any complications of pregnancy. It requires certain skills explained later in this chapter: lab work and analysis, routine urine checks, blood pressure assessment, fetal palpation and heart ausculation, and fundal hight measurement. Whenever significant abnormality arises, medical consultation should be sought for further instructions and prognosis.

Your first contact with a woman seeking home birth will probably be by phone. If the two of you are already familiar, your task will be to put aside preconceived notions and be open to new perceptions during this first discussion. Ask the mother specifically how she has come to be interested in having a home delivery; this will enable you to see how well founded her interest is and whether it is worth pursuing further.

If the initial information checks out well, go ahead with questions about her state of health, relationship with mate, previous pregnancies, medical problems, etc. Hopefully she will also ask questions about your orientation, experience, equipment, etc. If you decide to meet, an initial visit should be scheduled within the next week or so. Both parents should come to this visit, so schedule accordingly. Allow at least two hours time. There will be plenty to discuss, and physical examinations to be done.

Always remember, you must *never* try to talk anyone into homebirth. Wait until you feel that it is their decision to come to you. It is crucial that parents' responsibility for the birth be established from the beginning.

The Initial Interview

This very personal, in-depth meeting with the parents is your opportunity to understand their ideals surrounding birth and parenting, and to provide them with appropriate information. If they've had other children they will share their previous experiences. If this is their first they will be full of questions. Elicit reasons for choosing home birth from both of them. Pay close attention to the father's response, as it indicates his emotional orientation to the pregnancy. Notice priorities. Those primarily concerned with saving money must be made to see the responsibility and emotional commitment necessary for home birthing. And beware of those who tell you, "I hate hospitals." Parents stuck in a negative, reactionary vein need more insight. Present the benefits of home birth and then feel the response: what do these folks *really* want?

Other essential topics of conversation include your training and background, equipment and medical backup. Explain your style of practice, make clear your limitations and how you work with them, and discuss the nature of your relationship to the medical community. Discuss complications, and note any resistance to hospital transport. Carefully discuss the emergency complications which might result in damage or death. Of course you should stress that thorough prenatal care and careful monitoring of mother and baby will go a long way towards prevention. But if the worst happened, what would they do? If either

parent seems unusually fearful, it's good to ask them about their worst birth nightmare. This discussion provides ample opportunity to give physiologic explanation of complications, shifting many from accidental to predictable status. Explaining the significance of prenatal care in this diagnostic sense also impresses parents with the importance of keeping their appointments and letting you know if anything unusual develops.

The two most serious emergencies, hemorrhage and fetal distress, require detailed discussion. Explain possible causes of bleeding and basic procedures for controlling it. Also discuss your way of dealing with a depressed baby, including tools and techniques used to resuscitate. In general, it is the midwife's way to inform parents during labor of any unusual developments and to explain both standard procedures and alternatives. But in emergency situations there is no time for this, so start teaching parents now and continue throughout the pregnancy.

Who will be at the birth? The answer to this question will give you insight into the sexual and emotional nature of the couple. Are they private, exclusive, social or exhibitionist? Key people in the birth plans should be encouraged to come to clinic so you can assess the support system. Suggest possible roles and activities for each participant, including postpartum assistance.

Expectations: how do parents define your role at their birthing? Does the woman expect lots of guidance and participation or will the father be her main support? Based on your intuition of his personality and their relationship, do his projections for involvement seem realistic? Does he want to help with the delivery? How does the woman feel about this idea? If they want to do most of it themselves, do they understand the necessity of routine checks on mom and baby that need to be done from time to time? With this discussion you encourage them to express their personal style, which will give the birth experience its integrity.

Throughout the discussion there will be appropriate moments for passing along information, suggesting resources for further study or providing referrals to groups or individuals. This gives parents the idea that there is a lot to learn and that it's up to them to do some exploring. Recommend specific reading material (books, magazines, newsletters), film presentations or educational programs. Give a complete reading list (including periodicals) to parents as soon as you meet. Also refer them to local chapters of national organizations like La Leche League, Informed Homebirth and Parenting, etc. (see Appendix A).

Medical History

Medical history can either be taken orally or provided by the woman via take-home form. It should include a review of pertinent conditions and diseases, the significance of each depending on how long ago the problem existed and for what duration. Take a look at the list on page one of the Medical History Form in the Appendix; each item has a particular relationship to pregnancy and some of the problems are more serious than others. Diabetes, thyroid disease (hyperthydroidism), chronic lung disease, severe asthma, epilepsy, clotting abnormalities, congenital heart disease (grades 2-4) or kidney disease are definite contraindications for home birth. Conditions arising in pregnancy (or found to be pre-existing) that would rule out home birth are severe anemia, acute viral infection (rubella, cytomegalovirus, or chicken pox, for example), unresolved venereal disease, malnutrition, drug addiciton, moderate to frequent alcohol use or smoking (more than ten cigarettes daily). It's wise to have handy an obstetrical text which elucidates the effect of each of these on pregnancy, and essential to seek medical consultation if you are concerned or unclear about something in the history.

Gynecological history has an obvious bearing on pregnancy. Check first for any history of fibroids. These fibrous uterine masses may vary in size, but tend to grow considerably during pregnancy. They may be either external or internal; the latter may affect the pregnancy by impinging on fetal space or disturbing placental implantation. A sonogram is definitely in order.

Whenever there is history of uterine surgery, consult with your backup physician. If a woman has had procedures done to her cervix such as cauterization, cryosurgery or cone bi-

opsy, she may have considerable scar tissue which can retard dilation. Cervical adhesions may be softened by the use of evening primrose oil massaged into the tissue toward the end of pregnancy (see page 34).

What about previous Cesarean birth? Since research on vaginal birth after Cesarean (VBAC) has shown no significant dangers to either mother or baby, most midwives would handle VBACs at home were it not for an outmoded standard of care which identifies these births as high risk. Another five years and this will probably change, but in the meantime, the midwife doing VBACs at home may run the risk of losing her backup should transport be necessary.

However, do your best to refer the mother desiring a VBAC to a supportive provider. At the same time, refer her to a Cesarean Prevention chapter, or other such supportive organization in your area.

Contraceptive history is also critical. If a woman has used an IUD prior to conception, she may be anemic due to excessive menstruation and should have hemaglobin levels checked as soon as possible. The IUD may also cause scarring of the uterine lining, which predisposes to irregular implantation or possible difficulty with placental separation. Pelvic inflammatory disease, or PID, has the same effect. Scar tissue may also form at the cervical os (see suggestions above).

History of abortion should be thoroughly discussed. Was there any problem with excessive or prolonged bleeding afterwards? Under what circumstances was the abortion performed? What kind of emotional side effects were experienced? Many women feel a great sense of loss from abortion ("like tearing your heart out," one woman said) and need to talk it over. Some feel that the spirit or identity of the aborted fetus has returned in the baby they are now carrying. If the mother has had a saline or prostaglandin induced abortion she essentially experienced labor in the process and may have some very negative emotions associated with contraction sensations. Discuss this with her and anticipate some difficulties during labor.

Family history is most important to determine prevalance of hypertension, diabetes or genetic diseases. History of twins on the mother's side is significant if you find the woman large for dates.

A history of symptoms experienced with the current pregnancy indicate how normal and healthy the mother has been thus far. Incidence of bleeding or spotting is significant; it may indicate a propensity to miscarry that should be addressed (more on this in Chapter 3). A history of edema should be evaluated medically if experienced before conception or prior to 24 weeks gestation. Swelling may indicate a poor state of health in which edema is a pathological symptom predisposing to pre-eclampsia. If these conditions have been ruled out, evaluate the diet and recommend the elimination of any heavily processed foods laced with chemicals, which tax the kidneys. Recommend plenty of high quality protein, fresh vegetables and salt to taste. Occasional headaches by themselves are fairly common, but in combination with any two signs of pre-eclampsia, indicate serious danger and need for immediate referral. Visual problems are also an ominous sign (see Chapter 3).

Any report of flu-like symptoms requires close scrutiny. Particularly if the mother has experienced extreme fatigue, swollen glands or over-all aching, she may have contracted either cytomegalovirus or toxoplasmosis, although these serious infections are frequently asymptomatic. If exposed, the fetus may suffer severe neurological damage, particularly *after* ten weeks gestation. Cytomegalovirus is a fairly common infection, 60% of the general population has antibodies. There are no particular preventative measures, whereas a mother can minimize her chances of contracting toxoplasmosis by avoiding uncooked meat and contact with cat feces.

Any report of vaginal sores early in pregnancy may indicate an initial outbreak of herpes, particularly if the mother has no previous history. This can have serious consequences for the baby (see page 27).

A bonus in using the take-home history is the section of essay questions at the end, which forces parents to make definite statements of how they really feel and what they really want. Responses to questions about possible damage or death indicate how emotionally responsible and mature the parents

truly are. Responses to questions concerning *willingness to go to the hospital if necessary* are best to have in writing. Responses regarding parents' perceptions of the midwife's role may indicate ways in which the midwife can adapt her style to theirs.

Occasionally you'll encounter a woman who is unwilling to fill out take-home forms. In almost every case that I recall, this stance has borne out an emotional inability to accept responsibility for the birth. To write it down is to make a statement, to be honor bound to one's word. If part of the history is incomplete, send it home to be finished up.

Physical Examination

Every woman should have a complete physical early in pregnancy unless she has had one within the last year. I have not included instructions for this because it requires considerable hands-on training. Also, it can be done by a backup physician or other health care worker, whereas the routine checks and pelvic assessment described below are essential to midwifery practice. This does not mean, however, that physical assessment cannot be part of the midwife's scope of practice. An excellent reference for study is Barbara Bates' Guide to Physical Assessment *(see Appendix).*

The first checkup is an opportunity to ascertain the mother's general state of health. Beyond that, an essential purpose of this visit is to establish physical intimacy and trust. Keep this in heart and hands as you work with her. And record your findings as you go (see Prenatal Care Record Appendix D).

Begin by establishing her **estimated date of delivery** (EDD). You will need her last menstrual period (LMP), but make sure this was a *normal* period and not just implantation spotting. It helps to get the previous menstrual period (PMP) and the average length of her cycle, in order to accurately determine the LMP. Then count back three months from this date, add one week and adjust for the year if necessary. This is her estimated date of delivery (EDD). The baby's gestational age (GA), is simply the number of weeks since the LMP.

Next **check her weight,** noting her pre-pregnant weight and total gain thus far. This may get you back into a discussion of nutrition again. Assuming her starting weight was normal for her height and frame, an average gain is about a pound per week. Some women are very sensitive about changing body image, and need to be reassured that an ample weight gain is desirable and essential for the baby's health and their own endurance during pregnancy, labor and early parenting.

Then **check the urine** with a testing strip, looking for either protein or glucose. The significance of abnormal readings is explained in Chapter 3. It's important to understand and explain to parents whenever anything is unusual.

Next **check the blood pressure,** another sensitive area that is subject to fluctuation according to emotional state. Although medical texts state that only the systolic reading is influenced by tension or excitement, I've found that an overall high reading is fairly common at the first visit. Attributing it to the excitement of meeting, I tell the mother that it's normal and no cause for worry. However, an unusually high reading of 140/90, especially if combined with edema or protein in the urine, is indicative of pre-eclampsia and the need for immediate referral. Normal range is from 90/50 to 130/80.

Along with the blood pressure you should **check pulse and temperature,** to establish the mothers' baseline levels. For the same reason you should also **check reflexes.**

Optional but strongly recommended is a **breast exam.** When examining the breasts, look for *symmetry* of the tissue. Any mass or lump that stands out should be further screened by an expert.

Of the several standard techniques for performing breast exam, I prefer the following:

1. Begin by observing the woman's breasts while she is sitting upright. Look for symmetry, and for any puckering or pull around the nipple. Also have her place her hands on her hips and push against her hip bones, and observe as above.
2. Have her lie down and continue your exam by pressing your fingertips across the entire surface of the breast in a circular fashion, working inward toward nipple. Be sure to feel directly beneath the nipple, then squeeze it gently to check for any secretion. Colostrum, recognizable as a thick yellow discharge, may be evident after the first few months of pregnancy.
3. Use the same pressing motion over the upper chest (pectoral muscles).
4. Focus on the upper, outer quadrant of the breast, as this is the area that contains the most tissue and is therefore the most likely site for abnormal growth. Feel more deeply into this area by using thumb and forefingers to reach in and grasp underlying tissue, rolling it to assess structure. Repeat this motion on any other section of the breast that has thick tissue (will vary from woman to woman).
5. Last, feel along the side of the breast and into the armpit. With each step of this procedure, explain to the mother what you are doing. Then have her repeat the exam in your presence (one breast at a time). Since many women are intimidated by complex procedure, I usually simplify by suggesting that the woman not be afraid to squeeze her breasts, feel deeply and if she finds anything, check the other side to see if it's the same.

This is also a good time to discuss nipple preparation. Particularly if a woman is fair-skinned and her nipples pinkish, she may want to desensitize them. Going braless is one solution, though not a very practical one for pregnant women. But if a bra is purchased which has a seam running across the cup, the mother can open it to expose the nipple to the friction of clothing, and still have full support.

The mother may wish to put her shirt back on before you proceed with the **pelvic exam.** Invite her mate to sit alongside her on the bed if there's room.

Her internal exam is an intimate experience for her; she has probably had her share of rough, insensitive exams and is a little nervous. Proceed gently. Put on a glove, apply lubricating jelly to your fingers and go slowly, being guided by her muscular reaction and maintaining eye contact if she's open to it. Once you and she are comfortable, **check her cervix.** Note its condition (consistency, length, patency) and its position (central, posterior or anterior).

Confirm the EDD by doing a **bimanual exam** to size the uterus. Press up gently on the cervix while using your other hand to palpate the fundus (top of the uterus). As you bring your hands together you will get an idea of how large the uterus has grown. At ten weeks, the fundus barely clears the pubic bone; at twelve weeks it is generally a few centimeters above; at sixteen weeks it is midway between the pubic bone and the umbilicus.

If uterine size does not seem to conform to the EDD, re-evaluate the menstrual history. If the woman has used oral contraceptives prior to getting pregnant and has not had regular menses prior to conception, her dates may be off. Some women have bleeding for several months after conception at the time menstruation would ordinarily occur. If the uterus does not seem to be enlarged at all, do a pregnancy test before proceeding further. Nothing is more embarassing than doing prenatal care on a woman who is not pregnant!

Next **check her pelvic dimensions.** Take a look at the illustration below, but don't be overly concerned with pelvic type. This initial pelvimetry is for diagnosing any gross abnormalities in the bone structure which might present an obstacle to normal delivery. Remember that there is a natural softening of the cartilage at the end of pregnancy which can considerably alter any borderline dimension. And of course, it's all relative to the size of the baby.

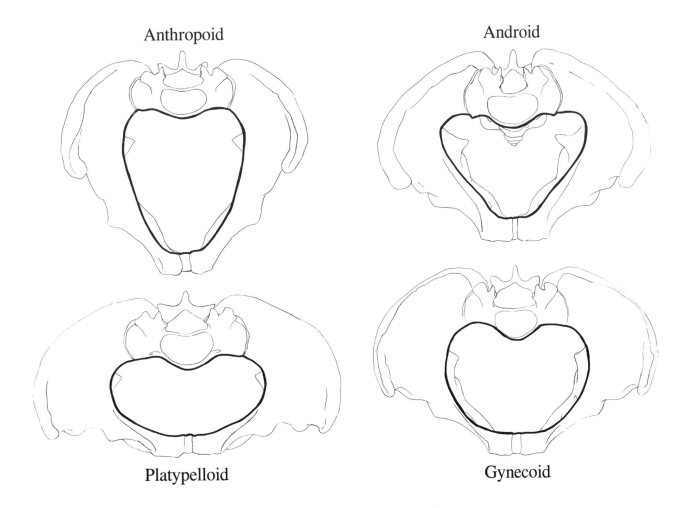

Anthropoid   Android

Platypelloid   Gynecoid

Basic Pelvic Types

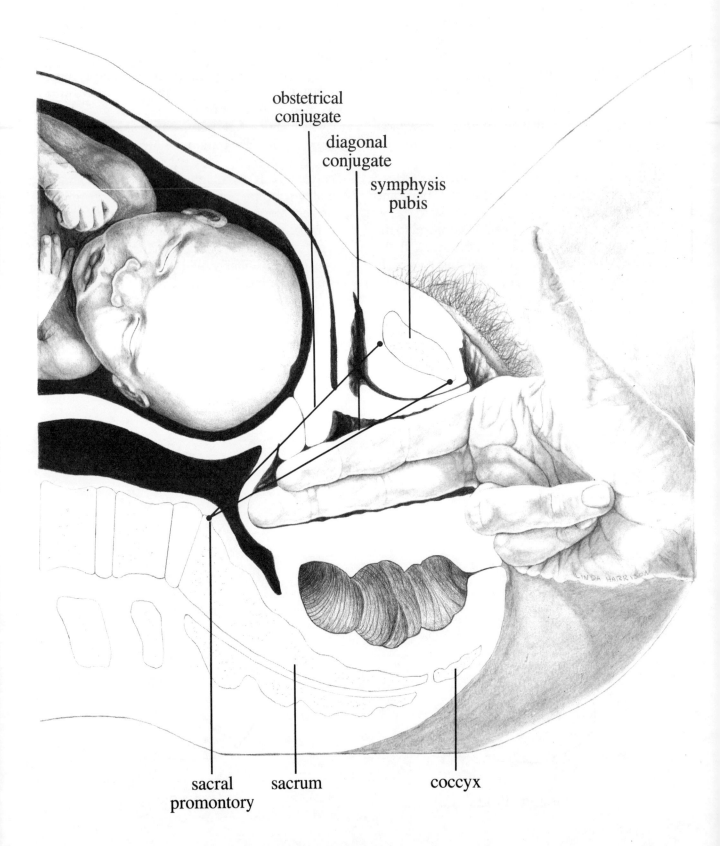

obstetrical
conjugate

diagonal
conjugate

symphysis
pubis

sacral
promontory

sacrum

coccyx

Measuring The Diagonal Conjugate

ischial
spine

Finding The Ischial Spines

There are five basic steps in doing pelvic assessment. **Assess the sacral curve** by finding the coccyx (aim straight down toward the bed) and then sweep your fingers all the way up to the sacral promontory (see illustration, page 14). The sacral curve should be deep and rounded, like a half circle. If the sacrum feels flat or heavy, note the possibility of android pelvis and reduced midpelvic dimensions. Sometimes the curve will be ample near the coccyx but will flatten toward the promontory. If such is the case, the baby may have trouble engaging because the inlet will be reduced. Make detailed notation of everything you feel; it may have a bearing on your management of labor. At least you may be able to anticipate potential problems and ways to solve them.

Next **estimate the size of the pelvic inlet.** First you must measure the diagonal conjugate, which is the distance from the outer edge of the pubic bone to the sacral promontory. To get the obstetrical conjugate (actual inlet dimension) you must subtract the thickness of the pubic bone (around 1.5 cms) from your measurement. Obviously, you're not going to insert a tape measure to do all this. So measure your reach beforehand, from the inside of the thumb joint to the tip of the middle finger. Adequate inlet is considered to be anything over 10.5 cms. If your fingers are not unusually short and measure at least 12 cms, you can perform this test with accuracy (remember, you must subtract 1.5 cms for pubic bone). Most of the time the sacral promontory cannot even be reached, a sure sign that the inlet is ample.

Next step is **finding the ischial spines.** This takes some practice, but once experienced, it's understood. The spines can be found by withdrawing your fingers almost to the introitus and then reaching directly to one side and then the other, at approximately 4 and 8 o'clock. The spines will be felt as bony prominences, blunt and barely noticeable, or may be sharply pointing and protruding. The latter may reduce the midpelvic dimension, which could cause problems with descent in second stage. A definite indication that you've found the spines is the woman's characteristic flinching response as you touch the sacro-spinous ligaments.

Next, as you slowly and gently withdraw your fingers, **palpate the pubic arch.** You should be able to fit two fingers under it and spread them slightly apart. Once your fingers are out, **determine that the outlet dimension is adequate** by making a fist and pressing it gently between the ischial tuberosities. Again, you should measure your fist in centimeters; it should be at least 8 cms. If it is less, adjust your estimate of the outlet accordingly.

This completes the pelvic exam. Don't hesitate to give the woman a reassuring pat as you're finishing up. Be sure to tell her what you're doing and what you're feeling for as the exam takes place. It's great if your partner can show points on a model pelvis while you're explaining procedures.

Next **do a fundal measurement** (if she's 18 weeks or more) by using a soft tape measure. Measure in centimeters from the upper edge of the pubic bone to the top of the uterus. To take this measurement accurately, dip in deeply at the very highest point of the fundus.

Now **palpate the baby for position and size.** Begin by feeling in the fundus to see if any obvious part can be identified. The head feels very hard and very round; the butt is softer, irregular in contour and smaller. Next, feel along the sides of the uterus for the back and small parts, and then above the pubic bone for the presenting part. Palpation is obviously an art learned by experience. I've noticed that midwives spend much more time with palpation than physicians do. Palpation is a very pleasurable and important part of midwifery practice, providing critical information regarding fetal size and weight, activity level and responsiveness to stimulation. Encourage the father to feel the baby too, and teach the mother how to palpate herself.

Next you should **take fetal heart tones** (FHT). The fetal heart should be audible by 20 weeks with standard fetascope; if not, check again a week later then refer for a scan. Normal FHT range is 120–160 beats per minute, but occasionally babies are considered normal up to 170. The heart rate is generally higher at the beginning of pregnancy, slowing 10–15 points as the baby grows. Also **check for variability.** This can be determined by listening for several 15 second intervals, then figuring out beats-per-minute for each and noting the overall range, e.g., 132–148. Variability occurs in response to

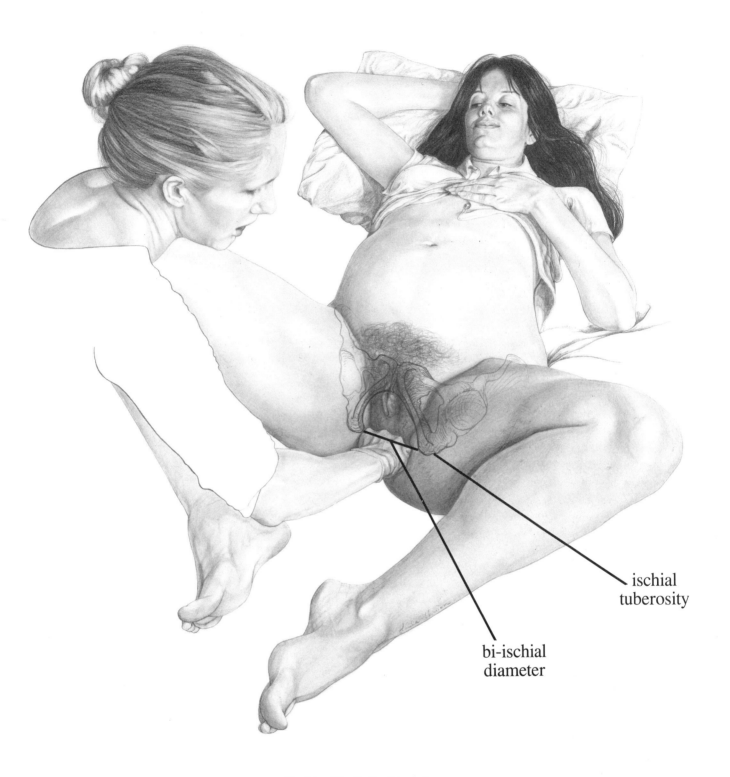

ischial
tuberosity

bi-ischial
diameter

Checking The Outlet Dimension

manual stimulation or baby's own movements. It is considered a sign of neurological health because it indicates that the baby can adapt to minor stress, which portends an ability to handle contractions during labor.

Letting the father, friends or siblings listen to the baby is a nice way to end the first visit.

Nutrition and Exercise

Nutritional advice should be based on a three-day record of food intake (don't forget to ask for this when you're on the phone if you want it at the first visit). Nutrition is just one branch of the tree of health, and should be evaluated with regard to exercise, activity level and lifestyle.

There are innumerable theories concerning nutrition, but it is not my purpose here to survey them. My own method of determining whether the diet is adequate does not include adding up micrograms of this mineral or that, but I do have a good working knowledge of the nutritional content of most foods and herbs and so can appraise a diet at a glance. However, it is a good idea to have as reference the handbook, *Composition of Foods*, available from the U.S. Government (Agricultural Handbook #8). This will aid you in settling disputes about how much zinc is in mushrooms, calcium in tofu, etc.

Above and beyond a good quality, well-balanced diet, I suggest the following daily supplements to compensate for devitalized soil, stress, air pollution, etc.: 1) Vitamin E—400 units; 2) Vitamin C—500 mg as maintenance dose; and 3) Iron—100 mg of a chelated, organic brand. If a woman complains of specific symptoms which indicate possible vitamin deficiency, look first to improve the quality of her diet and *then* suggest supplements! Devitalized soil aside, food comes first. The mechanics of supplement assimilation are still not fully known and understood. I heard recently of a mother who had taken very high quantities of vitamin C up to delivery; her baby became scurvied shortly after birth because such a tolerance for vitamin C had developed that withdrawal produced disease symptoms. A neonatologist in one of my childbirth classes suggested that likewise, neonatal hypocalcemia (low calcium level) might result from the

The midwife supports her client in purchasing and preparing the best quality foods possible.

mother ingesting large amounts of calcium during pregnancy to raise her pain threshold. Supplements should be supplemental!

Some mothers do not seem to need any supplements at all if their diets consist largely of freshly squeezed juices, raw foods and good quality protein. If these women are not anemic and show no other symptoms of poor health, then why insist? The irony is that sometimes a woman has the best available supplements and a fairly good diet, and still looks terrible. Another eats casually from excellent sources without much plan or thought, and is absolutely radiant. This indicates that food is not the only factor; it is how and when it is eaten that makes the difference. Mothers need to get in touch with their true inner voice of hunger, which will tell them what to eat and when. This only functions well in those not suffering from addictions to sugar, caffeine, alcohol or marijuana.

If obtaining food seems to be a problem, i.e., the mother is low-income and cannot afford the basics, refer her to a county agency. Sometimes a letter from the midwife verifying pregnancy and stating that the mother is at risk because of poor weight gain or inadequate nutrition can help her to qualify. Every midwife should be knowledgeable about the social services available in her community.

Getting in touch means getting in balance, and this is where a good measure of both activity and rest play a part. Activity should be *energizing* and rest *revitalizing.* The dismal notion of exercising until bored and exhausted need not apply, neither should the standardized "ten hours of sleep and nap every day" dictum. It's a question of individual need, which depends on sensitive interpretation of subtle messages from the body. A mother whose baby is experiencing a growth spurt and who is also having much personal stress in her life needs a combined remedy to suit her situation. Some instruction in relaxation, extra vitamins for stress and perhaps she will find the tranquility to examine what's going on in her pregnancy. Maybe there is a message to slow herself down coming from the baby, whose current development is making heavy demands on her resources. Maybe she does need ten, or even eleven hours of sleep for a week or two. It's a matter of self awareness.

What about heavy exercise and active sports? Mothers who are used to a high level of physical activity should continue, or taper off gradually as they receive messages to ease up. A sudden drop in the activity level can throw off body function, contributing to the development of constipation, circulatory problems or nervous irritability. For example, a woman used to jogging or aerobics can definitely keep it up unless she is fanatic and unlikely to sense when it's time to shift gears or stop altogether. A general rule of thumb is to avoid overheating and breathlessness. Yoga is my general recommendation for mothers inquiring about exercise because it is an integration of movement and rest. Yoga not only works the body but eases the mind. It's often been my experience that yoga at the end of a long day will energize me for the evening and dissolve my fatigue. Yoga recuperates the body by restoring subtle muscle and hormonal balances.

Mothers who work during pregnancy need special consideration. It's hard for them to be spontaneous; eat when they want, rest when they need to and move around when they feel like it. Bending the sharp edges of routine on the job might be a partial solution, but it is probably best to cut back working hours. Pregnancy is a precious time and preparation is essential. This takes a flexible schedule.

Encourage each woman to join a prenatal yoga or exercise class. These are great for bringing mothers together, while diminishing self-consciousness about changing body image.

Screening Out

Harsh terminology, but part of a process that involves parents' as much as midwives' decisions. On what basis do you decide that home birth is not appropriate for a woman or couple?

Exercising with others is fun, and helps you relax with your pregnant body.

Physical contraindications which may have become evident at the first visit include obesity, hypertension and contracted or abnormal pelvis. Psychological contraindications are more complex. An irresponsible attitude, hostility in response to suggestions or "know-it-all" closed-mindedness should give the midwife pause. A poor diet, particularly when the mother is adverse to changing it, is indicative of a general attitude of indifference. Excessive use of drugs, alcohol or cigarettes says the same thing. If you sense at the end of the initial visit that you won't be comfortable working with the couple, suggest that they check out other alternatives. This is also appropriate if you feel that they were not quite comfortable with you. But if you like the couple and they respond positively, make room for change. I've worked with women who began pregnancy smoking, drinking and using recreational drugs, and in a matter of weeks had cleaned themselves up quite nicely. Women who respond well to information and have the desire to set the health and welfare of the baby as a priority deserve the opportunity to try. Make your recommendations, provide handout reference material and see what happens at the next visit.

Lab Work

If the mother has had prenatal visits to a doctor or clinic, she has probably had the necessary lab work completed. She should make a *written request* for release of her records and have them mailed directly to you.

The **complete blood count (CBC),** is used to determine whether the mother has anemia or need for any supplements. Hemoglobin (HGB) and hematocrit (HCT) are the critical indicators. HGB values should be above 11.0 and HCT should be 33 or more. The HCT measures the percentage of red blood cells per total blood volume. Because red blood cells are the oxygen carriers, a low HCT means that both baby and mother will suffer some degree of oxygen deprivation. The mother will be easily fatigued and the baby will grow slowly. If the mother is anemic when she goes into labor the possibility of fetal distress is greater than usual. She herself is predisposed to less effective contractions, longer labor, postpartum hemorrhage and in-

fection. For the anemic woman even a moderate loss of blood is serious because the blood is poorly oxygenated to begin with. See the section on Anemia in Chapter 3 for more information.

Lab work also includes **GC and RPR screening** (RPR is also called STS, or VDRL). A positive GC culture indicates the presence of gonorrhea in the vagina or at the cervix, which can seriously infect the baby's eyes during delivery. Unless eyedrops are administered within two hours postpartum, blindness can result. Gonorrhea is often asymptomatic so every woman should be tested. The RPR is a blood test for syphilis, a disease which can cause miscarriage, malformations, prematurity, fetal death or neonatal infection. The desired result on the RPR is NR, or non-reactive.

A **Pap smear** is usually done at the same time as the GC. This tests for irregular cells at the cervix; important because pregnancy may cause more rapid growth of abnormal cells. It is not difficult to perform a Pap smear, and since the Pap should be repeated again at six weeks postpartum, you might want to learn to do this procedure yourself. The lab will supply microscope slides, cardboard slide holders and fixative; you will need long-handled sterile cotton swabs and speculum. You may prefer disposable plastic speculums so you won't have to bother with resterilizing, plus the mother can take hers home should she wish to look at her cervix in the future.

When placing the speculum use no lubricating jelly, the plastic speculums are prelubricated and jelly may invalidate results. Once the cervix is in view, take a cotton swab and gently rotate at the cervical os to collect secretion (the cells are contained therein). The os should be entered slightly to obtain cells from the squamocolumnar junction, the most likely site for abnormality. Roll the swab to deposit the secretion in straight lines along the slide. Then spray the slide with fixative, air dry and mark with client's name and date. The lab will also provide you with identification slips, and they will usually pick up weekly (or you may ship instead). The average lab charge for a Pap smear is $5–$10.

While you are doing the Pap smear, use a flashlight to check the cervix for unusual discharge or inflammation. If either is evident, the mother may have gonorrhea (which can be ruled out by routine culture) or she may have chlamydia. Chlamydia is the most common sexually transmitted disease in the United States. It is four times more common than gonorrhea, although the two often occur together. Frequently the woman will notice no symptoms, but her partner may have discharge or pain and burning with urination.

Chlamydia poses dangers to mother and baby. Untreated it can cause uterine infection during pregnancy, or might lead to sepsis in the event of prolonged rupture of the membranes (PROM). Chlamydia can also cause urinary tract infection. The baby has a 70% chance of contracting the disease during delivery, which can cause severe conjunctivitis or even pneumonia.

The prevalence of chlamydia, combined with its generally asymptomatic presentation, argues for routine use of eye prophylaxis (eye drops) for the newborn. Likewise it is probably prudent to do a **chlamydia culture or smear** at least once during pregnancy, probably near term. Although this is not yet routine (these tests were once prohibitively expensive) it will probably be standard before long.

The usual treatment is a full course of tetracycline, which is contraindicated during pregnancy because of its effect on fetal tooth enamel (causes discoloration). Erythromycin is nearly as effective and is safe for pregnancy. The woman's partner must also be treated, with no intercourse for 7–10 days and then condoms used for several weeks until an additional exam confirms that the infection is completely resolved.

Another possible cause of cervical (or vaginal) inflammation is Group B Streptococcus. This is a common vaginal infection which may have serious consequences for the baby. It is estimated that up to 40% of women have it in the vagina or at the cervix near term, and the transmission rate to the baby during delivery is as high as 75%. But fortunately only 3–4 babies in 1000 actually become infected.

The risk of infection increases with prolonged rupture of the membranes. If the organism travels up into the uterus, maternal infection can result (chorioamnionitis) which in turn can cause fetal contamination. This is a *serious* disease for babies; the fatality rate is as high as 90%! Often the first symptom is apnea (arrest in breathing) and spinal meningitis is another common manifestation.

Unfortunately strep does not respond very well to treatment during pregnancy. Antibiotics are standard, but even after a full course in the last trimester women often have positive cultures again at term. Nevertheless, it might be wise to **screen for Group B streptococcus** near term so at least you will know where you stand in the event of PROM. This is not yet standard of care but is an increasingly common practice.

Rubella antibody titre indicates whether or not the mother has immunity to German measles. The test is done by a diluting process which detects the presence of antibodies. For example, a rubella titre of 1:48 means that antibodies can be detected even though the sample has been diluted a number of times. It is proof that the mother has had rubella or has been immunized, even if she can't remember when. An unusually high reading (greater than 1:64) may indicate recent or current infection. In this case, a repeat is recommended and the woman should be referred to backup for consultation. If the mother has had a low titre (less than 1:10) it means she is susceptible and should be immunized *after* the current pregnancy and at least three months before the next, to minimize her chances of contracting the disease while pregnant. Were that to occur, her baby would have a 20 percent chance of heart, vision or hearing defects.

The mother needs her **blood type** too in case the need arises for emergency transfusion. This information is an absolute must for the midwife's records. The four blood types are O, A, AB and B, and the accompanying *Rh factor* is either + (positive) or – (negative). The Rh factor is an antigen present in the red blood cells; 83 percent of women have this factor and are Rh +, 17 percent don't and are Rh–. If a woman is Rh– and her baby is Rh +, there is a risk of isoimmunization. This occurs if some fetal blood enters her circulation (due to intrauterine trauma, premature separation of the placenta, or placenta praevia) causing her to produce antibodies against the baby's positive cells. This leads to severe anemia in her unborn child. The incidence of this is minimal with a first baby (as rare as the traumas that can cause it to occur) *unless* the Rh– mom has had abortions or miscarriages which might have allowed for blood transfer. Nowadays RhoGAM (anti-antigen injection) is given to every Rh– woman following abortion. But even a first time mother may have had early undetected miscarriage at some point. To play it safe, *every* Rh– mom should be screened for antibodies early in pregnancy, and again at 24, 28, 32 and 36 weeks.

It is now standard of care to administer RhoGAM *during* pregnancy. In fact, some practitioners routinely recommend RhoGAM for all Rh– mothers at 28–30 weeks, as there is a 2% risk of sensitization. RhoGAM injection during pregnancy conveys *passive* immunity, it will not protect a subsequent pregnancy. Such prophylactic use of RhoGAM is somewhat controversial; according to a recent article in *Mothering*, there may be risks of fetal injury, even death. Undoubtedly fear of lawsuit has led to the use of RhoGAM in this conservative fashion; the mother must make her own decision.

Immediately after the birth, you must take cord blood from the baby and draw blood from the mother to determine whether there is a need for RhoGAM and if so, appropriate dosage. To be effective, RhoGAM must be administered within 72 hours.

Urinalysis is also part of standard prenatal screening. Besides protein and glucose, a complete urinalysis detects the presence of bacteria, which may indicate urinary tract infection (UTI) if the value is + 4 or more. A value of + 2 or + 3 indicates the need for repeat screening.

It is important to remember that bladder infections are often asymptomatic during pregnancy. The urethra is so soft and dilated by increased progesterone that the mother feels no pain. For this reason, any woman with a history of recurrent UTIs should be warned to report the slightest symptom. Unchecked, a bladder infection can migrate to the kidneys and cause serious damage (see page 26). And the medication most commonly prescribed during pregnancy for kidney infection predisposes the mother to anemia, thus intensifying her risk status.

Increasingly common is routine testing for tuberculosis using the **tine test.** Tuberculosis is particularly common in crowded urban areas and among Native American, Asian and Middle Eastern populations. After the initial infection (which is often self-healing) a woman may remain infected and yet appear asymptomatic. Although congenital infection is rare, postpartum infection of the newborn is common as it comes in contact with the mother or other infected family members. If the mother has an active infection during the pregnancy she will be treated at once, whereas treatment will generally be postponed if infection is inactive.

Any woman with history of a positive tine test *should not* be tested again, as repeat tine could reactivate the disease. Refer this mother to a physician.

Certain women should also receive **genetic screening.** If both parents are of Mediterranean descent, the fetus is at risk for B thalassemia. Tay-Sachs disease can affect the fetus of Jewish couples. Or if the parents are Black, they may be carriers of the Sickle-cell gene. Parents who have previously given birth to children with defects will undoubtedly be concerned about the likelihood of recurrence. Refer all parents at risk to genetic counseling. This can be an area of tremendous anxiety and it would be irresponsible of a midwife to reassure a couple without being on good technical ground.

Every woman 35 or over should also be advised of her options regarding genetic screening. *Amniocentesis* can be used to rule out Down's Syndrome, or other chromosomal defects associated with advanced maternal age. The incidence of Down's for a woman of 35 is one in 365, approximately the same risk as miscarriage or infection caused by the procedure. But by the age of 40, the incidence increases to one in 100. Amniocentesis is performed by inserting a needle through the abdomen and into the amniotic sac, then withdrawing a sample of fluid. Ultrasound is used simultaneously to visualize the baby. The procedure cannot be performed before 14 weeks because there is not sufficient fluid; 14–16 weeks is optimal. Results can take several weeks.

Chorionic villi sampling is done earlier, at 10–12 weeks. This is an obvious advantage in case something is found and the woman decides to terminate the pregnancy. However, this procedure has a higher incidence of miscarriage than amniocentesis. It is performed by removing a small sample of the fetal side of the placenta. This procedure is still in the experimental stage and so is not yet widely available.

Alpha-fetoprotein screening is a blood test to detect neural tube defects only. These include anencephaly, microcephaly, hydrocephaly and spina bifida. Unfortunately the test has a 20% false positive rate, so that ultrasound and amniocentesis may be necessary for a final diagnosis.

Decisions regarding genetic screening are very personal and often agonizingly difficult. Should a woman decide against it, she will undoubtedly be reminded of her decision time and again as total strangers ask whether she has had "the test" and if her baby is a boy or a girl. Apparently amniocentesis is becoming increasingly routine; some physicians recommend it for any woman over 30! This is undoubtedly a result of the malpractice crisis. There is no easy answer, but a session with a genetics counselor can help a woman assess her risks realistically. The midwife should be prepared with up-to-date handouts and referrals.

It will undoubtedly become increasingly common for women in your care to inquire about AIDS testing. Please refer to Chapter 3, page 60, for details on this procedure.

Later in pregnancy (around 26–28 weeks) you may decide to have a **glucose screen** done. Most physicians do so routinely, to rule out gestational diabetes (for more information see Chapter 3). This test requires that the mother injest 50 mg. of glucose; an hour later her blood is drawn and if values exceed 140 mg/dl, she should be referred for further testing.

If a woman comes for her initial visit with no previous lab work and you are unable to do it yourself, send her to a public health facility or women's health center with a request for a Prenatal Panel (including Pap smear and GC). And take the first opportunity that arises for learning these skills yourself; your clients will definitely appreciate the continuity of care and you will enjoy the autonomy of practice.

Routine Checkups

The schedule for caregiving is fairly standard: up to 28 weeks gestation, every four weeks; from 28–34 weeks, every two weeks; from 35 weeks on, once weekly. The main reason for increasing frequency of visits is that complications are more likely to arise at the end of pregnancy when stress on mother and baby is greatest. Also, it is critical that you have more personal contact with the mother in order to forge the emotional bonds essential for the birth.

Routine at every visit are urine dipstick for protein and glucose, weight check, blood pressure reading, fundal height measurement, fetal auscultation and palpation (for position and activity). Also check on nutrition and exercise each time. At 28 weeks you may want to call for another three-day diet report, as needs for protein, calcium and iron intensify during the last trimester. The hematocrit should be checked routinely at this time, or whenever the mother complains of unusual fatigue or breathlessness. And you may wish to do a glucose screen if there is propensity to gestational diabetes. Otherwise your visits should focus on the more personal aspects of helping the woman and her family adjust to pregnancy.

There are many appropriate topics for discussion: reading material, childbirth classes and preparation, the father's role, grandparents, postpartum support, perineal preparation, nipple preparation, newborn care, personal hygiene, work and play. Take your cues from the parents, but see that visits don't get into a rut of discussing the same subjects again and again. It is stimulating to introduce a new topic for discussion and parents need perspective on the many-faceted experience of childbearing.

Don't forget to inquire about the mother's general wellbeing, as there are a number of physical complaints that may arise from time to time (see next section).

And always take good notes at each visit! Read the section on Charting in Chapter 8 for guidelines.

Common Complaints

Pelvic sensitivity and the vague pains noticed while walking are usually **ligament pains,** caused by the stretching of the ligaments which support the uterus as they adjust to its increasing size and weight. Many women don't realize that the uterus is suspended by

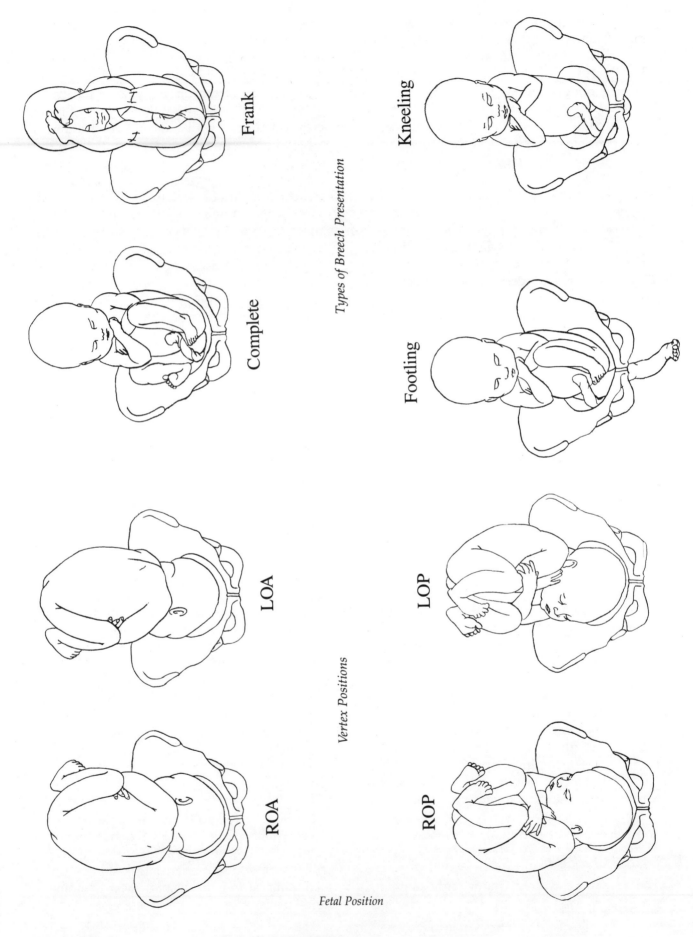

Frank

Kneeling

Types of Breech Presentation

Complete

Footling

LOA

LOP

Vertex Positions

ROA

ROP

Fetal Position

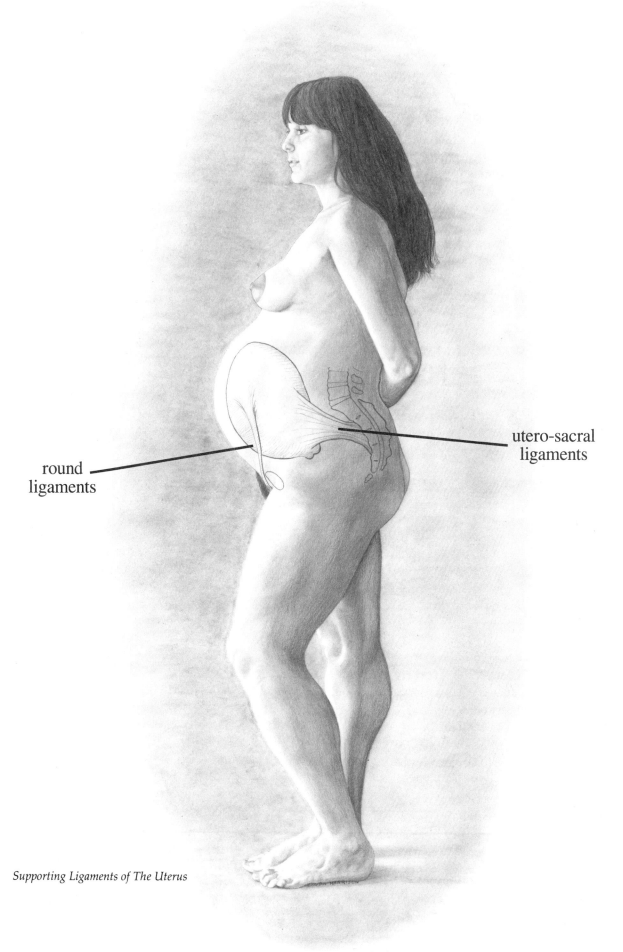

round
ligaments

utero-sacral
ligaments

Supporting Ligaments of The Uterus

ligaments which run from its base to the pelvic bones. The uterus is very movable, more a less a floating organ (see illustration page 25).

Morning sickness is generally due to hormone sensitivity, although it may occur in reaction to the new sensations of being pregnant. It is widely acknowledged that mental conflict or emotional turmoil concerning pregnancy can greatly contribute to nausea or vomiting. For this reason, ample B-complex is recommended for mediating stress; B-6 is especially important. Other remedies include soda crackers or plain yogurt upon arising. Many women report that small meals and nearly continuous eating seem to help. Relaxation practice can help, as does emotional clearing.

Should nausea progress to vomiting, keep a day-by-day watch on the situation. If vomiting becomes chronic, the mother has developed a condition known as *hyperemesis gravidarium* and is at risk for dehydration and malnutrition, which predispose the baby to serious complications as well. Persistent vomiting is a vicious cycle; often IV therapy is necessary to stabilize the mother's electrolyte balance so she can keep food down again. Refer the mother with hyperemesis to a backup physician immediately.

Indigestion and **heartburn** are often related to fetal growth spurts and the displacement of the stomach and intestines. The best remedy seems to be digestive enzymes (papaya and bromelain), taken whenever the problem arises. Special care must be taken not to overload the stomach before lying down. The manner or the mood in which food is eaten has something to do with it too. Digestion is so much slower than usual that food must be chewed very carefully. And since the gall bladder functions less efficiently during pregnancy, reducing fat intake can help.

Fatigue and **lowered resistance** have a relationship to nutrition and overall state of health. Review the diet; ask that a three-day intake sheet be brought to the next visit. Sometimes women get into ruts, both food-wise and activity-wise, and need to break away from old patterns. A wide variety of foods, especially fruit and vegetables, will provide the diverse vitamins and minerals needed for vitality. Varying daily activities and getting out more often will stabilize the mind and emotions. Encourage the woman to find out what works for her.

This is good preparation for creative, resourceful mothering.

If fatigue is extreme or persistent, repeat the HCT to rule out anemia.

Headaches and **general aches and pains** often respond to relaxing teas such as hops, scullcap and chamomile. Yoga is another remedy, as is emotional clearing by talking and feeling through problems.

If the mother complains of **backache** see that she is getting adequate but not overstrenuous exercise, and suggest pelvic rocks to keep the lower spine flexible. These can be performed on hands-and-knees, alternately arching the back like a cat and bringing it back to normal position. Or she can do the same motion standing, sitting, driving in the car, anytime.

If she indicates that backache is higher up, at waist-level, rule out the possibility of kidney infection (pyelonephritis) by *checking for CVA tenderness.* Do this with the mother in a sitting position, her back fully exposed. Using your fist, strike the area nearest her waist and adjacent her spine, on each side. (Obviously you must warn her first.) Pound gently enough not to actually *cause* pain but firmly enough to secure your diagnosis. It may help to work your way down the back (for comparison) or to cushion your blow by placing your other hand across the area first. If the woman jumps or otherwise indicates pain, note whether her sensitivity was left, right or unilateral. Refer the mother immediately to a backup physician. (If there is no CVA tenderness, chart this "No CVAT.")

Varicose veins of the legs and vulva are caused by the hormone progesterone, which relaxes smooth muscle and impairs venous return, especially from the legs. Some women seem to have a hereditary disposition to these. Standing for long periods makes things worse, but exercise helps by stimulating circulation, as does elevating the legs and buttocks periodically. Six hundred to 800 units of vitamin E daily may be helpful, but this amount should be tapered to 400 units by the seventh month because excessive quantities may cause retained placenta. Take E separately from other vitamins and with milk or cheese for best absorption.

Swollen ankles (in the absence of high blood pressure or proteinuria) may also result from impaired circulation or excessive periods of standing. The diet should be improved (more protein, fresh vegetables and plenty of fluids) and moderate exercise taken regularly. Elevating the feet and legs helps too.

Constipation can be caused by hormones or diet, but plenty of fluids and fibrous foods should take care of the problem. Often women eat well but mistake thirst for hunger, and must learn to distinguish between the two impulses.

Vaginal infections are common and bothersome. **Candidiasis (yeast)** frequently occurs due to alkaline vaginal pH (another effect of progesterone) and is characterized by a white, curd-like discharge. It can be controlled by inserting vaginal sponges soaked in acidophilus culture. Be sure to boil sponges first to remove mineral deposits then saturate with solution, squeeze out lightly and insert. Change every three hours. Yeast infection at term increases the risk of newborn thrush.

Trichomoniasis is characterized by a thin, malodorous, highly irritating yellowish discharge. The usual medication, Flagyl, is contraindicated for the first half of pregnancy. The following herbal douche is reputed to be so effective that it's definitely worth a try. Unlike vinegar, it nourishes (rather than strips) the mucous membranes. Although douching is generally not recommended during pregnancy it is safe as long as the pressure flow is minimal (bag should be hung low) and the water is warm, not hot. The nozzle should never be inserted more than three inches.

Douche for Vaginal Infections:

One part each of:

Comfrey root	Yarrow
Mugwort	Rosemary
Peppermint	Alum

Steep in a non-metal container using boiled spring water. Allow to cool. Douche with one pint strained solution twice daily for two days. On the third and fourth day, douche as usual in the morning but for yeast infections add one part acidophilus in the evening, and for trichomoniasis, one part golden seal in the evening.

Another remedy is the insertion of a peeled, un-nicked clove of garlic, changed twice daily. This can be used in combination with the douche.

Keep in mind that trich is contagious so the woman's mate must also be treated. His symptoms may be mild, but he can harbor the organism in his urethra and so he will have to take oral medication. No sexual activity until both are cured.

Whenever there is vaginal infection the diet should consist primarily of dark green vegetables, good quality protein and whole grains. Yeast thrives on sugar in particular so it should be completely eliminated, along with excessive intake of fruit (including dried). Eating plenty of acidophilus yogurt is a help, as is brewer's yeast.

Herpesvirus hominis #2 has reached epidemic proportions and has almost become a common complaint. These small, painful blisters are caused by a virus for which we know no cure. Herpes #2 is spread through sexual contact, but after the initial infection the virus remains in the nerve ganglia in the genital area: susceptibility to outbreak is increased during times of severe stress or fatigue, regardless of sexual activity. Some women run cycles of infection which are predictable; every three or four months, or as often as every six weeks. Make careful note of this information on the woman's chart. This virus has a *devastating* effect on the central nervous system of the baby; if a woman has active lesions at the time labor commences, vaginal delivery must be prohibited. However, inquire as to the number, severity, and location of lesions that commonly occur. Women who are infected only on the outer perineum or anal area may possibly have vaginal delivery if the sores are no longer open and can be kept from contact with the baby. If a woman has a history of herpes, most doctors want cultures done weekly from 35 weeks onward, to rule out cervical contamination. At the onset of labor, a slide test should be done to see if any lesions are present. Or if her membranes rupture prior to the onset of labor, the test should be done within an hour to rule out infection.

Treatments for herpes during pregnancy are basically comfort measures. Most important is to keep the affected area dry and cool. This means no nylon underwear or preferably no underwear at all. Hot baths may aggravate the infection. Intercourse is prohibited until all sores *on both parents* are completely healed. Local applications of cold milk, zinc oxide, A&D ointment, golden seal, ice, and calendula cream (marigold extract) are all reputed to be healing and soothing. Certain dietary changes are also important; one mother reported cutting her ordinary five-day cycle of infection in half by beginning stress complex and protein drinks at the first tingling intimation of infection. Increased lysine intake helps too. Complete elimination of coffee and alcohol will help purify the blood and speed healing. Any use of marijuana should also be cut back, as smoking uses vitamin C needed by the body to counteract infection.

If the mother has an *initial outbreak* in the first trimester, the baby may suffer neurological damage. The mother should be immediately referred to a physician.

Common Fears and Counseling Techniques

There are certain universal fears about pregnancy and birth which are bound to arise time and again. Almost every mother wonders if her baby will be normal and healthy. Most women have some fear of the sensations of labor, and wonder if they will be able to get through it. These worries are often alleviated simply by explaining how commonly they occur.

Besides these fears, there are also special concerns unique to our times and culture. The mother may have great anxiety about her changing role; she may fear total domesticity and the loss of her career-related identity. She may also find herself uncertain about her relationship with her partner: the more emotional she becomes the more nervous and erratic his behavior may be.

As she expresses these concerns, you may need to do a bit of counseling. Your primary goal should be to focus the mother on her own problem-solving capabilities. It is crucial that she feel affirmed in her distress. Validating the sensitivities of a pregnant woman, heightened and distorted as they are by the hormones of pregnancy, can be one of the heavier demands placed on the midwife. Or it can be a lot of fun, if you are genuinely interested and can give of

yourself in the process. In midwifery practice, it is most appropriate that the counseling relationship be one of developing friendship.

What are some basic techniques for counseling? *Mirroring* is number one; the midwife receives impressions and reflects them back without judgment or distortion. And then by *listening well* (not just with her ears but with heart and being) she may sense the moments of truth or reckoning in a woman and give her *positive reinforcement* for her realizations. Here's where a midwife's character comes through, and serves to inspire women struggling to accept newly revealed truths about themselves and their lives.

Personal involvement is essential. By being committed to help her client work out problems, the midwife inspires commitment in return. And by *eliciting commitment and responsibility*, she enables the woman to implement realizations and make them manifest, which is the ultimate aim of counseling. On a practical level, the time and energy saved at birthings by clearing up problems in advance definitely makes it worthwhile.

Midwives need to be needed. They are traditional healers; mothers, lovers, nourished by giving. But enthusiastic participation in counseling should always be tempered by respect for privacy and individual pace. This takes objectivity, and sometimes restraint. It helps to work in partnership; if one of you is emotionally involved the other is usually level steady.

Men with questions and concerns about parenting and identity may not communicate directly. Despite changes in recent years, it is still difficult for men to share and express deep feelings. Pride can be a contending factor, along with general embarrassment over matters considered too personal to discuss. The way of passing information should suit the situation; sometimes tact and discretion are necessary. Supplying reading material, handouts, etc. can be an effective solution.

Father Participation

Many fathers now desire a very active, vital part in the experience of pregnancy and birthing. Some want to catch their babies. This takes emotional and mental preparation: it requires intimacy between partners and a good understanding of labor and delivery mechanics. There is no reason why the father shouldn't catch the baby, barring complications or the last minute desire of the mother to have him by her side. For some women, the image of easing the baby into their man's waiting hands is both joyous and releasing.

Whenever a father expresses interest, provide a book or handouts with clear, reasonably detailed information on assisting delivery. At the same time, give instruction for perineal massage, so that touch sensitivity and communication are well established. When it comes time for delivery practice (a few weeks before the birth, perhaps at the home visit) use a model pelvis and a baby doll to demonstrate. While you're doing a vaginal exam on the mother show the father how to combine massage with perineal support. Or you can demonstrate by using your hand to simulate the birth outlet, with stretched skin between thumb and forefinger seving as perineum.

Some fathers see "making the catch" as a kind of virility test, a chance to master the mystery of birth. Be sure to emphasize the need for

sensitivity and awareness of what is happening to the woman; the man must at all times follow her lead. I remember one father who paid minimal attention to prenatal instruction and had a pretty rough time during the delivery. He massaged so vigorously that he actually pushed the baby's head back in as it began to crown! I put my hand over his to slow him down and gave him a few instructions; this calmed him enough to make his work effective.

Ideally, the father's preparation is mostly personal, an extension of sexuality. Here is Frank's story:

I wanted to share the birth process with my mate and felt that my involvement was necessary and my right as a father. Practicing exercises and massaging Bridget almost every night put me in tune with her body and spirit. By participating in this way I believed that my mind and body would appreciate the mystical aspects of birth when the time came.

My participation was not limited to

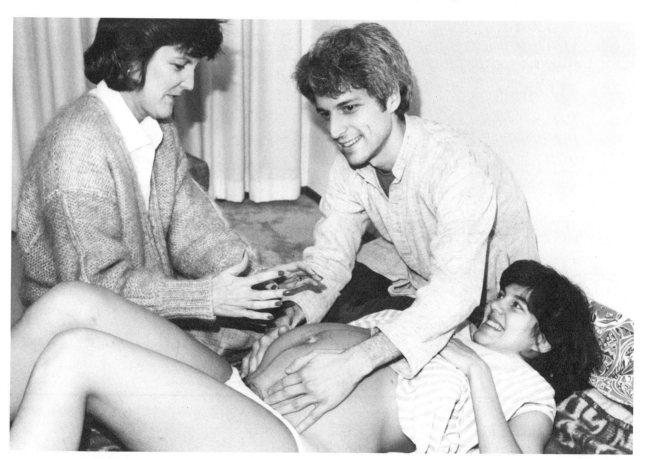

This father is discovering how to feel his baby's position.

prenatal classes, exercises, and reading material. This was our second pregnancy and once again my goal was to catch the baby and cut the cord. I had performed this mighty ritual during our first birth. That labor was only three hours; Bridget went immediately into hard labor-transition. Even though it was hard to absorb this rapid labor I still made the catch. Lydia was small, yet perfect to the touch. I caught her and held her close to my joyful, tired body.

I did not catch our second child. His shoulders were stuck and thus we needed assistance. His birth was twelve hours long, which let Bridget and me absorb ourselves at every stage. We touched, massaged, showered and supported each other in every way. This made up for not catching Paul.

During this second birth I felt fully in touch with Bridget sexually and spiritually. I noticed that my sensitivity was greater than before, and my love for Bridget and my family grew with every phase of the encounter. Patience, listening, and empathy were at their peak. I felt then that I truly understood both birth and Bridget.

Here's the joint perspective, with comments from both father, Eugene and mother, Pamela.

Eugene:
Every man should catch his own baby. I didn't realize that when my daughter was born eight years ago. We had her at home, I cut the cord, and it was the high point of my life. Yet it would have been even better if I had caught her.

I didn't because I was ignorant. I didn't know how easy it was, and nobody told me that I could or should. But when my son was born, I found out that catching your baby is the next best thing to having it. I urge all fathers to do it, to insist on it.

I enjoyed being down there between Pamela's legs. At my daughter's birth I was at her mother's side and didn't have the intimate perspective. This time I could see what was going on.

Pamela:
I was not sure where I wanted Eugene to be—at my side or at my feet. But as our cycle was near completion I realized that this was the only time we, the three of us, would be connected in that intense moment of birth. Watching Eugene's concentration, his hands and the message of love that they carried, and seeing my baby's head in the mirror helped me to stay focused. Soon I was feeling those irresistible urges to push and feeling my baby's body moving through the passage. First the head, then swoosh the body into the hands of the man I love. A beautiful baby boy was born so right. The connection is made and is never lost.

Eugene:
When Lenny slithered into my hands I immediately felt bonded to him. I was the first one able to see that he was a boy. That was a special thrill. Though Pamela carried Lenny and gave him up like ripe fruit, I was his first contact with the world as a whole person. In this first, total contact I knew he could feel my protective, loving feelings. And when I gave him to Pamela, completing the cycle, I felt truly satisfied.

Sibling Participation

Children who will be at the birth need preparation too. Have a few picture books for lending to families with young ones. Many parents worry needlessly that their children will be frightened by birth sights or sounds. To assuage these fears, send the family to a film showing or slide presentation. Mothers with small children can make "birth noises" for fun, so the little ones will be better prepared.

The atmosphere at clinic is important too. Here's one mother's story of her experience in preparing her three-year old daughter:

From the beginning of our second pregnancy we wanted to include Lydia in the birth. We felt that this would ease the transition from being an only child and lessen any jealousy that might arise. A home birth would enable her to comfortably share this joyous family occasion. Although some friends and relatives thought she was too young to participate, our midwife and other friends invited to the birth supported the idea.

Our preparation started with prenatal exams in the home of our midwife, Elizabeth. Lydia accompanied us on all of these visits, and with each one became more interested in the proceedings. We tried to explain each step to her and encouraged her to take part by imitating Elizabeth. The relaxed atmosphere and obvious enthusiasm of everyone in the room made her more comfortable.

In preparation for the actual birth we asked a friend who is close to Liddy to look after her during labor and to try to gauge whether she wanted to be in the room while the baby was born. We were happy that she slept through most of my labor because this reduced the chance that she would become bored, plus Frank and I were better able to concentrate on each other and the birth.

Liddy entered the room in the arms of a friend just as I was pushing the baby out. She was very calm, putting to rest our fears that the intensity of pushing might upset her. Even after the birth, much of my attention went out to Lydia who seemed a bit shy at first. But a few hours later when the four of us were alone, she warmed up considerably and has continued to show a deep affection

for her little brother. We feel that bringing her to clinic and letting her attend the birth has a lot to do with her present warmth and tolerance.

The Last Six Weeks

The quality and emphasis in prenatal care changes during this period. Parents begin to ask more questions as the birth becomes imminent, and the midwife spends more time palpating the baby for position, size and growth. She will also check for descent, and eventually for flexion and engagement. This can be done abdominally or by internal exam. Deflexion of the baby's head can be corrected if it is not too far down in the pelvis, in fact a deflexed head can and should be prevented from engaging. Simply press the occiput down into the pelvis while pulling upward on the sinciput (see illustration page 32).

Internal exams are not mandatory but can satisfy everyone's curiosity. When examining near term you should: 1) check the cervix for dilation and effacement; 2) note the station (level of descent) of the baby's head; 3) feel for general readiness and flexibility of the vaginal muscles. The cervix of a woman pregnant for the first time will usually be somewhat closed

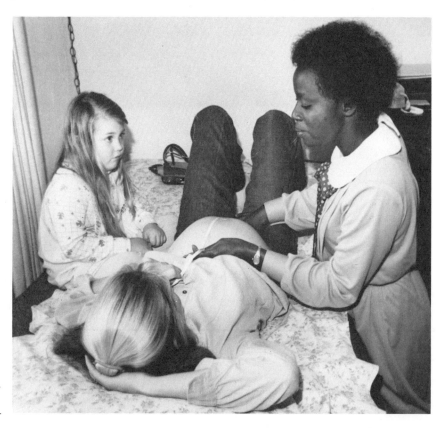

Children love to imitate the midwife's actions, which diminishes their fear at birth time.

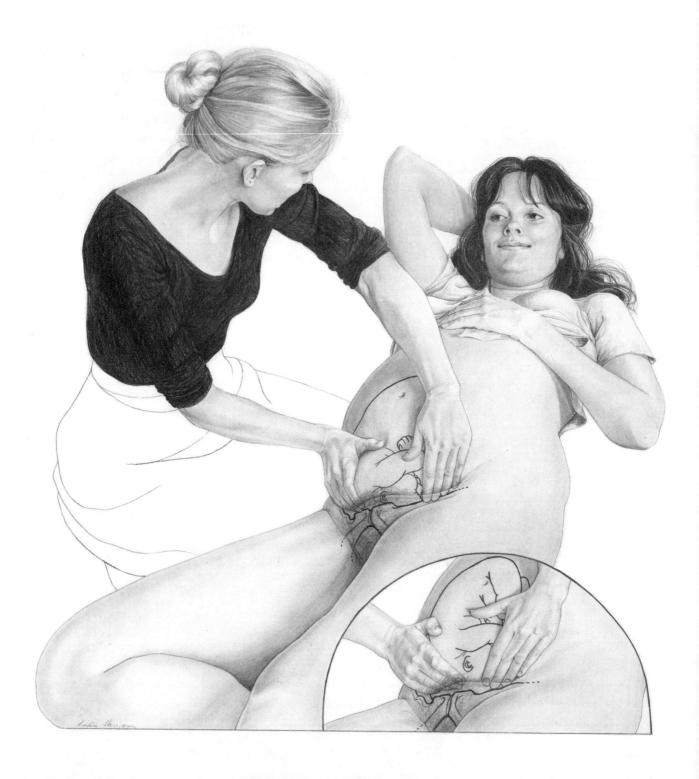

Checking for Flexion and Engagement

until labor begins, with perhaps a fingertip **dilation** (one to two centimeters). **Effacement** is more variable; this measurement of how thinned-out the cervix has become is recorded in terms of percentage. A non-effaced cervix feels thick, firm and about an inch long. A cervix already 50% effaced feels softer, "mushier" with a less distinguishable neck of only half an inch. Sometimes the outer surface of the cervix thins first while the part against the head remains thicker; then the cervical os is felt as a ring-like opening with clearly defined edge. Sometimes the forward part of the cervix will efface first because the baby's head is coming down at an angle (asynclitism) and is putting greater pressure on either the anterior or posterior portion. If the baby's head is still high and the cervix somewhat posterior, it's necessary to feel way in back of the os to accurately estimate

effacement. Sixty to 80% effacement is fairly common in the last few weeks before labor commences. Occasionally women will be 100% effaced before dilating (cervix paper-thin and smooth against the baby's head) but this is unusual.

If you find the cervical opening to be rather tight and rigid, or if you know the mother has scar tissue there from fairly recent infection or surgery, try massaging in a bit of evening primrose oil (available at the health food store). This will soften tissue and break up adhesions, preparing the cervix for dilation. (This can also be done in early labor, in case it is prolonged.) The mother can apply the oil herself once daily; assist her in finding her cervix in case she has never felt it before.

The phenomenon of **false labor,** which sometimes occurs in these last weeks, is char-

Estimating Station

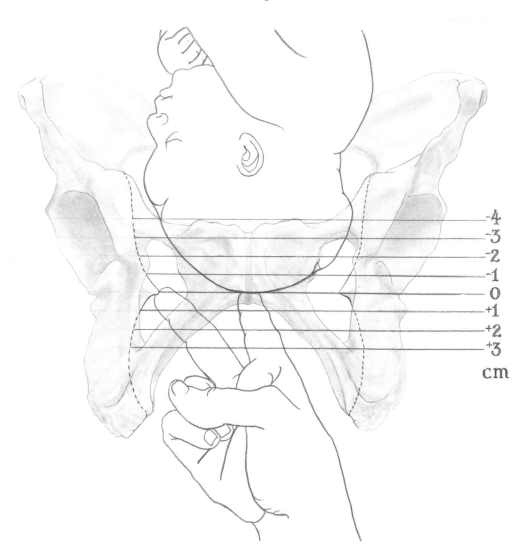

acterized by irregular contractions. Instead of lengthening and coming more frequently, they eventually just peter out. Little or no dilation takes place because uterine action is *incoordinate*, i.e., only certain muscle segments contract. Nevertheless, the term "false" is both discouraging and misleading, as these contractions usually accomplish some cervical softening or effacement. False labor is often stimulated by the head engaging or descending.

Descent is measured according to the relationship between the level of the presenting part and the level of the ischial spines (which mark the halfway point through the pelvis). If the head is about one centimeter above spine level, the **station** is termed −1. The head can be higher (−2, −3 or −4) and still be felt internally. If the tip of the head is exactly level with the spines it is at 0 station and considered engaged. Should the head be lower than that your finding would be + 1 or + 2 (rarely more than + 2 before labor begins).

Checking for station is difficult for beginners. It's essential to have some clinical experience with pelvimetry to be certain you can find the spines. Insert two fingers and place the middle one on the spine, while scissoring the index finger to find the presenting part. Try to keep both fingers on the same horizontal plane. Then note how many centimeters up or down you must move your index finger to find the top of the head, and you have your reading. After a while assessing station is based on a qualitative sense of how well the head fills the pelvis and is no longer such a mysterious and painstaking procedure.

Vaginal muscle awareness and control is essential for women who want to avoid tears. The mother must learn the difference between contracted and relaxed states of the vagina and perineum and should be able to create either at will. Usually she must put her own fingers inside and contract her muscles around them, in order to learn the exact motions to use. Being able to stop the flow of urine does not necessarily indicate a full range of control.

The advantage of **perineal massage,** like any massage, is that it increases circulation and makes tissues supple, healthier and more liable to stretch well. Some women may not feel comfortable touching or massaging them-

selves, but this can be changed with some instruction and gentle encouragement.

Sometimes women are more comfortable if their mates or lovers help them with this. Massage often flows into lovemaking and that's fine. The penis makes a great vaginal massager. But sex is not essential in preparing for birth, especially if there are heavy emotions involved that inhibit letting go. A woman's relationship to her baby is unique and distinct from her relationship to her man. She can feel more or less open to him sexually and still respond completely to the erotic sexuality of birthing her baby.

Sometime in the last couple of weeks it's also a good idea to take a careful look at the mother's external genitals, particularly her labia and perineum, so if tearing occurs you have some idea of how she looked beforehand. Many women have caruncles (hymenal skin tags) which can be confusing when trying to figure out how to approximate edges for suturing. There may also be scarring from previous repair that will require extra support during perineal distension.

Home Visits

Home visits are obviously an essential part of home birth services. It is good to do at least two; one early in pregnancy to see the mother and father in their own element, and another

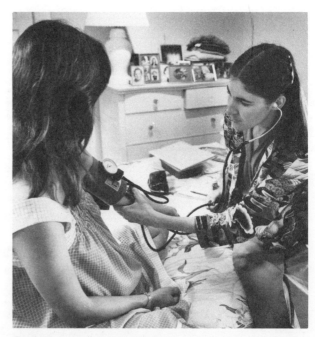

Combining a prenatal checkup with a home visit.

around 35 weeks to be sure that supplies are in and last minute concerns are covered. Sometimes an extra home visit is appropriate when a woman complains of problems at home. It's also a good idea when the father hasn't come to clinic for a while, whatever the reason.

The last home visit can also include a review of birthing skills, which is especially important if the couple has not had classes. Children of school age can be included in a dinner get together, winding up with feeling mom's belly and listening to the baby. And friends planning on attending the birth should be present too, so their roles can be clarified and they can get to know you.

Use this visit to appraise the birth room for order and cleanliness, and see that a table top or some other protected area will be available for laying out supplies. *Make sure there is adequate heating in the room,* or that a space heater will be available. And check out sleeping arrangements for baby; beware of the crib or cradle in a separate room. Emphasize the importance of skin-to-skin contact in the early weeks and banish taboos about having the baby in bed. You might come prepared with handouts or magazines to lend, should this discussion progress to baby care or other postpartum concerns.

If the mother has felt shy or awkward about perineal massage or vaginal exams at clinic, perhaps her own bed will make it easier. Her children might also watch these procedures so they won't be surprised during the birth.

This is a perfect time to clear up any unresolved fears about the birth itself. Because this is a longer visit and the woman is in her own environment, she may become more vulnerable than ever before and discuss her deepest feelings. Consider this visit time well spent, as the birth itself may be shorter and smoother because of it. The main purpose of this visit is to create an aura of certainty that home is in fact the birthplace, and that it will be workable and wonderful for everyone.

Last Minute Clients

What about mothers calling for help just weeks before their due date? In general, it means a last minute scramble to obtain the necessary information and a big push to develop a close relationship. If the woman has records of prior care, including lab work, it is not so risky. Previous care indicates that parents have at least taken basic responsibility, which is somewhat reassuring with so little time left to truly get to know them.

Without prenatal records you have no way of assessing maternal and fetal baselines. Particularly if there is some question regarding the date of conception, you have almost no point of reference except the baby's size for determining estimated date of delivery. These uncertainties place extra demands and liabilities on you. You must decide if the effort and risk can be justified.

Your decision to assist must be based on a strong feeling of rapport and an intuitive sense that parents are truly committed to home birth. If they are switching from another midwife, explore their reasons carefully to be sure they're not just chasing rainbows. Get right down to it: what do they want from you? Make a home visit as soon as possible and schedule longer clinic appointments. Remember, you must still give all your basic information about emergency situations and treatments, the mechanics of labor and birthing techniques. Some last minute clients expect a major discount; explain that providing their care will require a challenging condensation of services. Keep this in mind when negotiating your fee.

Tina, a midwife practicing in rural Hawaii, gave me this tale of a last minute situation. It also serves as an example of the way in which midwifery can overflow into personal, home and family life.

> This lady-in-waiting called me two days after her due date (I'd met her before) and I said sure, I'd find time to see her. But I made no promises, as I'm wary of "last minute goodies." She had no support, no man, not even a place to call home. She'd seen a doctor three times, but didn't feel comfortable or prepared for the hospital situation.
>
> There she was on my doorstep; I had just returned from one of my huge food shopping expeditions. So I put the groceries away, made some tea, sat down with the woman and felt out the situation. She looked pretty tense, had been having contractions all night but didn't want to go to the hospital. She didn't even know if she wanted to keep the

child. Very much alone, she felt she had other things to do with her life besides mothering. But she did have enough incentive to give the baby a good beginning with a natural birth and breast milk. She also was willing to give herself some time to feel out motherhood.

It was early afternoon, and I got the feeling that she was definitely in labor and would have her baby that night. But I didn't even know this woman, didn't even know if I liked her! All I knew was that she was confused and I wanted to help her. She *couldn't* have her baby at my place—too much traffic with five children. So I told her I'd go to the hospital to ease the doctor confrontation and serve as a support person and coach. She seemed relieved with my decision. She took a walk outside in the banana patch for about an hour and came back a different woman: resigned, courageous, strong. She began squatting for most of her now regular contractions. I suggested that she lie down and rest in the loft where it was quiet and where Adrian (my one year old) was sleeping. The older children came in from playing and we gathered around the table for dinner.

No sooner were the dishes cleared than we heard some serious "oh-oh-ohs" from the loft. I dropped everything and got ready to examine her, but she was already on her way down the ladder saying she had to go to the bathroom. She came back out to kneel on the living room floor and her water bag broke. 'Can I check you?' said I. 'No, no, no, oh, oh, oh,' said she, 'I've got to go to the bathroom again.' Then she re-

ally began complaining, she said she wasn't comfortable *at all*, couldn't see any point in all this discomfort, wanted to go to the hospital and get drugged out. She got off the toilet and leaned on the sink, but was still pushing.

Uh, oh . . . what's this? Oh god, quick, wash those hands, catch that baby, plop, flop, she's out, gorgeous! Her mother was stunned but finally uttered something, and the baby gave a cry back. Relief, release. I wrapped the babe in a towel, set another towel on the floor for them to lie on and waited for the placenta. I opened the bathroom door and there were some eager little faces to greet the baby; the children all heard that first cry. Haydon (nine and a half) announced that it happened at two minutes to eight. Chana (eight years) got a blanket for the baby. Nara (six) got my birth kit so I could clamp the cord, and also a bowl for the placenta. Then I announced bedtime but of course I wasn't heeded; the excitement was too much.

I assisted the mother with baby holding and bonding and the placenta came out fine. 'Now,' I thought, 'if I can just get them up off this floor and onto a bed in the living room to check for tears . . . hmm, well, she *was* standing and there *was* no support!' So after a good nursing session I suggested that she go to the hospital to be sutured and stay for a few days. She would rest better there and wouldn't have to think about her personal life for a while.

They came to stay with us for several weeks before finally leaving the island. We really fell in love with the baby—it was quite an experience for all of us.

Self-Care in Pregnancy

Prenatal care is not just something you receive from your practitioner every few weeks. It is what you should give yourself *every day*! Here are some of the main components of self-care, with a rating system to help you see where you stand. Enter one of the following after each catagory:

> 4: Do this automatically, naturally
> 3: Do this consistently but with definite effort
> 2: Do this occasionally, with some resistance
> 1: Just can't seem to do this, or haven't thus far

Nutrition
_____ Eat from the four basic food groups daily
_____ Take supplements that I know I need
_____ Drink at least 2 quarts of water, juice, etc. per day
_____ Pay attention to my inner voice of hunger and respond accordingly
_____ Treat myself to something I know is especially good for me and the baby
_____ Indulge myself in favorite foods (that are also healthful) for pure pleasure

Exercise
_____ Take fresh air and (if available) sunshine daily
_____ Do something to work up a sweat each day
_____ Stretch out my back, legs, shoulders and neck daily
_____ Do exercises specific to pregnancy several times a week
_____ Dance, move rhythmically and freely with music
_____ Do Kegels daily

Relaxation
_____ Completely let go at least once every day
_____ Practice progressive relaxation at least twice a week
_____ Have my partner (or someone else) massage me at least once weekly
_____ Dress in clothing that allows freedom of movement and is comfortable
_____ Deliberately release areas where I know I hold tension, several times daily
_____ Allow myself the necessary comforts to curl up and take it easy before bed

Emotional Wellbeing
_____ Let myself cry whenever I feel like it
_____ Vent my frustrations before they become explosive
_____ Feel free to be loving and tender with my partner, day-by-day
_____ Ask for support, acknowledgement, touch, sex from my partner whenever I need it
_____ Give myself time alone and find new ways to enjoy it

Intellectual Preparation
_____ Read something on pregnancy at least once a week
_____ Formulate and ask questions of my care provider

_____ Take stock of my status in pregnancy by reviewing my daily or weekly activities and looking for areas that need improvement
_____ Discuss technical aspects of pregnancy, birth and parenting with my partner on a regular basis
_____ Work on developing my birth plan by noting ideas and preferences as they arise
_____ Attend information sessions or film series on birth whenever possible

Social Preparation
_____ Meet with other pregnant women at least once a week
_____ Talk to mothers of infants or pregnant women in public places
_____ Observe infant behavior and family interaction whenever possible
_____ Ask for concrete support from friends and relatives for needs in pregnancy and postpartum
_____ Think about the changes having a baby will bring and formulate ways to adapt
_____ Support my partner in talking to other new fathers, reading about parenting, or discussing the baby with me.

There are several different ways to score this exercise. First add up your total score in each section; this will give you a general idea of areas where you are strong and those where you could use improvement. Your overall score can be viewed as follows:

110-144: yes, you are enjoying being pregnant and are taking good care of yourself.

80-109: you are doing OK, but could stand to focus a bit more on the pregnancy. Look carefully at your areas of resistance or no-go, and see what you can do to discipline or motivate yourself.

36-79: well, perhaps you are very busy with other things, but you definitely need to give your pregnant self some attention. Try combining an activity where you scored low with one where you scored high; for example, if you get outside every day but can't seem to take your vitamins, make it a prerequisite before leaving the house (like locking the door, turning off the lights, etc.).

You'll feel *much* better if you care for yourself regularly!

CHAPTER 3
Problems In Pregnancy

Problems may arise in pregnancy in either body or mind, often in both at once. But one must be wary of oversimplifying physical complications with a psychosomatic view. Some women simply have hereditary factors or physical history and it is pointless to psychoanalyze. On the other hand, even if psychological factors are clearly evident it may be that emotional disequilibrium over a period of time has caused complex changes in physical wellbeing. These may be rather difficult to unravel, and in the interim appropriate medical treatment may be necessary.

If a physical problem is not so extreme as to place the mother at risk, the midwife should suggest a remedy as holistic as possible, i.e., a combination of physical treatment and awareness practices. Safe leeway for experimentation will depend on keeping a close and continuous watch on the mother's condition. Whenever a pregnancy becomes complicated, prenatal checkups should be scheduled more often.

The following section on physical complications does not include all possible pathology of pregnancy, but only that relevant to the low-risk woman already established as a good candidate for home birth.

Physical Complications

Anemia

Anemia is a fairly common problem in pregnancy, partly due to the quality of the American diet and partly due to the physiology of pregnancy itself. Iron deficiency anemia (95%) is caused by a diet low in minerals, specifically low in iron. Oftentimes simply taking iron pills is not enough to cure anemia; many factors must be put in balance to solve the problem. For example, dairy products block the absorption of iron; vitamin C helps, but may be depleted by stress. A good general recommendation is to increase intake of fresh fruits and vegetables in combination with high quality mineral supplements.

Stress the iron-rich foods and give parents a list to take home. I highly recommend a supplement by Schiff called Org Iron, which is ferrous peptonate combined with vitamin C and B-complex, including B-12. Tablets are low dose (25 mg. each) and are therefore better assimilated than highly concentrated ferrous sulfate or ferrous gluconate products. A general rule of thumb regarding the assimilation of iron supplements is that only one-third of the dosage is absorbed, but it helps if intake spans the entire day. Otherwise the unused portion can irritate the kidneys and intestines and cause indigestion, constipation, and black stools. If the mother is a strict vegetarian she can try one of several brands of iron which contain no animal products.

For a woman with a low hematocrit in early pregnancy (32 or 33%) I recommend at least 200 mg iron daily, taken with about 500 mg vitamin C. Make sure to check the reading again in a month or so. For a woman with a very low reading I would recommend at least 300 mg iron, in combination with an iron-rich diet. Good food sources include prunes and prune juice, molasses, almonds, raisins, dark greens and of course liver, provided that it is organically grown. Keep in mind, however, that readings done around 28–32 weeks are often surprisingly low due to increased blood volume and and the temporary dilution of red blood cells, or *hemodilution*. All women should have their HCT checked around this time and should begin or increase supplements as necessary to bring the HCT to an optimal level by the time of the birth.

The problems facing an anemic mother are many. She will experience fatigue and a lack of vitality which will affect her enjoyment of the pregnancy. During the last six weeks of pregnancy the fetus stores iron for its first six months of life and if the mother's intake is inadequate, she may have to begin feeding solids before the time is really ripe. As is easy to surmise, the reduction in oxygen-carrying red blood cells can lead to difficulties in labor such as maternal exhaustion or fetal distress. And the baby of an anemic mother is often small and less vigorous in the early weeks. The greatest danger is the possibility of postpartum hemorrhage. The anemic woman will fade and become shocky much more quickly than one who has rich healthy blood and can withstand loss more readily. For all of these reasons, a woman wanting home birth should strive to maintain HCT of at least 35 throughout her pregnancy.

Sometimes a mother takes her supplements faithfully, improves her diet but still her HCT shows no elevation. Keep in mind that it takes time for the body to build red blood cells (two to three weeks at least) so allow enough time before retesting. Or, it may be that she has megaloblastic anemia (5%) which is deficiency of either folic acid or vitamin B-12. How do you determine that a woman has this problem? Take a look at her blood work and notice the figures given in MCV, MCH and MCHC categories. MCV (Mean Corpuscular Volume) indicates average size of red blood cells. MCH (Mean Corpuscular Hemoglobin) indicates the average amount of hemoglobin per cell. MCHC (Mean Corpuscular Hemoglobin Concentration) indicates amount of hemoglobin per cell relative to cell size. In regular iron deficiency anemia, the MCV is normal but MCH and MCHC are definitely on the low side. This type of anemia is also known as microcytic or small cell anemia. In B-12 anemia, MCV is usually quite high because the body is producing large (though immature) cells; MCH and MCHC are normal. This type of anemia is known as macrocytic or large cell anemia.

Seldom is anemia so severe as to register major deviation in any of the blood count readings but HGB and HCT. But, if iron alone does not solve the problem, folic acid (2 mg. daily) should be added as a precaution. And make sure the mother is getting enough B-12, because folic acid alone can mask symptoms of B-12 deficiency.

Food sources of folic acid include all dark greens like spinach, chard, kale, collard greens, etc. The darker the green, the better. Three large servings per day would barely be enough to remedy a minor deficiency during pregnancy. So advise a woman to combine food sources with a supplement. Vitamin B-12 is found almost exclusively in dairy foods and animal products and will therefore frequently be lacking in the diet of complete vegetarians unless they are taking a supplement. Besides causing anemia, lack of B-12 is associated with brain and nerve damage in newborns so it is *absolutely essential* for all vegetarian mothers to be certain of adequate intake. This is often a touchy point because most strict vegetarians dislike supplements in general and believe their diets to be perfect. They are often attached to some sort of dietary identity and are difficult to persuade. Suggest the addition of tempeh, a fermented soy product which is about the only source for strict vegetarians. Fortified nutritional yeast is also a help.

The HCT *can* rise remarkably fast on some occasions. Twice I've seen very low readings (28 and 29) rise in a matter of three weeks to 35 percent; in both cases the women were only a few weeks from their due date and were issued ultimatums. Sometimes a woman says she's made dietary changes and is taking her supplements, but is really lax. Explain the dangers carefully and be firm.

Problems With Weight Gain

Determining whether or not weight gain is excessive depends partly on pre-pregnant weight. Average weight gain is 30 to 40 pounds. Women starting out lean will often gain more, and women starting out heavy should receive counseling to evaluate dietary habits and enable them to keep their gain to a minimum. However, the mother should gain at least ten pounds by 20 weeks.

What causes weight gain in pregnancy? There is increased water retention due to hormones, fatty insulation deposited over belly and backside, increased weight in the breasts, increased blood volume and then the obvious weight of enlarged uterus with amniotic fluid, placenta and fetus. Most women will lose an average of 15 pounds at delivery or a few days thereafter; the remainder is used for sustenance during the first few months postpartum. Getting up several times nightly, making breast milk and dealing with the stress of a crying baby will definitely burn up the fat reserves!

When a woman seems to be gaining too rapidly, check first for a fetal growth spurt. It's not unusual to see a gain of five pounds in two weeks if the fundal height has jumped three or four centimeters. Or sometimes the mother gains *just before* the baby grows. You might also check the diet to see if she's made any arbitrary

Your pregnant body takes some getting used to, but once you feel the baby move it all makes sense.

changes due to something she's heard or read somewhere. If so, direct her back to her own fundamental needs. Check the diet for excess sugar, which may indicate a need for more protein. Suggest substituting vegetable snacks for high caloric fruits and juices. See what fruit she likes and find a vegetable with a corresponding vitamin and mineral content. Also recommend top quality, low-fat protein like tofu in place of low quality, high-fat protein like cream cheese. Be creative and sensitive to her response; feel her attachment to any particular food and try to work around it.

If a woman has pre-existing weight problems, it's obvious that eating is an emotionally based activity not fully in her control. She probably feels guilty about it and may have suffered criticism from family or friends. Don't dwell on the negative aspect, but make positive suggestions for increased activity. Brisk walking is a good beginning; prenatal exercise classes are ideal.

What about the normally underweight woman who doesn't seem to be able to gain much during pregnancy? These women are often hyperactive, used to running around constantly and "living on air." They need to be slowed down bit by bit, particularly if they show any nervous symptoms. Several of my slender clients ate excellent diets of fresh squeezed juices, raw vegetables and vegetable proteins like tofu and nutritional yeast, but the *quantities* were inadequate. Thin women frequently complain of feeling bloated, heavy or clogged-up if they eat more (particularly carbohydrates). But the body sets fetus as priority and will take from the mother if necessary, and herein lies the danger for the underweight mother. Will she have adequate reserves to handle her labor and take care of the baby?

Work to get her attention and make her liability clear to her. See that she has no neurotic anxiety over changing body image and is receiving lots of loving appreciation from her mate. See how sex is going and offer suggestions on comfortable positions where she can still be active. Emphasize physical changes pregnancy can bring: fuller rosier face, warm pregnant glow, etc. Suggest an extra meal at night before bed, and a good supply of snack food in her bag when she's out. And set a goal

Miscarriage (Abortion)

The proper technical term for miscarriage is **spontaneous abortion.** It refers to the loss of the fetus before 20 weeks, (after this it is called fetal demise). Far and away, the primary cause is abnormal development of the fetus or placenta due to chromosomal aberrations. Very rarely a mother may miscarry due to infection, *severe* malnutrition or an antibody effect against her partner's sperm.

Threatened abortion is presumed whenever a mother has vaginal bleeding in the first half of the pregnancy. There may also be cramping or backache. Keep in mind however that *one in four* women have bleeding in the first trimester, while only one in ten will actually abort. Usually if miscarriage is truly pending, the bleeding is *slight but continuous* for days or even weeks. **Inevitable abortion** becomes evident if membranes rupture or if the cervix is dilated.

Is it possible to forestall a threatened abortion and prevent miscarriage? There is no conclusive evidence that this is so. Certainly you should recommend that the woman be at bedrest, curtail all activity, etc. Particularly if there is cramping without bleeding, a glass of wine might halt uterine activity. But if miscarriage does ensue, console the parents with the fact that this is usually nature's way of passing an imperfect fetus before the strain on the mother becomes great.

If a woman wishes to go through her miscarriage at home, keep close surveilance as hemorrhage is possible. Two cups of blood is the maximum safe loss. Of course, home is the easiest place to handle the emotions. But if the process drags on for a number of days, the woman becomes susceptible to infection and must be careful with toileting, and should check her temperature several times daily. If bleeding or pain persist, the woman should see an obstetrician to determine whether the abortion is complete, i.e., everything has been shed.

Occasionally there may be bleeding for many weeks with no resolution. The mother may have had a **missed abortion,** wherein the fetus has died but is retained. Usually the mother notices that her breasts have returned to their normal size or that she has lost several pounds. For a time the uterus seems stationary in size, and then becomes smaller. But sometimes these changes are almost undetectable.

It is important to rule out a missed abortion as soon as it is suspected (using sonography) because there are certain coagulation defects that may arise as a result of retained products of conception. Disseminated Intravascular Coagulation (DIC) can seriously complicate an eventual termination, whether spontaneous or by D and C, although it seldom occurs before 20 weeks. But if the mother has noticed excessive bleeding of the nose, gums or sites of injury, she is at risk and may require complex medical treatment.

I've had one case of missed abortion in my practice. The mother came for her first visit at 18 weeks, reporting brown spotting for the last week or so. She did have a history of previous miscarriage, although she had also had a term baby which I assisted several years earlier. Her uterus felt normal sized for dates; I couldn't hear the baby with the fetascope but was not concerned, as this is often the case up until 20 weeks. At 20 weeks she came in again and reported what she thought was fetal movement, but had also been bothered by a continuous yellow discharge since her last visit. This time I was alarmed at not finding the fetal heart and although the uterus felt larger (2 cms more than the last visit) I sent her for a sonogram. She notified us the next day that she had had a missed abortion; it was unclear just when the fetus had died but development appeared arrested at 12 weeks. She underwent testing for DIC and was normal, but went ahead and had a therapeutic abortion because she couldn't stand the agony of waiting.

Emotional support and counseling in these situations are critical. Women often feel guilty or unsure of their abilities to carry to term in the future. Occasionally miscarriage is habitual and genetic factors may be at fault. Refer a woman or couple with this problem for consultation.

Ectopic Pregnancy

Ectopic pregnancy refers to implantation which occurs outside the uterine cavity. Ninety-five percent of the time the pregnancy implants in one of the fallopian tubes. Depending on the portion of the tube in which implantation occurs, the fetus may either be expelled into the abdominal cavity as it grows too large or may cause the tube to rupture, usually around 10-13 weeks. The latter is much more common, and is a serious, life threatening complication. If rupture occurs the mother will lose the baby and is at risk for severe internal hemorrhage, which may lead to shock or even death.

The primary cause of tubal pregnancy is pelvic inflammatory disease, which leaves behind scar tissue that may partially occlude the tube and cause reduced ciliation, or the formation of blind pockets. Ectopic pregnancies have more than doubled in recent years due to the prevalence of sexually transmitted diseases, trauma from the IUD and infection following abortion.

Symptoms of tubal rupture include extreme pain, usually on one side, and spot bleeding. A pelvic mass should be palpable on the affected side. A definite sign that the mother is suffering from tubal rupture and not miscarriage is that the degree of shock far exceeds what would normally be expected for the amount of blood loss.

If a mother in your care calls to report symptoms that lead you to suspect tubal pregnancy and/or rupture, phone your backup physician or local hospital immediately and have her call an ambulance for transport.

Hydatidiform Mole

This is an extremely rare complication of pregnancy (one in 1500-2000) which bears mentioning nonetheless. The hydatidiform mole is an abnormal growth of the chorionic villi, which ordinarily develop into membranes and placenta but in this case become a mass of clear, grape-like vesicles which completely fill the uterus. There is usually no fetus. The cause is generally fertilization by an abnormal sperm which inactivates the chromosomes of the ovum, although sometimes the ovum lacks chromosomes to begin with. It is much more common in women over 40.

Bleeding is the most outstanding symptom. It may go on for weeks or even months, although rarely past the first trimester. What distinguishes the mole from a threatened or missed abortion is that the uterus is often large for dates and feels woody hard or doughy to the touch. Fetal movements and heart tones are usually absent.

Abnormally high HCG levels are associated with hydatidiform moles, and hyperemesis occurs in 25–30% of all cases. The mole is also associated with gestational hypertension, if the pregnancy does progress to the second trimester. Since gestational hypertension rarely manifests before 24 weeks, development of hypertension early on strongly suggests hydatidiform mole. Usually the mole will spontaneously abort but sometimes must be surgically removed. About 10–20% progress to invasive cancer, so physician follow up and tests are necessary for about a year. If you suspect a molar preganancy, refer to a physician promptly.

Bleeding Late In Pregnancy

Occasionally vaginal bleeding a bit heavier than spotting occurs after intercourse in the last trimester. The cervix has increased vascularity and is often quite friable (easily abraded) which accounts for bleeding with friction. Or if the mother has a vaginal infection, the mucosa will be irritable and especially prone to bleeding during and after sex.

Another possible source of bleeding could be a ruptured cervical polyp. This is a small, tongue-like protrusion from the os, which is generally noticed when doing the initial exam or Pap smear. Bleeding from a polyp is usually sudden, then resolves quickly and spontaneously.

However, if bleeding occurs during the last trimester as either a steady flow or heavy spotting, the mother may have either placental abruption or placenta praevia.

Placental abruption refers to premature separation of the placenta. It may be caused by cord entanglement or hypertension, but often the cause is unknown. There are several types of abruption. **Marginal abruption** refers to separation at the edge of the placenta only, which will definitely cause blood to flow from the vagina. **Concealed abruption** refers to separation of the center portion of the placenta while margins remain attached, so that bleeding is concealed. **Complete abruption** refers to total separation of the placenta. These are all rare, particularly the last. And fortunately so because abruption may prove fatal for both baby and mother. If abruption occurs during labor and the woman is about to deliver, the fetus will probably survive and the mother will be fine. But if it occurs late in pregnancy or early in labor, Cesarean delivery may not be quick enough.

Symptoms of abruption are not always consistent. In cases of concealed abruption, bleeding is not evident but there is usually extreme abdominal pain. The uterus is woody hard and exceedingly tender to the touch. With marginal abruption, bright red bleeding is apparent but abdominal pain may not be noticeable, particularly in hard labor. In any case the mother should be rushed to the hospital, unless she is about to deliver. Administer oxygen and treat for shock with feet elevated, head down and body warmed with blankets.

On the other hand, repeated episodes of light bleeding or heavy spotting with no report of abdominal pain may indicate **placenta praevia** (or low lying implantation), some portion of which is being detached by the thinning and stretching of the lower uterine segment. There are varying degrees of placenta praevia: **total praevia**, in which the placenta completely covers the cervical os; **partial praevia**, in which the os is partially covered; **marginal praevia**, in which the edge of the placenta is just at the edge of the os, and; **low-lying placenta**, in which the placenta is in close proximity to the os but does not actually reach it. Prospects for vaginal birth depend on the location of the placenta at the onset of labor. If the placenta is low-lying only, vaginal delivery is probably possible but there is increased risk of maternal hemorrhage as the lower uterine segment does not contract very well.

Occasionally placenta praevia will manifest as early as 24 weeks. In this case the placenta will probably *migrate* upwards as the lower uterine segment develops late in pregnancy. I once had a case like this in my practice; I couldn't believe it was a praevia because bleeding occurred so early. The mother was put at bedrest for a number of weeks until a sonogram showed that the placenta was out of the way, and she had a perfectly normal vaginal delivery.

Diagnosis of placenta praevia must *always* be done by sonogram. To quote *Williams Obstetrics*, ". . . examination of the cervix is never permissible unless the woman is in the operating room with all the preparations for immediate Cesarean section, since even the gentlest examination of this sort can cause torrential hemorrhage." Enough said.

Gestational Diabetes

Gestational diabetes complicates approximately 5% of all pregnancies. Family history is absent in 40% of these cases, and sometimes no glucose is detectable in the urine either. For this reason glucose screening has become routine in recent years. Whether this is medically necessary or is simply malpractice protection remains to be seen. If a woman has obvious predisposing factors she should probably be tested. These include familial history, unexplained fetal death or stillbirth, obesity, recurrent candida (yeast), polyhydramnios, glucose in the urine, age over 35 years, large baby in utero or previous delivery of large baby.

Of all the effects of diabetes on pregnancy, a baby large for gestational age is probably the most obvious. Because glucose rapidly crosses the placental barrier, even mild degrees of elevated maternal blood sugar cause a critical rise in the baby. The fetal pancreas reacts by greatly increasing production of insulin, which leads to an increase in growth. The baby of a diabetic mother is therefore at risk during delivery due to its size, and may also develop respiratory distress or severe problems with hypoglycemia (low blood sugar) or hypocalcemia (low calcium levels) after the birth.

Negative effects of diabetes on the mother include a four times greater chance of developing pre-eclampsia, ten times greater incidence of polyhydramnios, and a high risk of postpartum hemorrhage.

There are several tests that are commonly used to screen for gestational diabetes. The most common is the *glucose screen:* a baseline blood sugar is taken, the mother ingests 50 mg "glucola and her blood is drawn again one hour later. If her blood sugar level is over 140 mg/dl, she is usually referred for a *glucose tolerance test* (GTT). After fasting the night before and up until test time, her blood is drawn to establish a baseline sugar level, then she ingests 100 mg glucose. In a three-hour GTT (the most common type), levels are taken at one, two and three hours. During this time the mother must not eat or smoke. If two of the following levels are met or exceeded, a diagnosis is made:

HEART & HANDS

1) fasting, above 95 mg/dl; 2) one hour, above 180 mg/dl; 3) two hours, above 160 mg/dl; 4) three hours, above 135 mg/dl.

There is another test called a *two hour post prandial*, which requires only one blood sampling taken two hours after a meal has been eaten. Normal levels are 120–140 mg/dl, but may range a bit higher.

If the mother does have gestational diabetes she will have to follow a special diet, very high in protein (125 grams daily) and obviously low in sugar. Non-stress testing usually begins at 36 weeks, and glucose testing is done weekly.

Hypertension

Hypertension, or high blood pressure, manifests in several ways. **Essential hypertension** is a pre-existing condition indicated by consistent readings of at least 130/90. **Gestational hypertension** develops during the pregnancy, generally as a steady rise in blood pressure after the 28th week. These two types can be confused if a woman has high blood pressure at her initial visit and she is already in her last trimester. In that case you must obtain some records of previous care, either from the pregnancy or before. Home birth is contraindicated for the woman with essential hypertension.

There are two assessments made when taking blood pressure: the *systolic reading* (higher number) indicates the pressure in the arteries when the heart is actively pumping and the *diastolic reading* (lower number) assesses the pressure when the heart is at rest. In a general sense diastolic pressure is a measurement of baseline physical tension, whereas systolic pressure indicates how well the system tolerates exertion. High blood pressure may cause a minor degree of intrauterine growth retardation, as vaso-constriction affects the flow of oxygen and nutrients to the baby. For the same reason, high blood pressure may cause fetal distress in labor.

What is the upper limit for normal blood pressure? The general rule is 140/90 but depends on the mother's normal pressure. A rise of 30 points above her baseline systolic pressure is considered diagnostic, as is a rise of 15 points in the diastolic reading. But be sure to use the average first trimester pressure when applying this rule; second trimester readings

may be considerably lower than usual due to vascular relaxation. Nevertheless, in my experience most women maintain their lower readings throughout pregnancy and right into labor. For this reason, I think that any woman who shows a *consistent rise* in blood pressure should be treated for gestational hypertension. Here are some suggestions:

1. *Exercise* is critical with moderate elevation, or whenever the pressure is just starting to rise. Exercise increases circulation and forces the vessels to dilate and stretch, which reduces the pressure inside them. The best exercise is one involving some exertion such as brisk walking, swimming or easy jogging. It's best to have the mother start out slowly but depends on what she is used to. (One of my colleagues advises all her clients to work up a sweat every day.) On the other hand, if blood pressure reaches a critical level (140/90), bed rest is necessary because the body is already so stressed that additional exertion does more harm than good. You've got to nip high BP in the bud.

2. *Deep relaxation* goes hand in hand with exercise. Some women live in a state of chronic tension and have little experience of complete release. Relaxation practice will help relieve tension in voluntary muscles, which will subsequently reduce tension in the involuntary system. A calm state of being also creates greater emotional stability, which helps prevent extreme reactions to difficult situations.

3. *No stimulants* whatsoever. These include coffee, chocolate, nicotine and cocaine. The last two in particular have been proven to cause vasoconstriction and low birth weight.

4. *Good diet and healing herbs* help immensely when used along with everything else. If a woman eats improperly and gains excessive weight she puts additional burden on her system. Adequate protein intake (at least 80 grams daily) is necessary, along with plenty of mineral-rich fresh fruits and vegeta-

bles. Contrary to popular opinion, salt is a necessary nutrient and should be used according to taste. (See Gail and Tom Brewer's excellent book, *What Every Pregnant Woman Should Know*).

Herbs like hops, skullcap and chamomile (listed in order of potency) should be used to induce relaxation; these are perfect for the mother with elevated systolic pressure who needs most to *calm down*. Increased fluids and high calcium intake are critical! And Chinese herbs and acupuncture are also helpful.

5. *Counseling* may be the first step if you're working with a woman who is so tense and distracted that she can hardly be responsible for herself. Getting at the roots of anxiety can release a lot of tension and help a woman enjoy her pregnancy. With a good attitude, the other aspects of working on her blood pressure won't seem so difficult or overwhelming.

I've had two experiences with gestational hypertension that bear repeating. The first mother made immediate changes in her diet and began exercising every day. Relaxation was difficult for her as she had a very active social schedule which couldn't be altered. But she tried to moderate her activities with a more relaxed attitude and meditation breaks. Her BP was down from 150/80 to 120/70 in just two weeks. Pride in her accomplishment motivated her to continue to care for herself. Toward the end of pregnancy her BP was up again to 136/80; she was experiencing much emotional tension and so began using relaxant herbs daily, and by the next visit her BP was down to baseline. During labor it was steady at 120/70.

The other mother developed hypertension at about 30 weeks, with blood pressure of 130/86. She was given suggestions concerning relaxation, exercise and diet but was decidedly indifferent. Her diet was not the best; she ate a lot of meat and refined foods and was about 35 pounds overweight when pregnancy began. At her next visit her blood pressure was 140/90 and when further attempts were made to help her, she became angry and defiant. By the next visit BP had risen to 140/100, at which point we rec-

ommended hospital birth and prepared to refer her. At this she began to cry and then expressed some strong feelings to her mate about his working too much and neglecting her. They went home seriously resolved to take our suggestions. When we saw her two days later her blood pressure was still 140/90 and unfortunately remained high for the next few exams, so we decided on hospital birth after all. She had her mag-sulfate IV (standard treatment) and delivered quickly without further complications.

Occasionally you will have a client who manifests a sudden rise in blood pressure just two or three weeks before term, with no other clinical problems. This is a message that her body has reached its maximum ability to tolerate increased circulatory demands, and she should give birth as soon as possible. If she is sure of her dates and her cervix is ripe, the baby appears to be term (by estimated size and recent growth pattern) and the head is engaged, suggest castor-oil induction. As soon as contractions begin you should attend her, checking frequently to be sure that BP is stable. It is also important to listen to the baby frequently to be certain that high blood pressure is not causing hypoxia.

Sometimes women who have been troubled with borderline hypertension show a drop in their readings during labor, a sign that the problem was not really pathological. And it is not uncommon for otherwise normal pressure to jump as high as 140/90 with the most strenuous transition contractions. But a *steady rise* during labor may herald pre-eclampsia and should not be allowed to continue at home (see Chapter 5 for more details).

Pre-Eclampsia

One of the main purposes of thorough, consistent prenatal care is to screen for pre-eclampsia. The exact cause of the disease is not known, but it is a dangerous metabolic derangement that poses a threat to the lives of both mother and baby. Signs include edema (generalized swelling), sudden and excessive weight gain, hypertension, protein in the urine and hyperreflexia.

It is probable that pre-eclampsia is the direct result of protein deficiency. Inadequate protein levels in the blood cause fluid to leak from the cells into the intercellular space; this results in generalized edema. Another effect is reduced blood flow to the kidneys, which triggers a rise in blood pressure in order to compensate. There is also reduced blood flow to the uterus, which accounts for fetal growth retardation in pregnancy and fetal distress in labor.

Nutritional guidelines for preventing pre-eclampsia include at least 80 grams of protein daily, combined with adequate carbohydrate intake and plenty of fresh fruits and vegetables. Borderline diets must *always* be followed up. Pre-eclampsia is established when blood pressure reaches 140/90 and an additional sign (see list in opening paragraph) is present. *Two signs are diagnostic.* A woman in this condition should be put to bed, resting herself on her left side as much as possible while the backup physician is contacted.

Check for edema first by observing the mother's hands and face. Swelling in the face causes the features to look coarse; the hands and fingers are puffy and inflexible and all rings are usually removed. Ankle edema is not particularly significant, but edema on the shins or breastbone is a definite sign. Check for **pitting edema** by pressing a fingertip into the skin, then seeing whether or not a depression remains. Pitting becomes significant when the depression is greater than 4mm. deep. The rating system is as follows: 2mm., +1; 4mm., +2; 6mm., +3; 8mm., +4.

Check for **hyperreflexia** by checking for *clonus.* Have the mother in a sitting position with knees bent; support or hold her calf with one hand while dorsiflexing the foot (bending toes upward towards knee). Maintain this hold for a moment, then release. Ordinarily the foot will fall back to its natural position with no extraneous movement; if you notice jerking while it is dorsiflexed or oscillations as it falls, the test is positive. (It is wise to check these reflexes at the initial visit to establish a baseline.)

When checking for **proteinuria,** keep in mind that vaginal discharge may wash down and affect your finding, so instruct the mother to get a *clean catch.* This is done by washing the area with a wet paper towel first, then parting the labia and allowing a bit of urine to flow before collecting the sample. Anything over a trace is significant.

Once a mother is diagnosed to have pre-eclampsia, her backup physician may assume her care or may want you to co-manage. She should be seen twice weekly, and should be advised to report any of the following danger signs that might indicate that her condition has worsened: 1) severe headache; 2) epigastric pain (pain in upper abdomen); 3) visual disturbances; 4) decreased output of urine or; 5) extreme nervous irritability.

One of my clients became pre-eclamptic at 37 weeks. I knew it as soon as she walked into my office; her face had that coarse look you so often read about. We had made a home visit early in the pregnancy at which time her diet was clearly excellent, but just last week had gone to the house again and had been served a vegetable dinner with absolutely no protein at all. I was concerned and intended to bring it up at this visit, but was obviously too late.

The remarkable thing in this case was the mother's blood pressure. It never went higher than 120/76, but was technically hypertensive as her first trimester baseline was only 98/56. We referred her immediately to Kaiser, her backup hospital, and alternated visits with them so she was seen twice weekly. Her condition remained borderline; sometimes facial edema and sometimes not, but her blood pressure remained elevated. She took bedrest as much as possible, and as soon as labor was established we transported.

What are the dangers of pre-eclampsia? Placental insufficiency and growth retardation may result from hypertension. There is also a higher incidence of premature separation of the placenta (about 8%) which can cause fetal death and may also jeopardize the mother by causing severe hemorrhage. If her condition progresses to *true eclampsia,* convulsions and coma occur in labor which may take both the baby's and the mother's life. A grim picture, but not without hope if changes are made early enough and if the woman and her midwife follow through responsibly.

Polyhydramnios

This is a term referring to excess amniotic fluid. It often occurs in conjunction with multiple pregnancy, toxemia or diabetes. It is also associated with fetal anomalies, particularly with atresia of the esophagus, anencephaly or spina bifida.

Polyhydramnios may occur suddenly and acutely, but this is rare. It is more common to notice a slight elevation in fundal height around 28 weeks with a steady increase in the weeks that follow. You will also note some difficulty in palpating the baby at a time when it should be snugly filling the uterus. Sometimes it is possible to confuse a thick uterine wall with excess fluid; in both cases heart tones will be difficult to hear and the baby confusing to feel. But polyhydramnios can be distinguished by a jelly-like, vibrational quality when palpating, in contrast to the solid feeling of uterine muscle.

A woman with noticeable polyhydramnios should be seen again in several days regardless of gestation. If you find an additional increase in fluid, she should have a sonogram to determine the cause. She may have twins, and that's something you should know about as soon as possible. Once polyhydramnios develops, hospital birth will probably be necessary. Polyhydramnios predisposes the woman to several serious complications of labor such as placental abruption, uterine dysfunction and postpartum hemorrhage, all due to overdistension of the uterus. Fetal malpresentations and cord prolapse are also common.

One woman I assisted who developed polyhydramnios did so before I had any idea she was carrying twins. The extra fluid really alarmed me; at 25 weeks her fundal height was 29 centimeters, a rise of six from her previous visit just three weeks earlier. She also had gained eight pounds in that time span. When I saw her again just five days later, her fundal height had increased three centimeters and she had gained three more pounds! She was very difficult to palpate. I had no intuition she had twins but did mention the possibility. Sure enough, the sonogram showed two babies plus the extra fluid, an amount which was considered normal for twins. Two weeks later she went into premature labor and no wonder, with a fundal height of 39 centimeters at only 28.5 weeks! Still many woman carrying twins show absolutely no excess fluid. It seems that good nutrition and good health enable the body to handle the stress of twin pregnancy more easily.

If you are co-managing the care of a woman with polyhydramnios, check her cervix weekly to see if there are any changes which might portend early labor.

Diagnosing Twins

A fundal measurement above gestational age should immediately lead you to check for twins. Begin by ruling out other possible causes of your large for gestational age finding, such as maternal diabetes, polyhydramnios, miscalculated dates or hereditary predisposition for large babies. Once done, consider your clinical findings. Have you noticed abundant small parts when palpating? Or a rather small head relative to fundal height? Sometimes twins may be missed if one is tucked behind the other's body.

Generally twins are discovered at around 30 weeks, with clinical confirmation through the auscultation of two heartbeats. But sometimes "two heartbeats" may only be one audible over a wide range, with an arm or side obscuring transmission in the mid-section. It is easier to be sure if the two sound distinctive, with a 10–15 point difference between them. Listen first

Twice the work, but twice the joy and fulfillment.

to each heart separately to determine quality and variability, then make your comparison. To confirm your diagnosis or at least ease your mind, a sonogram will tell you what you want to know.

It is imperative to pick up twins as early as possible because twin pregnancies carry extra risks and problems for mother and baby. Anemia is much more common, as is the incidence of premature delivery. Women with twins will need expert nutritional counseling and recommendations for moderating activity, as well as directions for recognizing and reporting any signs of premature labor.

In the area where I practice, delivery of twins at home is out of the question. However, I have diagnosed twins a number of times and have continued to give prenatal care, later attending the births in the hospital as patient advocate and coach. A midwife can provide special aid to women with twin pregnancy by focusing on the emotional and practical aspects of caring for two. And if she can help the woman maintain the pregnancy to at least 37 weeks, hospital management will be fairly relaxed, with early discharge.

The reasons for hospital birth are numerous. The most threatening complication is cord prolapse. This is more likely to occur if the first baby is breech. In fact, most physicians will do an automatic Cesarean if the breech is footling or kneeling. Cord prolapse is an even greater risk for the second baby, which is often high in the uterus after the first has been born. The second baby may also become hypoxic as reduced uterine volume causes reduction of the placental site and constriction of vital vessels. There is also an increased incidence of premature separation of the placenta for the same reason. Last but not least is the considerable risk of postpartum hemorrhage from an overdistended and tired uterus.

Only once did I seriously consider doing a twin birth at home. This woman was in excellent health, sensitive and cooperative, and both her babies were presenting vertex (head down). We all discussed and considered it carefully. My hesitation was mostly political; if transport became necessary I could lose my backup. The mother also had some doubts concerning her safety. Had this couple been really insistent, I might have assisted them.

You must be certain that parents are well aware of what to expect from the hospital experience. If the birth is to be vaginal, X-ray is standard to assess fetal position as is double fetal monitoring and IV (with pitocin added after the first baby is born). There are often many attendants besides obstetrician: residents, interns, student nurses and the neonatal team. Emphasize the emotional aspects of the experience and the support you will be there to give.

Breech Presentation and Transverse Lie

Because of my backup situation and the political climate in my area, I do not deliver breeches at home. If I had a choice I might do so after careful screening, and very selectively. There are two major concerns that must be addressed in order to determine risk status; these are cephalo-pelvic relationship and fetal position. The greatest danger in breech delivery is that the head will prove too large for the pelvis and will get stuck behind the brim, which can rapidly lead to death of the baby. Also serious is the risk of cord prolapse, particularly if the presentation does not fill the pelvis evenly or completely. If for example the breech presents with a foot dangling down or two little knees coming first, there is nothing to prevent the cord from slipping past.

Who would be a candidate for breech birth at home? A woman with a *large gynecoid pelvis,* having a *small to medium sized baby.* Particularly if she's had a baby already and her pelvis has been proven, the risks diminish. But the baby must be either *frank breech* (legs extended upwards over chest) or *complete breech* (legs up and crossed). And the *head should be well flexed* so that it can negotiate the pelvis readily. In order to make certain of all these factors, a combination of ultrasound and X-ray must be used. And even so, there are complications that can arise which require special expertise, for example, an arm impacted behind the head must be skillfully manipulated to effect delivery. These maneuvers are beyond the scope of this book; suffice to say, it is not advisable to attend a breech birth without someone already experienced in basic techniques.

Often before presenting breech the baby assumes a transverse position. Transverse lie is not unusual to about 26 weeks, but if the baby is also high in the uterus it's wise to listen carefully around the lower portion of the abdomen for placental sounds. These are swishing, wooshing sounds of blood coursing through the placental circulation, at the same rate as the mother's pulse. The purpose for this is to rule out placental praevia, an implantation over or near the cervical os which would prevent the baby from engaging either breech or vertex. Should the baby remain transverse past 30 weeks, a sonogram is in order to locate the placenta precisely.

Sometimes (although rarely) breeches rotate to vertex at the last minute, either during the last week of pregnancy or right before labor. However, I think it is best to have the woman try **postural tilting** for turning the baby if it remains breech beyond 30 weeks. Postural tilting simply means elevating the hips twelve inches (using pillows) for 20 minutes, three times a day. Ask the mother to do deep relaxation while tilting, and visualize the baby turning. If she feels major movement, have her come in to be checked.

If the baby has not rotated after several weeks and is beginning to feel rather snugly encased, another option is to try a version. This is a tricky maneuver for all but the most experienced midwife, as it requires great expertise in fetal palpation and a highly refined sense of touch. There is also some risk of cord entanglement or compression and for that reason the fetal heart must be *monitored continuously* by another experienced practitioner.

Have the mother drink a beer or glass of wine to promote uterine relaxation, and make sure her bladder is empty before you begin. Position her in a tilt and then *gently* attempt to massage the baby into position. Be sure to keep the head flexed and to rotate the baby in the direction it is facing. If *any* resistance is felt or changes in the fetal heart are noted, the movement should be stopped and the baby returned to its original position. Because of the risks involved in this procedure, it must only be performed with the informed consent of the parents.

Some mothers report massaging their babies gently into the vertex position by themselves; others mention talking with the baby or meditating on making the change. But if the baby has not rotated by 35 weeks, you might ask your backup physician to give version a try.

Since most use terbutaline or some other medication to completely relax the uterus, they are able to use a more forceful technique than the midwife.

If all attempts at version fail, prepare the mother for hospital birth, or possible Cesarean if the breech is footling or kneeling. (Also see section on Surprise Breech in Chapter 5.)

Prematurity

Most authorities consider the fetus premature if under 38 weeks gestation, although this limit is somewhat arbitrary. The chief concern for the premature baby is that the lungs may not be fully developed, which can lead to respiratory distress syndrome (RDS). But in the vast majority of cases the lungs are fully mature at 34 weeks. The discrepancy probably allows for a margin of error in calculating the due date; nevertheless, most midwives feel comfortable assisting home delivery as early as 36 1/2 or 37 weeks so long as the mother is absolutely certain of her dates, and clinical findings have been consistent with the dates all along.

The causes of preterm labor are as follows: spontaneous rupture of the membranes (which may be due to infection); cervical incompetency; polyhydramnios; multiple gestation; uterine abnormalities; faulty implantation of the placenta or *serious* maternal illness (urinary tract infections are sometimes implicated). Premature labor is also a possibility whenever the mother is large for dates. Particularly if she has a history of miscarriage or previous premature birth, follow her carefully by doing a *gentle* cervical exam at every visit after 24 weeks. If you discover softening or effacement, make sure the mother knows how to distinguish contractions from fetal movement and see her weekly thereafter. If you discover dilation of the cervix, she should be referred to a backup physician.

If contractions begin, the mother should be immediately at bedrest. Medications commonly used for stopping labor are ritodrine, terbutaline and fenoterol; these generally do the job but cause the mother nervous irritability and nausea. If the cervix is not drastically changed and contractions have just begun, you might have the mother take a couple of stiff drinks. Alcohol relaxes uterine muscle and inhibits the action of oxytocin.

One of my clients began premature labor at

35 weeks, her cervix was quite effaced and about 2 cms dilated (but this was her second baby). She took two shots of vodka in grapefruit juice, stayed in bed and was fine until the following morning, when upon arising contractions began again. So she repeated the same routine. This went on for five days, during which time I checked her daily and in spite of clearly palpable uterine activity, found her cervix to be stable. Contractions then stopped completely, she carried her baby to 41 weeks and delivered at home with severe shoulder dystocia, partial separation of the placenta necessitating manual removal and postpartum hemorrhage. An interesting trade-off of complications!

Another of my clients had a fundal height of 38 at 30 weeks, with twins and slight polyhydramnios. She began premature labor and was given ritodrine, but it failed to totally stop con-

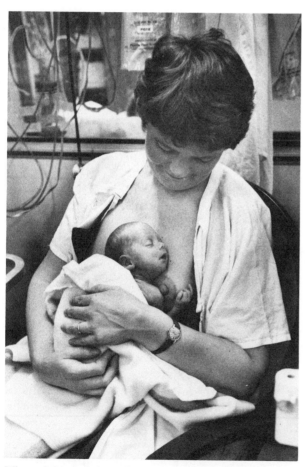

When a baby needs intensive care, the family must be creative, as well as assertive in finding ways to stay close to the baby.

tractions. She was however a student of yoga, and found that postural tilting several times daily would definitely stop uterine activity, probably by taking pressure off the cervix. The obstetrician at the hospital where she was being checked called in the nurses to observe her positioning. She carried her babies all the way to term.

Small for Gestational Age (SGA)

With regard to uterine size, causes of SGA include miscalculated dates, the fetus transverse or low lying, hereditary predisposition to small babies, and intrauterine growth retardation (IUGR). The first three are fairly easy to rule out but the last is a complication of pregnancy which requires special attention.

IUGR is suspected when fundal height has been normal up to 24 weeks gestation but then begins to fall behind a normal growth curve. Although babies do not always grow steadily (more often in spurts) the *overall* growth should average about one centimeter per week.

The causes of IUGR are numerous. Inadequate nutrition, anemia, chronic hypertension, smoking, hard drugs, alcoholism, fetal infections or malformations, prolonged pregnancy and abnormalities of the placenta and cord are all implicated.

Here is an interesting case history. This mother came to us at 27 weeks with a fundal height of 22 cms, fairly certain of her dates but carrying a very small baby for gestation. Her diet was poor and she smoked half a pack of cigarettes daily, but she made a commitment to improve. Her baby then began growth-spurting in subsequent weeks and grew steadily thereafter. (Total weight gain was about 20 pounds.) At 31 weeks she had a sonogram, with a repeat at 35 weeks to check for normal growth. Growth was adequate, but fetal size was so small that her due date was pushed back a month. This seemed odd and rather arbitrary, considering her menstrual history (regular menses, no bleeding after LMP) but if "sonogram says," we'd best believe it!

She went into labor at 38 weeks by original dates, but only 34 weeks by sonogram revision. Her cervix had been 60% effaced at her last prenatal, and labor commenced with ruptured membranes. What to do? Was the baby premature or simply on the small side? We palpated a four and a half to five pound baby and so decided on hospital birth, which was a real disappointment to the parents who had never believed in the revised date anyway.

After six hours of labor, she delivered a healthy, vigorous baby girl weighing five pounds, about 38 weeks by gestational age assessment. There was no evidence of prematurity, lungs were fine. The sonogram was obviously incorrect. There was some indication of fetal compromise in that the placenta was spongy, shredding and full of calcifications. But the baby was not at all wizened or emaciated and was really in top condition (9/10 Apgar scores).

Could this birth have taken place at home? It's really tough to decide when the baby is small and you can't be sure it isn't early. Premature babies face some *serious* risks. But with IUGR, the primary concerns are hypothermia (difficulty in maintaining body temperature) and hypoglycemia (low blood sugar) due to insufficient fat reserves. These are not immediately life threatening and can be dealt with at home, but the baby should be seen by a pediatrician within the first few hours.

If you are preparing to assist the birth of a small baby which you believe to be term, have oven-warmed blankets and an aluminum outer wrapper (space blanket) ready as insulation. Place the baby skin-to-skin with the mother, with blankets over all. It is crucial to keep the head covered at all times; use a stockinette cap so that the mother will not have to fuss with blankets and can maintain eye contact with the baby. Take the axillary temperature for several minutes at least once an hour until you are certain the baby has stabilized.

Check the baby's blood sugar level by doing a dextrostix (heel prick with test strip). If the level is below 45, contact a pediatrician. Otherwise, give sterile water and molasses (you can also use corn syrup), one teaspoon per cup. Repeat the dextrostix every two hours, so that you can evaluate whether the oral feeds are raising the blood sugar level. Be sure to chart each time fluid is given, how much, and how the baby tolerated it. If the baby vomits, intravenous feeding may be necessary.

This baby is also at risk for polycythemia (high hematocrit) which predisposes to severe jaundice. If the baby looks ruddy at birth, refer immediately to a pediatrician. Postpartum visits should occur daily for the first four days.

Large for Gestational Age (LGA)

Causes of LGA have already been discussed in other sections of this chapter. These include miscalculated dates, gestational diabetes, polyhydramnios and fetal anomaly, twins, hereditary predisposition for big babies, baby high in fundus due to placenta praevia or abdominal muscle tone, fibroids (internal or external) displacing the baby upwards or positioned atop the fundus, and postmaturity. Whenever the mother measures large for dates, each of these possibilities must be considered and ruled out. I recall a woman who came to me at 28 weeks with fundal height of 32 centimeters, wide abdominal girth (but not overweight) and plus-four (heavy) glucose in her urine. On palpating her I felt a good-sized head entering the pelvis, butt in the fundus and small parts all over (posterior position, I assumed). I sent her in for a Glucose Tolerance Test (the only screening for gestational diabetes at that time) and it was negative. Next week there was no glucose in her urine at all and two heartbeats were audible; a sonogram soon confirmed that she had twins!

The big baby is of particular concern as it may prove too large for the mother's pelvis and necessitate Cesarean birth. The only way to determine that the baby itself is causing increased fundal height is by careful palpation. How will a midwife know if a baby is growing too large for the mother, and what can be done about it?

One simple way of determining adequacy of the pelvic inlet is by checking for engagement. You must assess not only the station of the head but also how well if fills up or fits into the pelvis. If the baby is still high, check for ability to engage by grasping the head externally and pressing it back against the spine and down into the pelvis. If the head feels movable and inclined to slip in, things are fine so far.

I've had only one obvious case of cephalopelvic disproportion (CPD) in my practice. The mother was having her first baby, was certain of her dates and the baby had felt large all along. She had a small gynecoid pelvis, and was about 5'3" tall with 6' mate. At 37 weeks I remember feeling alarmed at the size of the baby's head and the way it seemed to be overriding her pubic bone and bulging out into my hand when I palpated. Upon discovering this condition of overlap, I told her to go ahead and have her baby anytime she was ready. Her cervix was ripe; 50% effaced. She finally commenced labor at 40 weeks, dilated completely but then pushed for two hours without ever engaging the head, and had to be delivered by Cesarean. Her dates proved correct as the baby showed no evidence of postmaturity. He simply grew too large for her pelvic dimensions.

If a similar situation arose again wherein we were certain of dates and the mother's cervix was ripe, I might suggest castor-oil induction as early as 37 weeks. Have the mother take two tablespoons initially with orange juice, followed by one more tablespoon in half an hour and the final tablespoon an hour later. It helps if the mother relaxes with a bath. I've used this formula (minus the bath) for cases of prolonged ruptured membranes where time is of the essence, and have had almost certain success with it. It is definitely worth a try.

There are certain risks which attend labor whenever the baby is exceptionally large. The overdistended uterus may not contract efficiently, which can cause prolonged labor, arrested progress or postpartum hemorrhage. There may also be some degree of shoulder dystocia. Be prepared!

Postmaturity

Fetal postmaturity becomes a concern when pregnancy progresses to 42 weeks, assuming the dates are correct. Sometimes there is hereditary predisposition (the woman's mother was always three weeks late, for example) but frequently there is no obvious physical reason. So what makes a mother "hold onto her baby"? This midwife's phrase suggests some of the possible psychological implications of postmaturity. Perhaps it's the last pregnancy the mother is planning and she's hesitant to let go. Or if it's a first baby, the mother may be frightened of the responsibilities of parenting. She may be hesitant to give up the special attention she's enjoyed during the pregnancy. Sometimes both parents are uncertain about chang-

ing roles and their vacillation will prolong the pregnancy. Or if a woman has felt obligated or otherwise compelled to work right up to her due date, she may be taking time to enjoy her experience at the last minute. When exploring these themes, it's important that the mother not feel accused or judged at this rather delicate time. Present your perceptions as suggestions rather than criticisms. Be sensitive in response to questions without overwhelming her with frightening information. Such a difficult time, those post-due weeks of waiting.

The risks of postmaturity are twofold. If all is well in utero and the fetus continues to grow, cephalo-pelvic disproportion may become a problem. Or if the placenta (considered to be a timed organ) ceases to function properly, the fetus may suffer deprivation as reduced placental circulation leads to weight loss, fetal distress or even stillbirth. To differentiate these two situations, *Williams Obstetrics* suggests using *postterm* for the baby who is late but otherwise healthy and *dysmature* for the baby clearly undernourished as a result of placental insufficiency.

Certain tests are recommended to check the integrity of the fetal-placental unit. Have the mother **count fetal movements** daily after meals, for about an hour and note about eight movements. Although critical for post-date pregnancies, all women should begin counting movements at 34 weeks and continue for the rest of their pregnancy. **Non-stress testing** can be performed in the hospital by external monitor, or the midwife can simply listen with a fetascope and have the mother report movements. The desired response is moderate acceleration of the fetal heart. But testing has lost popularity; research has shown no definite correlation between test results and fetal outcome. The **contraction stress test** is similar; it charts fetal response to uterine activity.

Recently it has been demonstrated that the most common cause of fetal distress in post-due labor is *reduced amniotic fluid* (oligohydramnios) with resulting cord compression, rather than placental insufficiency as was previously thought. For this reason, sonograms are recommended as early as 41 weeks to establish the baseline amount of fluid and are repeated weekly until delivery. You can also check for a diminished quantity of fluid by careful palpation. Depending on your findings you might consider castor-oil induction, particularly if the cervix is ripe and the head down in the pelvis.

Castor-oil induction is also appropriate if you feel the baby is getting a bit large for the mother's dimensions. The post-due baby's passage through the pelvis may be made more difficult by the ossification of the skull sutures, which renders the head less moldable in labor. Check carefully for overlap (see section on LGA) and beware of the previously engaged head rising up in the pelvis.

The most stressful time in labor for the dysmature fetus is probably at the onset. Uterine contractions are far more stressful than Braxton-Hicks, so fetal compromise will show up fairly immediately. Plan to attend the post-due labor from the very beginning, and take heart tones more frequently than usual.

Psychological Concerns

Begin by reading the section in Chapter 2 which introduces basic counseling techniques. And keep in mind that most emotional problems in pregnancy are primarily a result of hormonal changes. Vague complaints without focus, forgotton by the following visit, are typically hormone-induced. Nevertheless it's wise to ask the woman for a bit of background, particularly if complaints are repeated. You may uncover problems in her relationship, environment or health that were unknown to you before.

Occasionally you'll have a client who becomes increasingly unbalanced or extreme as pregnancy progresses. And as most midwives know from experience, the women who do best with birthing are those with their physical, emotional and mental aspects in harmony. Over the years I've come to believe that the main function of the midwife in promoting wellbeing is to identify any aspect of her client that is weak or undeveloped and then look for ways to stimulate growth in that area. The woman thus encouraged to work on herself during pregnancy will generally have a better birth experience and will be a better parent.

For example, a woman with an extremely physical nature may become quite anxious over certain changes in the first trimester. If she is used to competitve sports or marathon running, she will probably find the fatigue, nausea and softening of her body to be extremely annoying, even frightening. If she is not counseled otherwise she might push past body signals for rest and threaten miscarriage, or later in pregnancy, premature delivery.

I had one such client, a black belt in karate and marathon runner who broke down and cried, saying, "My body just doesn't *work* anymore!" I explained that pregnancy is a transitional state, that tremendous energy is available for the growth process but that it cannot be forced. I recommended reading to help her understand the overview of physiologic change in pregnancy. During labor she had a tough time surrendering to dilation but *loved* pushing, which was to be expected.

The more emotionally based woman will generally enjoy the early changes in pregnancy, particularly her heightened feelings (although she may drive her partner a little crazy). But she may forget to eat, may not exercise much and may need to follow a *schedule* in order to maintain her health. Reading for solid information must be encouraged. This type of woman usually dilates easily (after a rather dramatic prodromal) but often dislikes pushing. She prefers to sustain her experience, rather than bring to completion. Help her prepare for 2nd stage by assigning squatting practice, perineal massage and activities that require her to *exert* energy, lap swimming for example.

The mentally oriented woman often chooses alternative birth because it seems like the intelligent thing to do. She has probably read *everything* on the subject, and appears to be utterly well informed. Although she will generally practice what she has read regarding diet and exercise, she may tend to repress her emotions. Ask this client how she feels and she'll probably give you a simple "fine," in contrast to the emotional type who will talk for twenty minutes on every nuance of her emotional state. It may be very difficult to go any further before labor, although massage is one way to trigger emotional release. I had one such client whose mother was planning on flying out for the birth; she arrived a few days before the due date. Days and then weeks went by, and my client insisted everything between them was "fine." Well, the day after her mother left she went into labor. And she labored beautifully and with total control; in fact, she didn't want to be touched or assisted by anyone (including her husband). Caring for the baby was her biggest challenge; she kept trying to get him on a schedule!

Of course, most women are not as extreme as the above examples. Most are a blend of the two types primarily, with the other underdeveloped or a bit neglected. If you can help a woman identify the latter and find a way to activate that part of herself, she will experience a tremendous surge of power and excitement which will carry over into the birth.

There are also particular life situations that predispose certain women to difficulties during pregnancy. The following sections explore these situations in depth.

Single Mothers

It has become increasingly common for women to choose to parent alone. Some women speak of having mating recognition with their partner in conception, and yet know that this is it for the time being. This perspective is very different from that of the woman who has become pregnant accidentally by someone she barely knows, and yet has decided to keep the baby. And the woman who is estranged from her mate but is still attached to him emotionally has yet another psychological set.

No matter what their circumstances, most single mothers feel vulnerable because they have no intrinsic support person. Most fear the exposure and impersonality of the hospital experience, with no one to protect them. They need close personal attention to help them through labor, and through the early days of parenting.

What are the common emotions experienced by single mothers? Particularly if a woman has been with her mate for a while and is recently separated, pregnancy is a confrontation with loneliness and solitude. All pregnant women have feelings of uniqueness and singularity, but with an interested mate there is the comfort of intimacy. For a woman alone, pregnancy may make her feel isolated in a way she hardly

knows how to cope with. Single women speak wistfully of feeling the baby move and having no one to share it with. Being alone at night with the baby kicking and disturbing her sleep often sets a mother to feeling anxious or depressed about her impending responsibility with everything in her hands, in her keeping. The task which faces all single mothers is to accept and transmute these feelings of anxiety into positive, growth-producing emotions.

How can you help a single mother cope with her needs for loving companionship? First of all, help her to cultivate self-esteem. See how she spends her time and whether or not she gets out socially. Encourage her to talk through her doubts about herself, while stressing her positive aspects and accomplishments.

Single mothers will obviously require more time and energy than those with mates. But rather than assuming total responsibility as

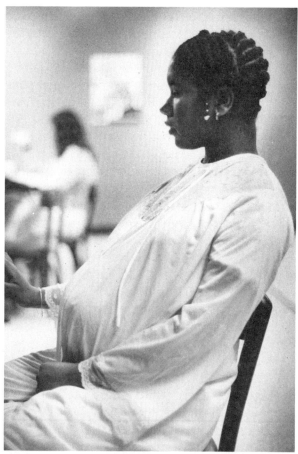

Single mothers must give themselves credit for the courage and strength it takes to go it alone.

confidant, try to connect the mother with others in her position. Keep in mind that after the birth is over she will be a parent with a whole new set of emotional needs, and you will remain a midwife with many others counting on you. It is a definite mistake for a midwife to allow a single woman to form a dependency on her.

What are some common fears and concerns about single parenting? Number one is that the emotional and physical stamina required will be just too much. Some single mothers prefer to keep the prospect of parenthood veiled, and float through the pregnancy with little thought to what lies ahead. Your role in this case is to help her explore her emotions concerning her baby. Ask her how she thinks she'll be feeling for the first few weeks after the birth, what she will do when the baby cries, or how she will dress, bathe and care for the baby. More than anything else, the single mother needs a relationship with another who has recently given birth who can instill some reality. She may even be able to help with chores for the first few weeks, or will at least stress the importance of finding someone who will.

What about fears concerning the birth itself? Most intense is the fear of overwhelming sensation and loss of control. An important point to keep in mind is that birth is a sexual experience, and the single mother may not be having sex at all. So it's wise to broach the subject of sexual-sensual intensity in birthing by discussing her sexuality in the present. The midwife can help by being as relaxed as possible. Explain the physiology of the birthing process and the way the vagina adapts and expands to suit the baby's contour. Sometimes it's easiest to talk this over while showing the woman perineal massage, and it helps if she can do a bit of self-massage in your presence. Then you can ask her about masturbating and orgasm. Can she let herself go and really experience orgasm all to herself?

Your aim is to help her find a comfortable-but-charged energy about her sexual self. She needs to understand that all of labor is a sensation-filled event and that she should expect to make noise and move sensually and uninhibitedly in your presence. Any unresolved sexual-emotional tension with her partner should be reviewed. Ask her what their sexual relationship was like, how he treated her sexually after he knew she was pregnant and what kinds of feelings come up if she imagines having sex with him now. Does she feel open to having sex with anyone else?

This brings up a major concern for the single mother: is there love and romance after birth? Are women with babies at all desirable to men? Who wants a woman with another man's child in her arms? Let her know that in today's world, single parenting is widespread for women *and* men alike. Single fathers often take half the responsibility for the child or children, and thus are discovering the joys of childrearing while discarding concepts of this task as mere drudgery or woman's work. One advantage for the single mother is that her lover will probably feel somewhat relieved of the usual (though often unspoken) pressure to reproduce that is definitely part of every powerful relationship. As one mother put it, "there are oodles of guys who would love a ready-made family." And a man may feel a certain security at finding his lover to be a capable mother, even if they are not yet planning to have children. Enable a single mother to feel more confident about her prospects for partnership and she will feel more positive about her overall situation.

Working Mothers

How work affects pregnancy depends on the woman involved and the kind of work she is doing. Certain women feel that work alone can satisfy their need to be productive or serve others. Often these women tend to center outside themselves, and may need help focusing on the pregnancy and the developing baby. The midwife should encourage the mother to stay tuned to her feelings throughout the course of her workday.

Does she have problems sleeping? During her free hours, is she preoccupied with concerns stemming from her work? And how is her sex life? Answers to these questions will shed light on how well the woman is supported, and whether she is able to unwind and experience periods of introspection and surrender that will prepare her for labor.

The most common problem for working mothers is continual stress. Stress increases the need for vitamins B and C, calcium and protein. It will often manifest as aches and pains at night, or insomnia. If a woman is working under stress she needs an excellent diet and daily emotional and physical release. Relaxation practice and meditation help, as does a measure of exercise.

If work is a financial necessity and she must continue even when the signs say that it's time to quit, suggest that she lie down and relax as soon as she gets home and keep her weekends completely free. This should also be discussed with her mate so he can support her. I urge all working women to quit their jobs about a month before their due date. Those women who work to term are frequently overdue, as if making up for lost time.

Often working women imagine that they will go on with their careers immediately after the birth. Stress the importance of taking time out for the baby. Emphasize the need to establish a good milk supply by getting plenty of rest. Refer the woman to a mothers' support group. This can provide interesting and intelligent discussions on the issues of parenting, and reassure the career woman that her identity as a mother can be exciting and socially significant. *Explain how a few months of undivided love and attention will provide an intimate foundation for the family that will make parenting much easier in the long run.*

An important catalyst is the bonding period immediately following birth. Most career women are very concerned with their image; help create a positive one of her as mother by commenting on the beauty of her baby, how great she looked during labor and how wonderful she is with the baby in her arms.

If the mother must start work soon after the birth, see that she is in touch with other working and nursing mothers. La Leche League, Int'l. can provide referrals and phone counseling. The mother who expresses ambivalence about working and continuing to breastfeed needs to find support *before* the birth. Otherwise she may unconsciously begin withholding nursings during the early weeks, so that her baby will be forced to wean and she will be free to go back to work.

An exception to all the above is the woman who chooses her own work hours, who is in tune with her pregnancy and whose work is so appropriate to her nature that it is health-affirming. For example, one woman I recently assisted had been an artist for many years and had been given a grant to do murals around the city. During pregnancy she planned and directed work on her projects but was free to rest whenever she wanted. Instead of distracting or exhausting her, her work enabled her to stay happy and well.

The working women category also includes women in school. More so than women working a regular eight-hour shift, students can really deplete their resources with late night studying and can accumulate tremendous physical tension from sitting still and concentrating for long periods. The student/mother needs to assess her best times of day for effective, relaxed study, then use these *and no others.* Help her take a realistic view of returning to school after the birth, with due caution to the danger of being preoccupied with subject matter (even if in-class hours are limited) when she really needs to be paying attention to her baby.

Mothers over 35

It used to be that any woman over 35 having her first baby was considered high risk. The main concern was that labor might be inhibited or complicated due to rigidity of pelvic bones and muscle tissue. Now the standard is changing: as more and more women delay childbearing and in the meantime maintain greater health and fitness than even before, age is no longer such an issue.

In evaluating the first-time mother over 35, take into consideration her overall state of health, her vitality and general attitude. She should also have a complete physical to rule out heart and lung problems more common with age.

Every woman deserves to be seen on an individual basis and should receive a truthful assessment of her situation. You can increase the likelihood of smooth birthing by giving personalized recommendations on nutrition and exercise, massage and relaxation. As for stamina, an older woman who really wants her baby and has determination can manifest a phenomenal endurance that is more than enough to see her through delivery.

This brings us to the benefits of working with older women; usually they have experienced enough personal growth and self-affirmation to relate to pregnancy deliberately and responsibly. With adolescence far behind them, these women are apt to have learned how to care for themselves effectively. They listen and respond well to your suggestions by taking the initiative to implement them. On the other hand, some have focused so intensely on themselves alone that the idea of bending the edges of routine to adapt to someone else's needs is rather unappealing. Sometimes conception occurs because the woman fears her time is running out and that it's now or never for baby-tending and diaper-washing before adaptability and patience are gone for good. Anticipation of disrupted schedules, unwashed dishes and hurried meals (along with general self-abnegation) can make this kind of woman feel either panicked or depressed.

You can help by showing her that age can be an advantage because it provides the emotional scope and stability to make her a more dependable parent. Let her know that the most effective mothering depends on honesty and personal integrity. And urge her to connect with other mothers, especially if her social circle is comprised mostly of childless couples. The greatest asset the older woman has is a well-seasoned sense of humor. Appeal to this with examples of the trials and tribulations of parenting, stressing the universal aspects. The woman of experience will relate well to this perspective; her context and ideals are generally broader than the younger woman using motherhood to work out her own personal identity.

What about the older woman having another child? I once assisted a 45-year-old woman having her third baby; her others were in their teens. Her physical condition was that of a woman ten years younger. Her body was in perfect shape, she had flexibility, good muscle tone and an excellent diet. Her physical exam showed her to be completely healthy, her heart was fine and blood pressure lower than average. So why hesitate? As it turned out, she had a four-hour, problem free labor. And her recuperation was perfect; she had plenty of energy postpartum.

Attitudes are also changing towards the grand multipara, or mother bearing her fourth or fifth child. Long considered at risk for postpartum hemorrhage due to lax muscle tone, recent research shows that this is no longer typically true. With attention to nutrition, exercise and rest, physical condition can be optimal regardless of previous childbearing.

Estranged Couples

Working with an estranged couple is complex; you strive to reconcile differences between the two while at the same time encouraging the woman to develop her autonomy should reconciliation prove impossible. The latter is important no matter what happens. Focus the discussion on basic needs not being met in the relationship and on her ultimate ability to take care of things alone if need be.

There are many variations on the theme of estrangement. Perhaps the couple has been together for a while but has not stabilized, and is vacillating on whether or not to marry. Be prepared for tearful clinic sessions and continual repetition of problems. Often your own counsel will repeat itself too. Hopefully there will come a time *before* the labor when the couple decides one way or the other. If not, it's important to advise parents of the difficulties that emotional ambivalence can create at birthings. You may need to suggest that the woman decide to labor without her mate present if they can't work things out. This is not a matriarchal stance but a practical one based on the fact that it is the *woman's* body which must be free to open up unhindered in order to give birth naturally and safely. Emphasizing this fact to both parents may make them realize the need to reconcile, or it may make them see that it's simply impossible.

Group experience in birth class may help couples with problems as other expectant parents profess similar ambivalence. But sometimes it's better to suggest that the mother take another support person to classes (like a close woman friend) if it seems likely that the father won't come through. Let this be the mother's decision though, as her intuition is more powerful than your projection. If there is even a slim chance that her mate might be at the birth, make sure that he's fully prepared both physically and emotionally.

In the meantime, give the estranged woman the same opportunities and topics for discussion as a single mother. It's a lot for an expectant mother to contemplate all these different possibilities, but only by keeping doors open will options remain available.

How to reach out to the father? Seldom have I had an estranged father call seeking advice or assistance; more often than not they simply drop out of the picture. A well-adjusted father could be invited to speak at the birth classes the couple is attending. Sometimes the midwife's husband can lend a bit of paternal authority to the situation, or could take a more brotherly approach.

If the couple does pull together and the father is at the birth, it is critical to encourage his participation as discreetly as possible. All the little things, such as supporting the mother in difficult positions, helping with perineal massage, and feeling the baby's head while it's crowning are intrinsic to paternal bonding. Along these lines, ask him beforehand if he would like to help with the delivery (even though it seems unlikely) or if he would like to cut the cord. These questions are often enough to stimulate genuine participation.

I've received several middle-of-the-night drunken phone calls from distraught fathers, which are obviously a bit disturbing. Tell the father to call again if he must, but be careful to keep your message platonic. Absolutely resist any temptation to play into the situation with feminine charms. Your position is that of a friend, neutral ground and resource for both parents.

Another situation you may encounter is that of the woman who is no longer with her mate but has a new man who seems committed to staying with her throughout the pregnancy and perhaps beyond. Sometimes this relationship is based on love but often it's based on curiosity; it may be difficult to distinguish between the two. Sad to say, it's not uncommon for the man in this situation to suffer intensely from postpartum blues, compounded by the knowledge that the wet, crying baby lying beside him in bed is not really his own. This type of couple needs to discuss the realities of early parenting, and you must persist through the usual joking affection to get at the issues. Have they discussed his role after the birth; will he be known as daddy? Is he prepared to deal with sleepless nights and lots of baby crying?

Does he understand the emotional needs of the woman for support in the early weeks, and does her realize how breastfeeding will probably temper her sexual desires for some time to come?

At some point when you are alone with the mother you might want to discuss the possibility of her parenting alone. Just ask her what she would do and how she would feel if she and her man started to grow apart after the birth. Remind her of the time alone that she experienced before, and suggest that she not lose sight of her self reliance if the going gets rough.

Lesbian Mothers

Lesbian women have certainly been subjected to more than their share of prejudice and misunderstanding. But when a lesbian decides to become a mother, society really reacts. Fortunately, many of the myths that cast lesbians as poor parents have been debunked in recent years and now it is clear that their children benefit from being carefully planned and very much wanted.

Artificial insemination is available through both physicians and midwives. Sperm is obtained from sperm banks for 94% of inseminations; otherwise, fresh sperm is secured from known or unknown donors. Rarely, the donor may wish to co-parent or may want some knowledge of the child. But because the relationship between mother and donor is usually tentative, legal contracts are advisable. In some states the donor surrenders all claim to the child if insemination is done through a physician. Otherwise custody battles could ensue in the future.

The relationship between a lesbian mother and her partner may be quite conventional, monogamous and committed. If so, the couple should be treated as a unit and offered the same support as a heterosexual couple for handling the stresses of pregnancy and early parenting. Occasionally, the lesbian mother is treated like a single mother in childbirth classes even though her partner is present! You may need to speak to the instructor on behalf of the couple, or refer them to another educator who will respect their relationship.

Some of your lesbian clients may want to be closeted, while others are definitely "out."

With the latter, you might advise your backup physician in advance of transport if such becomes necessary, or certainly in advance of any consultative visits.

The birth certificate poses a special problem. If the mother indicates that she was artificially inseminated, the state may later try to track the father if she ever applies for aid. Better to leave the space for father's name blank, or write "unknown." Only the mother can be listed on the certificate in the capacity of legal guardian, her lesbian partner cannot. In most states her partner cannot adopt the child either, although states where this is allowed may grant reciprocity to others. And if anything were to happen to the mother during delivery that rendered her disabled or incompetent, her partner would have no authority *unless* she established power of attorney in advance. Then she would be treated as next of kin.

The actual insemination process is often drawn out over months and is quite costly. The success rate quoted by most sperm banks is only about 19%. If two inseminations are performed monthly, it takes an average of six to nine months to conceive. This gets expensive, at $50–$100 per insemination. Again, this points to the fact that lesbian women desiring motherhood must be very committed.

Probably the biggest concern just now regarding insemination is AIDS. Sperm banks screen their donors carefully, which is obviously a critical consideration since the virus can survive freezing. In fact, the very existence of AIDS argues against using a casual donor.

If you meet with a lesbian client early in pregnancy who may have been exposed to AIDS, suggest that she be tested at an *anonymous testing site*. (These are available in every state and most every county.) Self-testing through the mail is not recommended as results are unreliable, and lists of participants (and their results) are made available to public health departments and insurance companies. If the woman is found to be sero-positive, her baby has a 50% chance of contracting the virus and she may wish to terminate the pregnancy.

Encourage the lesbian mother to find others in her own community for support. She will need practical cooperation with childcare and possibly childrearing, if she is single. It is a so-

bering fact that many lesbian mothers *do not tell* their midwives the truth, but pose as single mothers. Check your attitude and remember that the key to understanding is tolerance.

Relations With Parents

The family in today's world has taken a bit of a beating. What with family members often living far apart and communicating seldom, it's no wonder that most expectant parents think little of how their feelings for their own parents might affect the birthing. Many women are quite surprised to find memories of childhood and unresolved emotions surfacing as pregnancy progresses. Not all will delve into their feelings, but most will at least want to contact Mom to get her perspective on the birthing experience and her suggestions for dealing with the baby.

This desire to get in touch says something about family bonding, which often remains unconscious until maternal and paternal surges turn the wheel and complete the cycle of biological relatedness. First-time expectant parents commonly express some negativity about their upbringing, but frequently confuse a happy childhood with the recent difficulties of adolescent challenge and breakaway. Becoming a parent really begins by defining oneself as an individual, and letting go of old anger and resentment (reactions of attachment) towards Mother and Father.

When working with someone having problems in this area, urge them to forgive their parents for all the things they did or didn't do and encourage them to use positive memories of childhood to generate their own approach. *By accepting their parents as imperfect, they acknowledge the same condition in themselves.* A most difficult aspect of first-time parenting is reckoning one's ideals with one's actual situation in life. Stress that parenting is a *process* and that the birth will revitalize and activate forces and abilities that have been sophisticated almost out of existence, or simply repressed.

Prospective parents may also have to contend with one another's idealism about bringing up a child. One parent may assume a purist standpoint with all sorts of preconceived notions of what the child will or will not be exposed to, while the other maintains a more pragmatic, "wait and see" attitude. It's difficult to mediate these disagreements, but once again your own example of a time when compromise was necessary, or the tactful, graceful thing to do might be appropriate. It's not necessary to squelch idealism, but do try to instill a little reality so parents realize the value of flexibility. Often parents with somewhat rigid ideals about parenting are also over-positive about the birth going perfectly and need to broaden their perspective.

Some men and women with decidedly unpleasant experiences of childhood may confide to you that they don't really like children, and wonder how in the world they will be able to parent with these feelings. Most prospective parents suffer from our cultural bias favoring

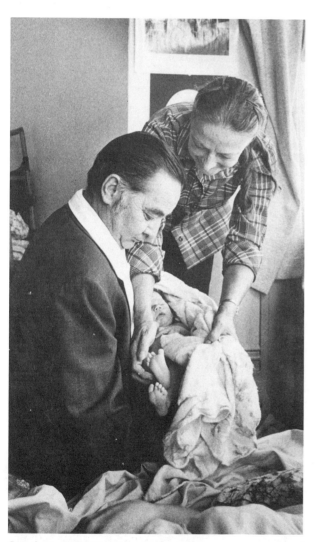

Grandparents thrill to the miracle of birth.

young-adultism. With little or no exposure to the world of babies, toddlers and little children, they fear their enthusiasm is a lot lower than it should be. The hardest thing for parents to grasp during pregnancy (which becomes apparent at the time of birth and bonding) is that this baby is not just some abstract, alien little infant but *their* baby, with all kinds of hereditary, spiritual and emotional linkage.

Much of the fear around having children has to do with the fear of perpetuating cultural role models. Many men remember Dad as an authority figure and imagine that becoming a father will necessitate a tightening up and constricting of emotional energies in order to "be the boss" and stay on top of things. The pregnancy may be viewed as a sobering and serious event, a paring down the self to society's specifications. Typical reactions to this kind of pressure are extreme overwork, unpredictable rounds of heavy drinking, staying out late or periods of depression. A woman reporting any such symptoms in her mate should be asked to bring him to clinic, or you may want to make a special home visit. Deal tactfully with the male ego in this state of polarization by approaching the matter intellectually; take an objective look at relevant social patterns. If you delve emotionally as is so easy and stimulating when counseling a woman, most men will close up and become defensive and awkward.

Women struggle with the model of self-sacrificing and consistently-giving madonna. What with the hormones of pregnancy moving them up and down, most wonder how they'll ever be stable enough to handle the baby. Sometimes a fear-and-repression process sets in long before the baby is born. If this phase slips by unattended, the mother will start to suffer from depression.

The most important and liberating news you can give clients caught in these patterns is that *it is possible to be a person and a parent at the same time*, and it's better to express a full range of emotions with spontaneous intensity than to vent them later as distorted or even violent outbursts. Explain that parenting means relationship, with the same guidelines for openness and assertiveness that work in the adult world. This information often brings tremendous relief. Performance anxiety begins to slip into the context of things past. The more that prospective parents relax and trust their instincts, the easier it is to deal with relatives and society at large.

Sexual Problems

Problems with sexuality often stem from concepts and expectations regarding proper masculine or feminine behavior. Our culture has had heavily polarized role models in the past and even now, while professing equality of sexes, the feminine aspect is seldom expressed in our society. Women are struggling to work and play in a man's world and still retain their femininity while men feel both fascination and resentment at seeing their long-standing superiority swept aside.

Concerning intercourse itself, most problems spring from an inability to communicate needs and desires. By discussing various positions appropriate for different phases of pregnancy, you expand the horizons of what's normal and acceptable. In this respect, discussion with other expectant parents is ideal because participants are all undergoing similar changes and adjustments.

A woman's desire for sex will vary considerably during pregnancy. At no other time in her life will the emotional component have so strong an influence on her response; her emotions in turn are influenced by the stage of pregnancy through which she is passing. The first trimester is often a time of all-barriers-down intimacy and tenderness. This is partly a reaction to not having to worry about birth control. But there is a certain intimacy that flows from conception itself, from the knowledge that she and her man have really become one and that the fruit of their union is living inside her. Of course this is bound to be modified by any feeling of ambivalence about the pregnancy; a woman with conflict has enough on her mind to keep her from desiring intercourse. And sometimes normal nausea and fatigue interfere with sexual response.

Once the baby's movements can be felt, a woman may feel withdrawn at times and quite preoccupied with the baby. Her growing size can hinder ease with certain sexual positions; the most comfortable ones have her on top or lying on her side with her partner behind her.

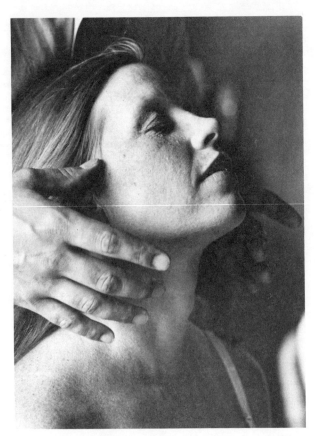

Women need to tell their partners the truth about what feels good, then let go and enjoy it!

In the last trimester, comfort can be a problem in almost any position, and when the birth seems imminent, she may once again be focusing on her relationship with the baby. In order for sex to seem right at this point, the mother must never feel that her man is attempting to turn her attention away from the baby, but rather that he wants to make love to them both. Because his attitude will affect her so intensely, the mother is right to be selective about intercourse.

It is very important though that she make an effort to keep her sexual circuits open; it has everything to do with the sensual scope of her labor. The compelling intensity of contractions necessitates the same kind of free verbal expression running the range from demand to plea that happens when she is about to reach out for orgasm. How can the midwife help with this? Sometimes a rather graphic demonstration will give the idea: start with some intense breathing (the kind she'll be using at the very end of first stage) combined with moving surrender in your body. Then add a few appropriate moans or pleas while peaking "Squeeze my shoulders . . . mmm," or "There . . . push harder!" and you'll have made your point. This might trigger some embarrassed laughter but you will have imparted more information on the real nature of birthing than any amount of technical training can give.

Many women complain that their partners are insensitive and move too fast or ignore foreplay. The best suggestion for these women is that they initiate sex contact themselves, and explicitly show their partner what they want to feel. If intercourse begins with the woman on top she can control the timing and set the tone of the experience.

Sometimes shy women are afraid of their own passions and recoil from these suggestions. Draw a parallel to labor as a sensual experience centered in her body which will call on her to take the lead. Help her redefine her sexuality as a sharing of her own power, rather than her skill in pleasing or submitting to a partner. Emphasize the need to pleasure herself with hot baths, relaxed meals, massage, etc. Yoga or dance can help release tension, get her in touch with her rhythms and show her that she has her own resources for making herself feel good. Comfort with her sexuality will influence not only her response to labor but her handling of the baby, her recuperation postpartum and her commitment to breastfeeding.

Psychological Screening Out

Despite your best efforts, sometimes a client continues to have serious emotional problems that cause you to question the wisdom of doing her birth at home. Be sure to talk it over with your partner, who may see signs of actual improvement that you have overlooked. On the other hand, you must guard against excessive optimism, lest it obscure your reason and responsibility. Pay careful attention to your emotional aftertaste when working with the mother and try to distinguish the exhilaration of extending yourself as counsel from her actual response.

If it is obvious that you are getting nowhere and there is nothing left to try, it's a sign of wisdom to suggest hospital birth with yourself as support person. Sometimes the mother is re-lieved at this suggestion, and it becomes evident that fear of the responsibility of birthing at home was part of the problem all along. When a woman's psychological aspects are jumbled her chances of developing complications increase dramatically, and it's best to take those chances in the hospital. This amounts to psychological screening out.

The only way to learn this discrimination is by experience. After a few long, drawn-out, three or four day labors with all your skill and effort seemingly coming to naught, you begin to develop stricter standards. It's part of your responsibility to others in your care to avoid personal trauma and burnout. And if you decide to risk out, hold firm. Once hospital birth has been decided on, apparent last minute improvements are probably due to increased security with more conventional plans. Don't be tempted to reverse yourself just because things are looking better. This takes the wisdom to let things be, and to forego your own desire for a certain kind of experience or level of involvement.

Keep in mind that these home-changed-to-hospital births often require an incredible amount of coaching. The labor may not be any easier in the hospital, but at least some of the weight is off your shoulders. Maybe you'll decide to be more stringent in your initial screening after several of these experiences, although it's likely you'll be drawn into these situations from time to time. The important thing is to be aware of your choices and to stay free of illusion.

Be sure to discuss your borderline emotional cases with your backup doctor before birth time comes around. Otherwise the development of an emotional crisis in labor might cast a bad light on your judgement. It's a challenge to discuss the link between mind and body with a conventional physician, but explaining your client's psychological profile before the birth will at least make the emotional events of her labor more comprehensible. Your efforts to communicate in advance may also assure you more authority in the hospital, and may give the parents a chance for a better experience.

Danger Signs in Pregnancy

Report to your midwife immediately if you notice:

1. *Vaginal bleeding.* In the first trimester, can indicate threatened, spontaneous or missed abortion (miscarriage), molar pregnancy or ectopic pregnancy. In the second trimester, can indicate placenta praevia. Likewise during the third trimester, or may be due to placental abruption.
2. *Initial outbreak of blisters in the perineal or anal area during first trimester.* This may be herpesvirus, contact midwife at once so culture can be taken.
3. *Severe pelvic or abdominal pain.* In first trimester, may indicate tubal pregnancy. In last trimester, may indicate placental abruption. Both are emergencies; contact midwife at once.
4. *Persistent and severe mid-back pain.* May indicate severe kidney infection. Not an emergency, but don't wait until next visit to report.
5. *Swelling of hands and face.* Particularly if face looks puffy or coarse, notify midwife. May indicate pre-eclampsia.
6. *Severe headaches, blurry vision or epigastric (chest) pain.* May indicate pre-eclamptic condition becoming critical. Notify midwife at once.
7. *Gush of fluid from vagina.* If in first or second trimester, may indicate miscarriage. If in late second or third trimester, may indicate premature delivery.
8. *Regular uterine contractions before 37 weeks.* May indicate impending premature birth. Don't wait to see if they will go away, lie down and call midwife immediately.
9. *Cessation of fetal movement.* May indicate fetal demise. The baby should move about three times an hour. If less, or less than usual, report to midwife.

CHAPTER 4

Labor and Birth

The first principle of attending births is to maintain an open mind and pay good attention to what's happening in the present. Regardless of any turmoil or conflict that existed prenatally and perhaps remains unresolved, the birth is the main event and every effort must be made to come to it clear and clean of preconceptions. This quality of freshness will be well appreciated by the birthing woman and her partner; it's the spark for getting things off to a good start.

Early Labor

Every woman should be instructed toward the end of her pregnancy about the beginning signs of labor. Encourage her to call you if anything *at all* seems to be happening. Even a desultory round of false labor or incoordinate contractions may precede the real thing, and knowing that it's happening will enable you to get your personal life in order and prepare yourself for the birth, even if it doesn't happen for several days. Most women call eagerly to discuss their warm-up signals, which gives you an opportunity to allude to the reality of labor's intensity. Every woman needs to do a final amount of letting go before labor really gets in gear. If she is experiencing strong Braxton-Hicks with minor cramping, encourage her to breathe into her sensation and relax with it. And don't hesitate to tell her how very much stronger her sensations will become.

The obvious signs that labor is impending include the "show" (mucous plug coming away), ruptured membranes (water bag breaking), or regular, strengthening contractions. Many women lose globs of mucus in the last week or so, but only if secretions are blood-tinged can

you assume that some cervical change is actually occurring. Sometimes the plug is lost and labor takes a day or two to commence. Be sure that a woman knows the difference between normal, pink-tinged mucus, and abnormal, excessive bleeding which might be related to placental problems.

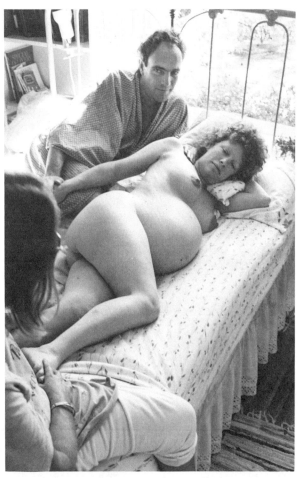

This midwife makes her presence felt by holding the woman's feet, without intruding on the couple's privacy.

If a woman has lost her mucous plug and is having no contractions, advise her to go about her normal routine, eat high quality, non-constipating foods and get plenty of rest. Make it clear that there's no need for her to do anything to get labor going, and that this is her time to let flow her sensitivities while taking the best care of herself. See if she's experiencing the usual pre-labor burst of energy, and encourage her to sleep so she will have energy for her work later on. But share in her elation too, as this will help her release nervous tension and get down to business.

Sometimes labor begins with the amniotic fluid leaking, or gushing out completely. Occasionally it's difficult to be certain that a slow leak isn't in fact urine that the woman is losing involuntarily due to constant pressure from the baby's head on her bladder. Insert a sterile speculum, place a bit of nitrazine paper in a ring forceps and hold it at the cervical opening. Then take your pH reading (amniotic fluid is alkaline). Sometimes a woman reports a big gush of water followed by little or no leaking. It may be that a *hind leak* high in the membranes has released just enough pressure to allow the baby to settle snugly in the pelvis, effectively sealing off any further flow of fluid. But sometimes a bit of amniotic fluid does filter down and is trapped behind the intact membrane still encasing the baby's head. These are the *forewaters*, which can feel like an intact water bag.

Once the membranes are ruptured, serious considerations arise. There is definitely a possibility of infection if germs in the vagina or outside enter the sterile uterine environment. On the other hand, the body has its own defense by replenishing amniotic fluid, which with its down and outward flow tends to discourage bacteria from moving upwards. It's essential for a woman to be meticulous in her toileting and to put nothing in the vagina. She must have plenty of liquids to replenish the supply of fluid. And to ward off infection, vitamin C (250 mg every three or four hours) can be taken prophylactically. Temperature should also be checked every few hours. If you are not with the mother yourself, be sure to have her check the odor on her pad periodically (it should smell clean and fresh) and have her report any change. If the fluid is anything but clear she

should call, as a green or yellow tinge indicates meconium and possible fetal distress.

There is quite a debate concerning ruptured membranes and safe time limit before infection becomes a possibility. This will be covered in the next chapter; just remember that women reporting ruptured membranes should always be acknowledged as being in labor. One midwife says she always responds with, "Good, you're in labor!" and then explains that the bag was probably broken by contractions, with more soon to follow. In managing ruptured membranes, you must juggle any attempt to stimulate labor with the need to conserve the mother's resources for the hard work to come. Don't make the mistake of encouraging her to get labor going if it is not really established. If it's near bedtime or the middle of the night, suggest that she have a strong cup of relaxant herb tea and get some sleep. Her mate might want to give her a massage, but no intercourse or finger-genital/mouth-genital contact.

A picture of relaxation: note loose mouth and easy jaw.

The labor which begins with contractions alone is a bit harder to confirm; many women have warm-up rounds of contractions for weeks before actual labor. Commonly called false labor, this rather negative terminology can only make the frustration of starting and stopping worse. Explain that incoordinate uterine action is at fault, and that even if these contractions don't do any dilating they still have the effect of flexing and strengthening the uterine muscle.

There are several classic false labor patterns. One is typical of the woman whose baby is large and not engaged. She experiences "lightening" or "dropping" with considerable stretching of the lower uterine segment. This usually causes some cervical effacement, but little or no dilation. What this mother calls contractions are often just twinges associated with descent, having no pattern of dispersal or duration. Suggest that she take a hot bath and relax.

The other type of false labor is more like the real thing, with some pulling discomfort or cramping. Contractions come every 10 or 20 minutes, but never seem to get any stronger or closer together. In fact, the sensations are spasm-like and quite uncomfortable. This is typical, incoordinate uterine activity — nothing to worry about, though rather distressing. Suggest a glass or two of wine, which will slow or stop things altogether if the time is not really ripe.

Genuine labor is characterized by contractions which gradually increase in intensity and come closer together. It's hard to lay down definite guidelines for determining true labor; it's more a matter of wait and see. Contractions may remain somewhat erratic in spacing and duration for many hours, but if there is cervical (menstrual-like) cramping, chances are it's the real thing. There are many types of early labor patterns; it seems a general rule that women who commence with contractions five minutes apart will deliver sooner than those contracting every twenty minutes. But always keep in mind that a woman can shift gears to active labor very suddenly, so be conscientious about staying in touch, and be sure to inform the parents of the signs of heavy labor so they know when to call. If a woman is able to make her own smooth transition from early to active la-bor, she might well call too late for you to make it on time.

This brings up the question of when to go to the birth. Once they've notified you initially, most women want to know when to call again. The best answer is "whenever you feel the need for company, or if something changes." It's important to let the mother know you are there to help her through any rough periods, regardless of her actual dilation. Explain your willingness to come and go, and reassure her that there's no such thing as calling too soon.

Certain things can happen at the onset of labor or early on that demand your presence and observation. For example, if the baby was high at the last prenatal (particularly if the head was floating) and the mother calls to inform you that her water bag has ruptured, you should go right over and listen to the fetal heart to rule out any degree of cord prolapse. Likewise, if you have any question about the baby's ability to handle contractions due to an SGA or postdates condition, you should be there when labor starts to check fetal response. A report of meconium-tinged waters necessitates your presence to rule out any immediate fetal distress. And maternal conditions such as hypertension need to be supervised carefully right from the start. In general, any borderline findings in the last few weeks necessitate your earlier involvement in labor and more diligent supervision throughout.

Otherwise, leave it up to the parents. Those with psychological problems may need you to make an early visit for some emotional reassurance. Often women call around two centimeters of dilation to report some "really intense" contractions and are afraid that if the cramping or back pain is so sharp already, they'll never be able to handle it near the end. This is a fairly universal response, this reckoning with the forces. Explain that later on her body will just take over and work automatically, and she'll find resources for coping that she doesn't even realize she has, if only she'll surrender and let it happen. You might suggest a hot bath for getting used to her sensations, as long as her water bag is intact. And *relaxation;* often women forget to use their relaxation techniques in early labor. Recommend that she go about her usual activities, leaning against something and releasing her pelvis and hips completely during a contraction. Often by maintaining good phone communication you can guide a woman through early labor without the need to go and see her. This becomes especially important if you are doing many births or are tired from a recent delivery.

When a woman calls be sure to keep her on the phone for a few contractions; listen to her breathing as a gauge of labor's intensity. Notice how quickly she recuperates. Active labor is characterized by a definite pause which lasts some time after the breathing stops, and before conversation resumes. If you get the feeling that she's sinking in deeper with each contraction and note that the pause period is increasing, it may be time for you to head over regardless of her subjective evaluation of sensation.

Complaints about environment deserve attention too. It's impossible for a woman to relax and dilate if her home is chaotic; beware of loud partying noises in the background. You may need to help her clear the house of distractions, by explaining to well-meaning friends

that it will be a while yet and she needs a chance to concentrate. Friends can also be sent on last-minute food runs, or can do a bit of cooking if the mom is still hungry. The birth room itself should be orderly, well-ventilated and aesthetically pleasing, with ample fluid supply by the bed, massage oil, towels, heating pad, etc., all laid out and ready for use. Many women will take care of this themselves, manifesting a nesting instinct in early labor, but those who are somewhat frightened might need help getting organized.

Encourage a woman to keep eating as long as she feels hungry. Emphasize high calcium (raises the pain threshold) foods that are easily digested, like yogurt and kefir, and carbohydrates for energy. And remind her of her need to keep drinking (preferably juice or tea with honey) and to urinate frequently. *Your suggestions for activity depend on the time of day;* if it's morning, she can do whatever suits her, if it's late in the day, she ought to try to rest, or at least lie down for as long as is comfortably possible, and if it's nightime she should use herb tea or a glass of wine to get some sleep.

The Midwife's Role in Early Labor

If you do go over during early labor, you should start your labor record (see Appendix E) with notes on the onset of labor and uterine activity. Take initial vitals: blood pressure, pulse, and urinalysis. Palpate the baby for position and listen to the FHT. Do everything but the FHT between contractions so as not to disturb the mother. You should listen to the fetal heart *during and immediately after* a contraction to check fetal response (see page 71). And you may want to palpate the uterus during a contraction, to assess the intensity and strength thereof.

In early labor vaginal exams are optional, but often desirable to establish for everyone present just exactly what's going on. Some women react very intensely to early labor, and may appear to be further along than they are. Check whenever in doubt.

Your goal in doing vaginal exams during labor is to be as gentle and undisruptive as possible, while obtaining as much information as quickly as you can. Use sterile gloves with lubricating jelly; later on, if the membranes are

Pep up a lagging labor by getting out in the fresh air.

ruptured use a squirt of Betadine or other antiseptic. Start your exam as soon as a contraction has ended and once you have the woman's OK to go ahead. Check first for **dilation,** being careful to make your assessment of centimeters without stretching the cervical opening when you spread your fingers. Then note the **placement of the cervix:** is it central, anterior or posterior? Is it stretchy and yielding or tight-rimmed? Usually the cervix stays posterior when the head is above –1 station, and swings forward as the baby descends. Now check for **effacement,** estimating by percentage how much of the cervix has been thinned out and taken up into the lower uterine segment. Next, notice **how well the cervix is applied to the baby's head;** it should feel smooth against it. If it is loose like an empty sleeve, and you can slip your fingers inside between it and the baby's head, it's a sign that the head is not fitting well into the pelvis or is malpresenting in some way.

Next, estimate the **station** of the head and get a general feel for how well it's centered in and filling the pelvic space. Last of all, if the cervix is thinned out or dilated enough, you can feel for **sutures and fontanelles** (see diagram below). Generally the sagittal suture is the most noticeable because it is most subject to molding, and so can be felt as a bony ridge when the fingers are swept across the surface of the head. Follow the suture line, and when you find the fontanelle, try to determine whether it's the anterior or posterior. If you've felt the head to be well-flexed by palpation, you're probably feeling the posterior fontanelle; it's the smaller of the two, about the size of a fingernail, whereas the anterior is more the size of a thumbnail. By noting the location of the fontanelles and the direction in which the sagittal suture is running, you'll discover the exact position of the baby's head.

You may not be able to get all of this information in one exam and may need to check again

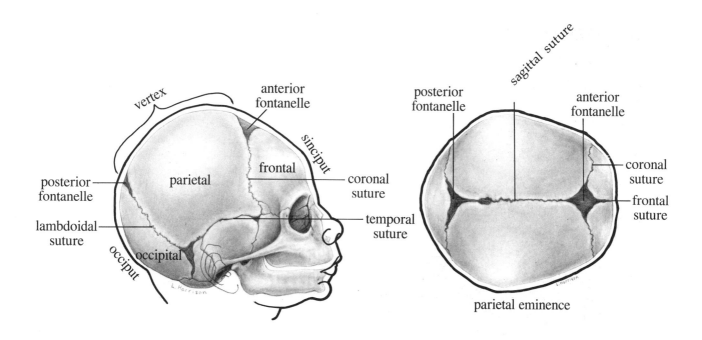

Fetal Skull

after the next contraction ends (start over with a fresh glove). Most important are **dilation** and **station,** which indicate whether you need to stimulate labor or effect further descent of the baby. Finding the sutures is most critical if there seems to be a holdup in progress or a rather long drawn-out latent phase. For example, when the baby is posterior the head is usually deflexed and not well applied to the cervix. And without adequate pressure on the cervix, contractions will get no stronger and labor may arrest (more about this in Chapter 7).

Interpreting your findings depends on what's happening with the labor and how the mother is responding. If she is only two centimeters and is losing control, she may need a change of scene and new input to really get her going. If it is late at night and contractions are not particularly compelling, a finding of three centimeters with high station is an indication for rest and/or sleep for everyone involved.

Active Labor

Sometimes you'll get the feeling that stronger contractions and hard labor are knocking at the door but the woman is keeping them at bay. Up to about four or five centimeters (and sometimes beyond) women have the power to control labor's ebb and flow and can choose the time when they let the forces take over. Difficulties occur if the uterus has already worked to a certain intensity and the mother continues to tighten up against it. This is often the case when a woman is groaning and rocking at only two or three centimeters of dilation.

Women often need special guidance at this point. It is definitely a time of shifting gears, a time of giving up notions of how it was supposed to be. Sometimes the slow deep breathing which has thus far been so effective begins to sound jerky and labored; this is your cue to introduce a slightly accelerated chest breathing with emphasis on rhythmic ease. At this stage, movement during contractions (even pelvic rocking) can create muscular tension; show the woman how to let herself be still, how to "melt" her body while focusing on the rhythm of her breath. Enable a woman to make this change, and her frantic huff-and-puff agitation will be replaced with a peaceful demeanor which permeates the environment and sets a tone of readiness for harder labor.

Touch is very important. If a woman is still fully dressed, offer to rub her lower back; most will welcome this. Use olive oil and let your strokes be strong, smooth and sensual, timed to the rhythm of her breathing. Transmit energy through your hands; it will ground her and give her focus.

Positioning can make a big difference in comfort; what works best depends on the position of the baby and what the woman likes. If the baby is well down in the pelvis, already engaged, then lying on her side with pillow support and lower back pressure is usually OK. If the baby is not yet engaged, a more upright position will employ gravity to assist descent, and will also create maximum pressure on the cervix to keep the contractions coming. Walking serves the same purpose. If the baby is really high (–2 or –3 station), squatting down with each contraction and walking between is good for progress. But it is tiring, and needs to be interspersed with periods of sitting or reclining with pillow support.

Some women feel vulnerable lying down, particularly those who need to have a certain amount of control. Sitting cross legged with shoulders and hands loose and yielding can give a woman the feeling of steering through sensations; a straight spine keeps tension from building up in the back. Having someone to sit

Moment of reckoning as labor forces intensify.

A good position for relieving back labor discomforts, and for encouraging the baby to rotate.

behind and squeeze her shoulders or push on her lower back will help a woman stay loose in this position.

If the baby is large, posterior and not yet descended, the mother should take the hands-and-knees position, with pelvic rocking to encourage rotation. Massaging the woman's buttocks using long, downward strokes will remind her to focus low in her body and keep her breathing relaxed.

If the woman's mate is ready and willing to get involved but at a loss for what to do, help the woman find what's comfortable, and show her mate how to facilitate this. Of course you must be sensitive to what the father is feeling; perhaps he's a bit shocked by the intensity of labor and needs to observe a while before jumping in. Because men are so often concerned with performance and women are so unused to being assertive, this may take some time. But give them their privacy as soon as you are sure they are comfortable together. An advantage to letting them labor alone is that it fosters intimacy which will enhance their experience and make your job easier overall.

Medical Duties During Active Labor

What are the midwife's medical duties during active labor? She must keep a closer eye on the mother's condition, checking blood pressure hourly if it's been normal prenatally, or every 20 minutes if it has been, and remains, border-line high. Be certain that the mother is well hydrated and urinates hourly. An occasional tablespoon of honey will help prevent signs of clinical exhaustion.

If labor has been long in the active phase without much progress (three or four hours), do a urinalysis to check for ketones. A ketone reading indicates a mother is dipping into her fat reserves for energy; a trace is fairly normal in labor, but a higher reading indicates a disrupted electrolyte balance and the need for better hydration. An IV might be given in the hospital; at home, you can replicate the formula with something called labor-aide. Here is a recipe: 1 quart fluid (water); 1/3 c. honey; 1/3 c. lemon juice; 1/2 t. salt; 1/4 t. baking soda; 2 crushed calcium tablets. Better yet, have her eat if she possibly can; even a piece of toast will help immensely. And keep track of her pulse; it should stay within 10–15 points of normal range. If it rises, check her temperature as well. Elevation of these vital signs may indicate an exhaustion level difficult to reverse, which requires transfer to the hospital. Exhaustion is most often a problem when the woman has been vomiting and is unable to keep anything down.

Fetal heart tones should be taken with increasing frequency, at least every half hour. If anything unusual arises, listen constantly until the problem resolves or some further decision is made as per management. Even in routine monitoring you should listen throughout contractions, continuing to listen for about 15–30 seconds after the contraction ends to get a thorough picture of response. Normal response may include some speeding up of the heart rate at the beginning of the contraction or at its peak, but the heart should retain a steady beat with no thready or erratic tonality. Heart rate over 170 is known as **tachycardia** and is generally cause for concern, but this depends on the baby's normal baseline; a rise to 170 is serious for a baby normally at 130 but for the baby averaging 160, 170 is not so alarming. Sometimes the FH will dip and bob during the contraction; this pattern of **variable decelerations** may be caused by some degree of cord compression, which varies depending on the strength of the contraction and any re-positioning response of the baby's head. The best thing to do for this problem is *have the mother try a new position.* This often relieves the pressure on the cord and gets the pattern back to normal.

There are several more ominous patterns; one is **flat baseline** with no apparent variability, and the other is **late decelerations**. With the latter, the FHT dips at the peak and does not return to baseline until the contraction ends. If the baby is really compromised, you may also notice **slow recovery**, with the deceleration extending past the end of the contraction. This pattern may indicate placental insufficiency or fetal acidosis; in either case the oxygen reaching the baby is not adequate to see it all the way through a contraction. If you pick up a pattern like this during first stage, you should give the mother oxygen and transport.

One of the most important things a midwife can do for the parents at this stage of labor is *pay attention*, keeping a constant eye on progress while discreetly facilitating. Some midwives are simply too little involved, allowing a mother to languish in an ineffective position so

that progress arrests and she loses strength, all in the name of non-intervention, but occasionally, a woman needs to arrest temporarily in order to integrate sensations and prepare to go on. This is the **plateau phenomenon**; labor may plateau at four centimeters, six or seven centimeters and then again at nine plus. It's interesting to note that each of these is a turning point in terms of new sensation. Four centimeters marks the transition from outward to inward focus, six or seven centimeters may be accompanied by transitional symptoms of such intensity that the mother hesitates to go further, and nine plus is the change-over from dilating to bearing down. By understanding these points you can assist a woman to get through them, but remember that there is no harm in letting her hold back a bit to collect herself. An arrest for a few hours time is OK if the mother's condition is good and her morale is up. If on the other hand she deliberately chooses a non-dynamic position which hinders progress in an effort to keep her sensations manageable, remind her with humor that labor is not always comfortable, stronger contractions get the baby born and she should go on

Skin-to-skin contact is tremendously reassuring to the laboring woman.

HEART & HANDS

while she still has energy. Sometimes the atmosphere in the room becomes stale and a walk in the fresh air is in order. Especially depressing to a laboring woman is a room full of dozing friends and tired birth attendants. Clearing people out to sleep elsewhere, opening windows, turning up the lights, getting out the ice chips, etc., are all good catalysts for stimulating progress.

Heavy Labor-Transition

Heavy labor ensues once a woman has made the shift to stronger sensation, and has reached a deeper level of surrender. The phase from six or seven centimeters up to transition is often characterized by great concentration and quietude, creating the illusion that time has stopped. If labor has been long thus far, this can be a difficult time for everyone to stay awake and alert because the rhythm of contractions is so hypnotic. This is generally a good time for the father to take a break, and for the midwives to spell one another. By now the mother is so immersed in her work that she will hardly notice these comings and goings, so long as there's a hand on her lower back and a comforting voice nearby.

This is the phase of labor when women often report (afterwards) that they experienced sensations which intimated death and dying. The yielding up of the body must be as complete as the woman can make it, while the breathing rhythm and force of energy carry to the outer reaches as every contraction ends. To observe women at this time is a privilege; most have a softness, a rosiness and glow about them as the social mask falls away and their true nature is revealed. The sleepy, far away quality between contractions is for many an experience of bliss and renewal. Birth attendants must respect this phase for what it is; a peak, out-of-the-body experience which prepares and rejuvenates the mother for the back-in-the-body, re-entry phase of pushing and delivery.

Usually by now a woman has few demands to make, having learned to bear the sensation, and wants mostly to concentrate on being as open as possible. If ever you notice her faltering with breathing, a word or two, or gentle touch will usually guide her to focus.

Whenever there is a marked shift in the

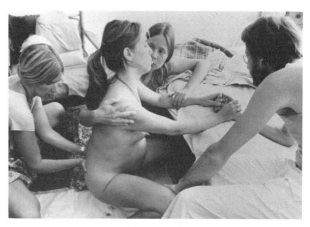

Perfect support for a woman in transition: one midwife holds the mother from behind, the other does breath coaching and the father gives his total attention.

strength of contractions, *check heart tones frequently* to see how the baby is adjusting. Otherwise, your medical surveillance remains about the same, with 20 minute checks on the FHT and attention to fluid intake and elimination. Assist the mother to sip tea or water as each contraction ends, before she slips away. Bendable straws make this easier. The hardest part of carrying out your tasks now is to avoid disturbing her concentration and comfort. Obtaining clear fetal heart tones, for example, requires that she lean back somewhat and this can be rather disorienting. If you have a doppler, you may wish to use it now (see page 165 for more on the use of dopplers).

Don't forget the importance of vaginal exams. What with the unrelenting rhythm of contractions, it's possible to forget to keep track of how well the woman is actually progressing. Sometimes you can tell by her posture, breathing and expression that she's moving ahead and there's no need to check, but if you're uncertain, give her an exam. If you find she has not progressed, make suggestions on breathing and positioning which will facilitate, so as to conserve her energy for the final stages.

Often vaginal exam is prompted by transition symptoms such as restlessness, complaining, shifting of focus or loss of control. Check immediately whenever these manifest; if the woman is eight or nine centimeters dilated she should be helped into an upright position so that maximum pressure is placed on the cervix, encouraging rapid dilation. There seems to be a tendency for the cervix to become edematous at this point if deprived of this pressure. The squatting position is perfect, although it often causes quite a bolt of new and stronger sensation for the mother. Taking fetal heart tones in this position is difficult, so take them before squatting is begun. On the other hand, if a woman is having an overwhelming urge to push and still has a few centimeters left to go, squatting may be too much to integrate. Still, give it a try while coaching her with blowing breathing. If she's pushing involuntarily, try a less compelling position like standing and leaning, or kneeling.

Understand that transition sensations are often difficult or impossible to integrate. Transition means turning point, time of change; it's not a time for having it all together. Convey your own understanding and acceptance of this to the mother, and she'll feel easier about manifesting powerful, explosive or awkward emotions. Physically, there is the overwhelming conflict of sensations, one message being "let go and bear down," and the other "no, it hurts, release and open." Psychologically, there is a shift from universal to personal awareness once again, a call and beckon back into the body. Delivery begins to come into focus.

It's especially important to watch the woman's body language, making sure her shoulders and neck are loose and relaxed and that her physical focus is low in the body. Sometimes women are confused by directions not to push and think they must hold the baby back, but such tension retards dilation. Phrases like "be really open and let that force move through you, just let it be, let it down" sometimes work. Meanwhile, try squeezing the mother's shoulders and breathing with her.

If this is a woman's second or subsequent baby, she will probably give birth quite soon after complete dilation (ten centimeters). Prepare for delivery by straightening up the room a bit and clearing the floor area. This is critical in case of emergency when you need to move fast. And make sure there are no open flames or candles lit, in case you need to set up your oxygen. Remove the blankets from the bed and set them aside so they don't get bloodied or wet. And here's a tip from a very experienced midwife: place several strips of masking tape on your pants legs to make notes in case of emergency. This saves you from having to fumble with the chart or worry about getting it dirty.

Scrub up well with Betadine or other soapy antiseptic, using a nail brush and working well up your forearms. Then set up for delivery, laying out a disposable underpad or toweling on which to place your tray of instruments, your bulb syringe and DeLee suction device, your 4x4 sterile pads and bowl of hot water (add Betadine) for washing the outlet and giving perineal compresses. You should have syringes and drugs for controlling hemorrhage (pitocin and methergine) readily accessible. Tear off the tops of the gauze pads and have them ready. And then, with a squirt of olive oil, you are ready to check the mom whenever she first manifests that irresistible, groaning, bearing-down urge. This way, you're all prepared for the birth and can devote your energy to managing the perineum and assisting delivery. Setting up during transition is also wise for the woman who is birthing a small baby through an ample pelvis, especially if her labor has progressed rapidly with contractions very close together.

One more thing; make sure the mother *urinates* before she enters second stage. A full bladder can hinder descent, and could lead to postpartum hemorrhage.

Second Stage

Second stage begins when the cervix is finally out of the way . . . fully dilated, at last! Almost every woman feels relief and excitement at this point, as she shifts from passive surrender to active participation with bearing down urges. This is the major turning point in labor, the time when identity and body consciousness return anew, along with a burst of energy and enthusiasm.

There is still some debate regarding the proper style of working with second stage contractions. The old school method advocates strong, sustained pushing with every contraction and is at odds with the newer method of sensitive, variable effort and breathing according to what each contraction demands. Another approach is the "breathe through" style of continuous breathing with no pushing effort whatsoever, said to conserve energy and assure maximum oxygen flow to the baby. The truth is that all these techniques have their place, according to whatever labor requires. Much depends on the size of the baby, its position and the dimensions of the mother's pelvis. Other factors include the woman's internal muscle tone and whether it's her first or second baby. *Adaptability* is the key; it's no exaggeration to say that some contractions are so powerful and compelling that to experience the involuntary squeeze sensation without a good breath held behind it is totally obliterating, enough to leave a woman gasping for air and feeling desperate. Then again, contractions may be so mild that breathing through is sufficient. Generally, variable intensity in 2nd stage will last only as long as the baby's head remains at 0 or +1 station. When it moves lower and puts pressure on the rectal and pelvic floor muscles, the urge to push is well established and remains fairly consistent in strength from contraction to contraction. However, the pattern will change once more and return to variable intensity as the perineum starts to distend and the mother receives messages from her body on how much to push, and when.

With this sequence of changes evolving in such a unique fashion, it's obvious that the mother should be the judge of what to do as long as there is no undue arrest of progress, or sign of fetal distress (covered later in this section). Your role is to offer guidance as needed. If she suddenly experiences an overwhelming urge to push and is floundering, help her to get a breath, then tell her to center her energy and guide it down. Massaging her shoulders will keep her from holding tension high in her body, up in her chest and throat. Many women make a lot of loud, moose-like bellowing sounds with each exhale, basically an involuntary mechanism. Just have her keep her noises low-pitched grunting sounds rather than high pitched wailing or screaming. Some women do scream out with the first involuntary urge and that's OK, but don't let it become a habit, as it definitely drains energy. Also screaming (as opposed to bellowing) tends to cause tightening of facial and throat muscles, with corresponding tension in the pelvic floor. So tell her to "keep it loose," and guide her with an example of squeezing or bearing down with a released jaw and smooth brow. Keep in mind that the feeling of a baby's head pushing through the vagina is some incredible stimulation!

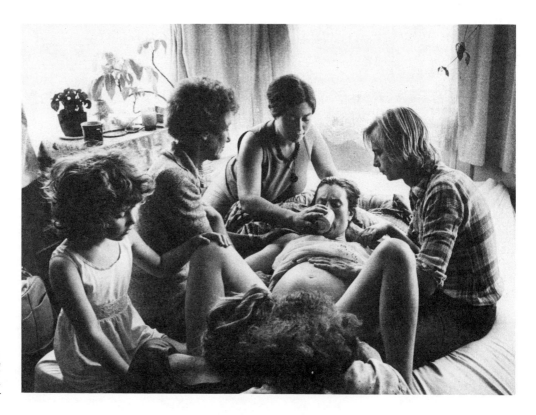

A woman in second stage gets a boost from having her friends and family gathered round.

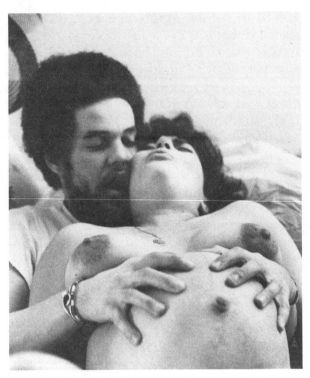

The uterus rises tall with a strong contraction, and the parents feel the passion of second stage.

Encourage her, give her your gutsy appreciation and do whatever you can to help her settle down into the sensation.

Vaginal and perineal massage can be very helpful at this point. It's best to do a bit of massage fairly early in second stage for the sake of getting the mother focused low in her body, at the same time identifying any specific areas of tension. Olive oil is a good viscous oil, and will provide a smooth continuous coating over vaginal secretions. Pour a freshly opened bottle into a squeeze-type container for easy application.

Although it is most effective to work without gloves, this cannot be recommended because of the possibility of AIDS transmission. AIDS can be transmitted through vaginal discharge, blood, amniotic fluid, and even breast milk. *You must protect yourself, your family and other clients by using gloves when in contact with any of these secretions.*

Start out slowly and be sensitive to response. Unless a woman really loves the massaging, do it only *between* contractions so you don't interfere with her efforts to interpret her contraction sensations and establish a rhythm. Concentrate on the areas closest to and immediately surrounding the descending head and just work your way down.

For working on tight internal muscle bands, the best strokes are either smooth sweeps of the entire band, or else deep pressure penetration on the tightest areas. Both are good; the first thins out and stretches, the second breaks up and un-knots the tension. Often only one side of the musculature is tight. You need not focus on the perineum while the head is still high, unless the muscles are drawing closed or remaining rigid during a push. Then it's good to massage the outlet, including the labia. Some women like clitoral massage in labor, some request it and some do it on themselves, but others find it over-stimulating and irritating. Work gently and take your cues from the mother's response. It's very important while doing massage to communicate your findings to her. So strongly do most women desire not to tear that the response to a comment like, "You're a little tight right here, now really try to let go," can be rather miraculous. Every woman should be instructed during pregnancy in techniques for releasing internal tension (using images like breathing out or exhaling from the vagina) and should develop a conscious ability to release vaginal muscles at will. This skill facilitates progress in second stage and a controlled, yet spontaneous, tear-free delivery. Perineal massage is less critical in preventing tears than the mother's attunement to her own sensations.

There is another remedy for women who are tightening up with their pushing. This is a pressure technique: use two fingers and push downward from inside the vagina against the rectum. This stimulates the mother to bear all the way down through her bottom. You might find this technique useful for women with very large babies, who have not established bearing down and seem to be stuck with the baby still high. By stimulating the pushing urge, you can gain the mother's response and cooperation, enabling her to move the baby down sufficiently to activate her natural urges.

The father should also be encouraged to do massage if he's planning to assist with delivery. Touching the baby's head internally and feeling it press down with a push will convince him that the birth is imminent. Many a father gets nervous at this first feel of the baby, and you may need to steady him with an arm around the shoulders and some very clear instructions on exactly what to do. Put your fingers close to his, showing the pace and movement of the strokes. Excited fathers tend to overdo it at first, but with some positive feedback he'll probably relax and start to enjoy it. Check from time to time to see how well tense areas have responded to his touch, and assist as necessary.

Medical Duties During Second Stage

What are the vital duties of the midwife at this time? Second stage is a rather trying one for the baby, especially if contractions are persistently strong and the baby is being subjected to much head compression. Your top priority is to listen to fetal heart tones every other contraction, listening both during and immediately after each ends. As the head moves onto the pelvic floor, listen with every contraction. The information gained will tell you what you need to know concerning management of second stage, i.e., whether or not the mother needs to accelerate her efforts to get the baby born. Strong pushing is not always the answer; change in position, deeper breathing or greater relaxation may be the key. There is definitely a limit to the tolerance of the baby when being subjected to hours of strong pushing, so listen well and often, and stay focused on facilitating (without forcing) progress.

Luckily, the fetal skull will usually mold and adapt to the musculature and bones of the pelvis. This may not be true for postmature babies in which the ossification of sutures has begun to occur; neither is it so for very large or malpresenting babies who can give only so much in proportion to the mother's internal structure. In these cases, head compression might cause **early decelerations** (FHT dropping at beginning of contractions and returning to baseline by the end). Drops of 10 points are OK in the early part of second stage; drops of 20 points are common toward the end during perineal dilation. A dip down to 100 beats per minute is not unusual, and neither is a dip to 80 during the last few contractions, but a dip to 60 indicates that the baby needs oxygen and so should be born quickly. More important than the dip itself is the recovery following the contraction; if the heart

rate bounces back up as soon as the contraction ends there is less cause for concern. If it stays much below 120, you have **bradycardia** (abnormally low baseline) and a baby that should be birthed immediately, or transported if delivery is not imminent. Whenever there is fetal distress, listen almost continuously, and have your partner cover coaching, massaging, and setting up for delivery.

It is unusual to get a pattern of early decelerations before the head has reached +1 or +2 station; in fact, this is not a good sign at all. In this situation, encourage the mother to squat and push effectively, as your goal is to shorten the period of head compression and hasten the delivery. It may be that the mother has a prominent sacral vertebra or prominent spines obstructing one plane of the midpelvis, and once past that point the pressure may ease up. You have to play it by feel; a large head remaining stationary may require some incredible pushing effort to pass through, but the mother must compensate by breathing deeply between contractions. Administering oxygen when the heart dips due to head compression is not physiologically indicated and seldom does much good. Oxygen *is* the remedy for late decelerations and slow recovery.

It is also possible to pick up variable decelerations in second stage (sporadic dips and peaks in the FHT) which generally indicate cord nipping, pinching or entanglement. Occasionally cord sounds can be heard (swishing or swish-squeaking at the same rate as the fetal heart) in the vicinity of the clearest heart tones. If the head is still high, try reversing or changing the mom's position; if the cord is pinched alongside the baby's head, change of position may relieve the pressure. But if the head is well down, listen constantly and be prepared for cord around the neck at delivery (clamps and scissors open, handy and ready for use).

Often the water bag breaks with the first few strong pushes, and you may be alarmed to find water stained with **meconium**. However, if the heart tones are within normal range, there is no need for panic. The meconium may be "old mec," evidence of temporary trauma earlier in labor or perhaps in the days preceeding birth. Be ready to do a gentle but thorough suctioning of the baby's mouth and throat with a

DeLee catheter (rubber tubing with catch-compartment) *as soon* as the head is born and *before* the baby begins breathing. Meconium aspiration is a serious matter which can cause neonatal pneumonia, and so must be prevented by doing a careful and thorough job of suctioning (see page 82).

In case of a long second stage (over two hours) or a very vigorous, shorter one, the mother should drink ample fluids or take tablespoons of honey as needed for energy boosting. Women often get very tired with a long second stage and need to be encouraged to *rest completely* between contractions. The mother's position makes a big difference; gravity positions like squatting or standing work best. But sometimes women refuse the most effective positions because sensation is so intense, and say they can't do it, can't take it anymore: "When is it going to end?" Remind the mother that her baby is almost here, and soon she'll be holding it in her arms.

The other extreme of second stage is rapid delivery. One push may bring the baby all the way down to the perineum, and the next involuntary effort may birth the entire baby, head to toe! If the mother has had a baby already and her second stage was 20 minutes or less, she is definitely a candidate. Women who deliver like this often complain that they never experienced the satisfaction of real pushing; if you anticipate a quick descent, position the woman on hands and knees during transition so she enters second stage without the force of gravity. This may not slow things down for long, but it will give a woman a few valuable moments for integrating her sensations, and you a bit more time to prepare for the birth.

Assisting Delivery

Delivery positions should be discussed prenatally, as many women have definite ideas and preferences. The best positions are probably hands-and-knees and semi-sit; squatting with adequate support is a possibility too. Lying on the back is contrary to the laws of gravity and not good for the baby, due to compression of the maternal vena cara with resulting oxygen deprivation. Lying on one side with leg raised has an unbalanced, passive quality that affects the mother's feeling of control and active participation, although it does reduce strain on the perineum. It seems that most women prefer the semi-sit position, which allows them to see what's going on and to reach down and lift the baby up as it's coming out. The main advantage for the midwife is easy access to heart tones. The parents experience an emotional bonus if the father sits behind the mother so they are completely in touch and united as they witness the birth.

Hands-and-knees does have some strong points, particularly for women with large babies, or for women who have had a prolonged period of pushing with the head quite low (indicating some disproportion in the mid-pelvic and outlet dimensions). This is because hands-and-knees opens the pelvis to its greatest capacity, and promotes good muscular relaxation. This position is a well-known remedy for delayed delivery of the shoulders; simply having the mother assume hands-and-knees will often bring the baby spontaneously, without any need for further maneuvering.

Many women find their position instinctively just as delivery is about to occur, so it's best to be ready for anything. One woman spoke of spending her pushing stage primarily in hands-and-knees, having found a certain comfort in that position and a style of working with her contractions, but at the last moment her midwife insisted that she flip over to semi-sit. Perhaps the midwife had never assisted a woman on hands-and-knees, but the mother recalled feeling quite disoriented, and believed that her subsequent loss of control and extensive tearing with delivery were due to this last-minute change. Every midwife should visualize and prepare to assist either position, so she can follow the mother's lead in this respect.

Once delivery is imminent, the time of utmost concentration has arrived. No matter how many birthings a midwife has assisted, there can be nothing matter-of-fact about assisting delivery, especially if she is close to the mother and is willing to let her participation be guided by love. *Every delivery is unique!* There are particular skills for making it smooth, but the midwife's main responsibility is to concentrate, to sense and respond on all pertinent levels with an attitude of *devotion*. This is the essence of midwifery care; you are assistant

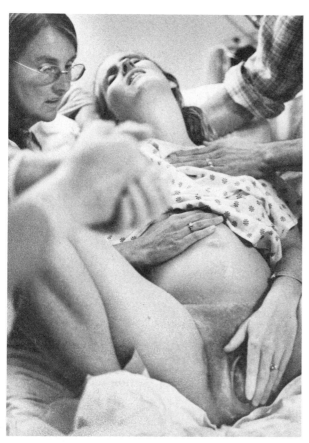
The magical wonder of touching your baby for the first time.

not only to the parents, but handmaiden to forces much greater than yourself.

Now for the specifics of preventing tears. One of the most critical and most appreciated techniques is the application of hot compresses to the perineum. These stimulate good circulation, promote relaxation and provide relief from burning, tingling sensations. You can use a sterile gauze pad, sanitary napkin or a clean washcloth soaked in a solution of hot water with a squeeze of Betadine or other antiseptic added. Compresses are especially important if the perineum blanches during distension. They are also a help for mothers who are involuntarily contracting the outlet muscles. If it looks like the delivery will be fairly rapid you might not have time to give compresses, but you might have your partner or apprentice do so while you concentrate on your other responsibilities.

As the head moves toward the outlet, massage any muscle bands inhibiting it, beginning with the start of the contraction and then easing up at the peak to allow the head itself to stretch through the area on which you've been working. Use plenty of oil! If the mother is heavy or has a lot of fatty padding, place two fingers of each hand inside her and pull down and outward at points four and eight o'clock, literally making room for the head to descend. Once the head has receded and sensation is passing away, finish with half-circular strokes on the perineum itself, between points three and nine o'clock. Apply another compress in the interim and resume your massage as the next contraction begins.

Don't forget the urethral area, as tears in these tissues are both painful and difficult to suture. It's enough to gently oil the surface area; massage is generally uncomfortable.

Now while you are going through your routine of perineal massage and compresses, remember to check the baby's condition. Ultimately this is the factor that determines how much time you can spend on keeping the perineum intact. Your fetascope should be conveniently hanging around your neck, and if you have the type with a forehead brace you can listen to the baby during a contraction and keep your hands free to support the perineum at the same time. However, most midwives work in pairs so these tasks can be divided, allowing each partner a chance to rest occasionally or to focus on the emotional needs of the couple.

At this time of maximum head compression, an early deceleration pattern with dips to 100 beats per minute should not cause concern. Most worrisome are decelerations with poor recovery or persistent bradycardia. Oxygen for the mother can help, but if the heart rate dips *and stays* below 100, the baby should be born immediately. Inform the mother that she needs to get the baby out quickly and that you need her full attention and cooperation. Tell her to let go and *relax completely,* and that you'll cue her when to push. Sometimes this advice is enough to dissolve the last little bit of resistance and the baby births spontaneously with the next contraction. Otherwise you may need to do an episiotomy; if so, do it only at the height of a contraction, directing your scissors down the midline of the perineum and clipping about an inch. More about episiotomies in the next few pages.

Sometimes it becomes very difficult to hear heart tones during second stage. Eventually your fetascope will rest right at the edge of the pubic bone, and as the baby moves lower still, the heart tones may become inaudible. This coincides with the phase of perineal stretching, which usually lasts for only a few contractions, but may occasionally take longer. So the problem presents itself: how can you continue to take your time carefully easing delivery, if you have no clue to the baby's well-being? Fortunately there is another indicator you can use, and that is the *color of the baby's scalp*. Also important is the rate at which the blood returns when the scalp skin is gently depressed. Both of these indicate whether the circulation and oxygen concentration in the baby's blood are adequate. Once, while attending a hospital delivery, I heard the obstetrician say, "I'll hang my hat on pink scalps." This test must be modified for babies of Black parentage due to a naturally dusky skin tone, but you can still check the rate of venous return and pay special attention to the color which appears immediately after doing the depression. A pinkish-blue is a good sign, blue is not the best and white-blue is ominous.

Now, back to the mother and her distending perineum. Assuming that the baby is doing all right, heart tones OK or scalp color reassuring, you can afford to relax and take your time in helping the mother to stretch out. Most important at this point is to *engage the woman in sensitive breathing*; as soon as the head is bulging forward, encourage her to pant, and show her how to stay with it without tightening up or holding back. Both books and birth classes propose that panting be reserved for the actual crowning, but experience teaches that if the baby is coming down quickly, it ought to be started much sooner. Anyway, there is nothing to lose by having the mother pant through one contraction; it gives you a chance to see how much force her body is exerting by itself so that you can decide how rapidly delivery is approaching and what you should do. If she pants through one contraction and there's no descent, have her resume pushing with the next. By getting her accustomed to panting before her sensations are totally overwhelming, you give her the power to ease up or come on according to what she feels. If ever she complains of the burning or tingling which are signs of extreme stretching, it's time to have her pant.

And what about perineal massage? Well, your emphasis changes to support, because by now the head is filling the opening so that you can barely fit your fingers inside. As soon as the head starts to bulge the outlet forward, apply a gauze pad firmly to the perineum and hold it in place with your other hand. This prevents fecal matter (which can cause contamination) from reaching the vagina.

As the head approaches crowning, apply some oil to the entire outlet, running your finger around and restroking any whitened areas gently and repeatedly. Then, when the head recedes between times, apply more heat via compresses.

Once the head begins to work its way outward, with a circular circumference presenting and not much receding during rests, it's time to forget about massage and use your free hand for guarding the urethral area and for controlling the rate of expulsion (the other hand stays on the perineum). By positioning the wrist edge of this hand right at the top of the outlet and letting your fingers extend down over the head, you can simultaneously ease the head under the pubic bone and keep the head in a well-flexed positon. The perineal hand maintains counterpressure and also encourages flexion by holding back the sinciput (forehead) while the parietal bones clear the upper part of the opening. Thus you assist the smallest possible diameter to crown through the outlet; a most critical aspect of preventing tearing.

This two-handed juggling act of easing the pressure back and forth between top and bottom, guiding, letting stretch, gently restraining, etc., must obviously be learned by experience. Here is a general guideline, though: if you feel that a tear is unavoidable and something has got to give, let it be the perineum. Never let up on your control with that upper hand; many novices make the mistake of guarding the perineum so well that they actually cause periurethral tears by pushing the head upward. And, most important of all, *hold on* to the perineum as the head is born over it. Don't let go!

HEART & HANDS

Sometimes an arrest occurs in this perineal phase. Perhaps the head has been on the perineum for several contractions, the mother has been panting during them, you've tried compresses, but no progress. A couple more contractions, and episiotomy comes to mind. Sometimes this arrest is due to tension in the mother's tissues, sometimes it's due to a large or deflexed head, and occasionally there is residual, almost unconscious psychological resistance which may be caused, ironically enough, by the fear of tearing! You might try having her push between contractions, for if she is fighting the force of sensation and the pressure on the perineum, she may be able to relax better and push more effectively between times. If this doesn't work, you should do an episiotomy. Position your fingers inside to protect the head, and have your scissors inserted and ready to cut as the head comes forward with the next contraction. Episiotomy can cause bleeding, so apply a clean gauze pad with pressure to the area that has been cut.

Sometimes it's necessary to extend an episiotomy to accommodate an extremely large head, but generally, no matter what size you cut, the tissues will be vulnerable to tearing beyond the apex. To help prevent this, you need to support and apply counterpressure to the base of the wound, just as you would guard and protect the midline of the perineum.

As soon as the baby's head is out, do a quick appraisal of color and in-the-body quality. Note how energized, how physically alert it appears to be, how vital. And look for signs of stress: white-blue head with clenched mouth usually indicates a baby that needs to be birthed quickly, and one that may need some help in getting started. Regardless, wipe any excessive amounts of blood and mucus or meconium away from the eyes, nose and mouth, and then do suction as indicated. A large rubber ear syringe (3 oz.) should be used when moderate secretions are noticed. Be sure to squeeze all the air out of it before inserting in the mouth, or you will force mucus and

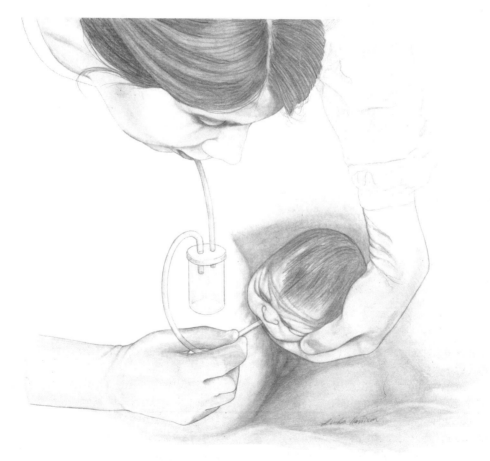

Using the DeLee Mucus Trap

fluids further down the throat and possibly into the lungs.

The DeLee trap is a must for thick mucus or meconium, because you can go deeper and see what you are getting out. First check to see that the lid is screwed on tightly so the device will work correctly. Then insert the tubing about four inches into the mouth, and withdraw slowly while sucking sharply, over and over (see illustration, page 81). Be sure to tell the mother not to push until you are finished; you can also have your assistant hold the baby back as a precaution. If you are still bringing up meconium as you finish suctioning, you should repeat the procedure until the fluid is clear. But work quickly, particularly if the baby appears depressed.

If the baby has no fluids bubbling at its mouth there is no reason to do anything. Suction need not be done routinely.

Next check around the neck for any loops of umbilical cord. To do this, slip your finger (sensitive side out) along the back of the baby's neck, and if you find cord simply flex your finger, grasp, and pull it over the head in one quick movement. Remember, this all must be done before the next contraction. If you find that you cannot pull the cord free or that there is not quite enough slack to slip it over the head, perhaps you can create a loop large enough for the shoulders and body to birth through. As a last resort, quickly clamp the cord twice with curved hemostats (curved so they don't poke into the baby), cut between them with blunt scissors and unwind the cord away.

It is crucial when the cord is tight that you remind the mother to keep panting, and tell her firmly not to push until you let her know that it's OK. You might also make the announcement "tight cord" as soon as you discover it, so your assistant can have your instruments ready.

By now the shoulders should be ready to deliver. If there seems to be a delay with the next contraction and the baby's head is getting suffused with blood (turning purplish) it's time to get the baby out via the mother's pushing efforts. Don't wait on this; as long as the baby's chest is compressed inside the mother's vagina, venous return from the head will be im-

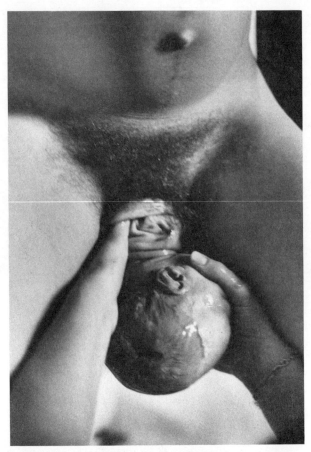

A woman in France giving birth in an upright squat, very effective for promoting pelvic relaxation and bringing the baby down.

paired, and intercranial pressure can build up to dangerous levels. So, encourage the mother! If you have an assistant, have her support the perineum as you catch the shoulders, or support it yourself if the father is doing the delivery. The head should be gently grasped on either side, guided downward until the first shoulder appears and then immediately lifted up and outward (45 degree angle) so that the lower shoulder will not drag and cause a tear. Shift hands to catch the baby and lay it gently on the mom's belly. If it is doing well (starting to breathe) place it right in her arms, facing her, but if it is pale or gurgling, place it up by her breasts where she can touch it but with its face downward. This will promote drainage of fluids and make suctioning easier. And cover the baby immediately with two or three flannel blankets (preferably oven-warmed) to help maintain its temperature.

Keep an eye on the baby and do Apgar scoring (see Appendix H) at one and five minutes. Be sure that the baby is kept warm; its first set of blankets are usually dampened with fluid and need prompt changing. Help the mother to get comfortably positioned so that both she and the baby can relax together. See that she is warm enough and has something sweet to drink, and then ease back to your tasks and give the new family a chance to bond.

These are the mechanics of normal delivery; about 90 percent of all your birthings will follow this basic pattern. Emotionally, though, every delivery is unique, depending on how involved the woman has been with her labor, how alert or tired she may be and generally, how happy she is to be having a baby. For the woman who has really found her way with labor, the moments of delivery are a time of complete concentration and inner focus. Intensity builds in second stage until sensation is continual (baby's head and body in the vagina, putting constant pressure on the nerve endings) and so overwhelming are these feelings that the mother generally surrenders her own body image to an awareness of her baby's form. This is for many a spiritual and sexual experience of union, merging . . . the orgasm of delivery.

There are some women who cannot easily surrender to so much sensation and fight for control, and others who simply won't stand for it and insist on pushing indiscriminately. These women should be warned about their likelihood of tearing, and should then be guided to reach down and feel the baby's head with the skin stretched all around it. Often this brings a sigh or moan of surrender as connection with the baby finally occurs, and delivery usually follows soon after.

Regardless of how sensitively a woman delivers her baby, the sudden sensation of emptiness that follows can come as both a relief *and a shock*. It is of greatest importance that the woman be given her baby immediately, so the shock does not deepen into numbness that will hinder her ability to bond. The practice of keeping the baby down on the mother's thigh until stable, or that of routine suctioning, cleaning, and cutting the cord before giving the baby to the mother, are unnatural methods which definitely disrupt the pleasure and needs of the mother, father and baby. No ex-

ceptions to this; even the baby who is born "floppy" should be lifted onto the mother and attempts at stimulation started with baby resting against mother's skin. This gives the mother a chance to connect with her baby and express her concern for its survival and well-being.

Third Stage

The key to a safe and easy third stage is *watchful observation*. Many a bonding period has disintegrated because the over-zealous midwife insisted on cord traction or squatting for the placenta before the time was really ripe. And then again, many a prolonged wait for the placenta, with disruptive anxiety as the overtone, has been caused by a non-attentive attendant missing crucial signs that the time has come to act. Watchful observation means exactly that; participation is indicated by specific signs and signals rather than by routine.

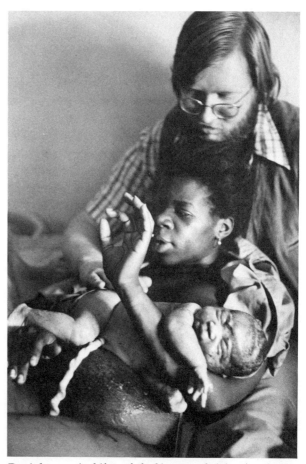

Don't be surprised if you feel a bit stunned right after the baby is born; it's such a tremendous release!

As soon as the baby is delivered and is warm and stable, your task is to attend to the mother and to see that her third stage is safely completed. The umbilical cord should not be cut until it has ceased pulsation. Rest it between the fingers of one hand (your thumb has a pulse) to check for this. When you clamp, put one clamp fairly close to the mother's outlet and the other about eight inches away. Have the father or assistant cut between them; several inches from the clamp nearest the baby.

By keeping an eye on the clamp nearest the mother you can watch for signs of placental separation; the clamp should move downward with the characteristic lengthening of the cord as the placenta descends. While you attend to the cord, keep an eye on the outlet for any sign of abnormal bleeding; usually there is very little blood until the characteristic gush-flow that signals separation. Occasionally the placenta will separate only partially and blood will pool behind it, so you should keep a hand resting constantly on the uterus in order to check for

any bogginess or increase in size which might indicate that this is happening. Do not massage or prod the uterus, as this stimulation can cause isolated sections of muscle to contract, thus predisposing to partial separation. *Keep your hands still.*

Delivering The Placenta

Nine times out of ten, the placenta separates all at once and as you notice the cord lengthening, the mother says she feels like pushing. This is an opportune time for her to squat, or if she is resting with the baby and doesn't feel like moving you can assist her with expulsion. The best way to do this is by using *controlled cord traction*, which simply means applying mild, guiding traction to the cord while at the same time *guarding* or protecting the uterus from prolapsing downward. Sounds complicated and a bit dangerous, and indeed it can be if the placenta is not fully detached. When in doubt, make certain the placenta is separated by donning a clean glove and following the cord up-

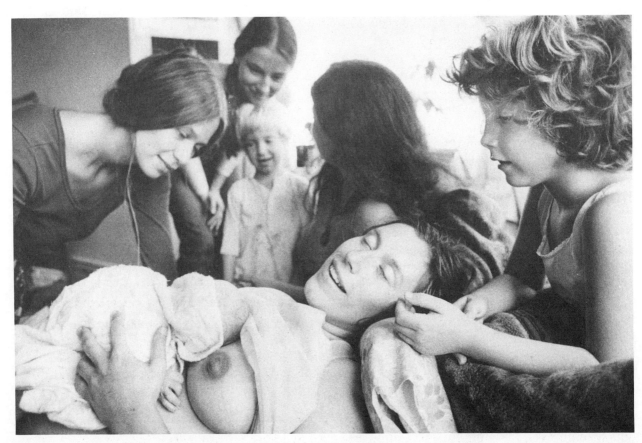

The ecstacy of delivery. One of the reasons for natural birth is this feeling akin to orgasm, of building up and completion.

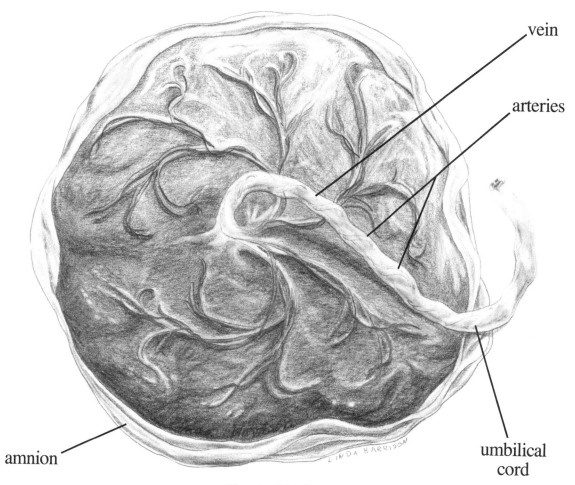

vein

arteries

amnion

umbilical cord

Placenta: Fetal Side

ward with your fingers; if it is in the vagina or at the cervical os you can go ahead. Apply traction by following the natural L-shaped curve of the birth canal. You can guard the uterus by pressing the edge of your hand in above the pubic bone and upwards towards the mother's head (see page 116). Do this with contractions or with the mother's pushing efforts.

What's the average time span for delivery of the placenta? About 20 minutes; often separation occurs in minutes but the membranes remain adherent, needing the weight of the placenta to pull them downward. When the placenta begins to slip out, it's best to catch and support it because if the membranes are adherent they may shred or tear should the placenta simply fall into the basin. If the membranes do seem stuck, you can coax or tease them out by moving the placenta with a give-and-take, circular motion. Or you can twist the placenta around and around so that the membranes form a rope, then coax outwards.

Once the placenta is expelled, check immediately to be certain that the uterus is well-contracted and give it a few quick squeezes to expel any clots which might have formed. Then settle back for more observation, watching for bleeding and feeling the uterus periodically for firmness. If you do notice softness, asymmetry in shape, or excessive bleeding from the outlet, rub up a good firm contraction and encourage the mother to nurse her baby, if she's not already doing so. Slow trickle bleeding must be watched very carefully; give herbal tincture of shepherd's purse/alfalfa/cohosh/ immediately. If blood begins to flow steadily or come in spurts, it's time to resort to emergency measures (see Hemorrhage, Chapter 5).

Check the placenta as soon as possible after it has been delivered. You can do this right there at the bedside, still keeping a watchful eye on the mother. If she is bleeding and you are working on controlling it have your assistant check, as retained products may be the cause

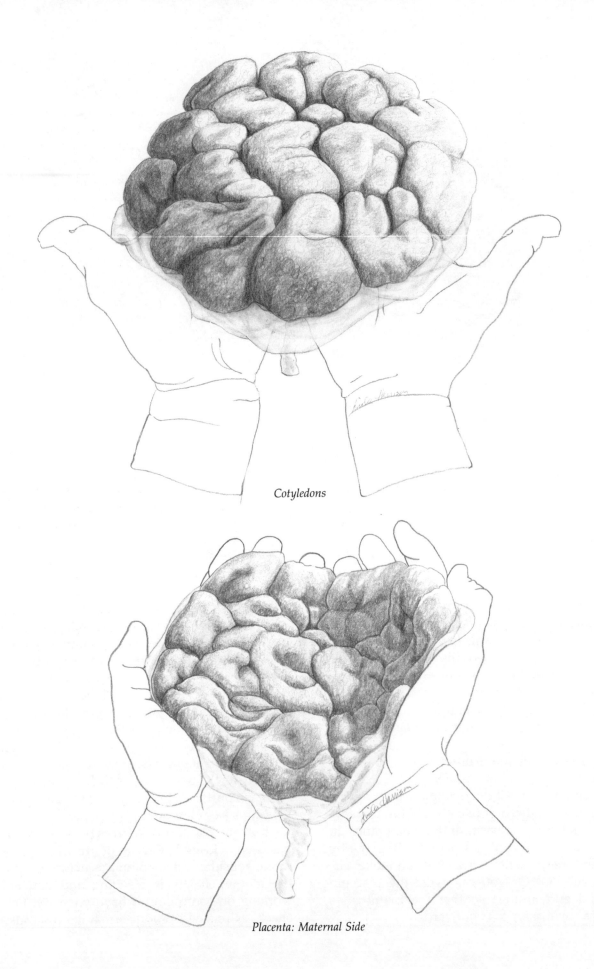

Cotyledons

Placenta: Maternal Side

of the problem. If this is the case, no amount of massage or pitocin will control the bleeding for any length of time. The cardinal rule for dealing with hemorrhage is to *determine the cause of bleeding* so you know how best to respond.

When examining the placenta start with the fetal side first, noting the cord insertion, and then checking for any venous pattern in the membranes. If you do see any veins leading off into membrane and ending abruptly, it's probable that a **succenturiate lobe** (mini-placenta) is still retained in utero, bound to cause a heavy bleed. This must be removed manually, either by you or by someone in the hospital, in order to control/prevent hemorrhage (see Chapter 5).

Next turn the placenta over and examine the maternal side. Start by pulling away the clots, then hold it in your hands so that it opens convexly, exposing rents and separations clearly. Then cup it together, and see if the edges of the rents and spaces join evenly and match up. Check all around the edge of the placenta to make sure that it blends cleanly into membrane and nothing appears to have been torn away. You'll learn to do this first exam fairly rapidly and can save a more detailed examination for later, when mother and baby are stable and settled and you have free time.

Once the placenta has delivered, attend to other tasks such as clamping and re-cutting the cord next to the baby, getting the baby and mother warm and cozy and cleaned up, and facilitating breastfeeding. If you have a partner, she can handle the baby while you attend to the mother. But if you are working alone you need to establish priorities; the cord can wait, a few extra blankets will keep the baby warm until you have time to change the originals, cleanup can be delayed, but the *mother's comfort* is very important. If she has slouched down in her pillows, have her mate or someone else help her into a comfortable sitting position, with enough support under each elbow to enable her to cradle the baby easily. Once she is relaxed and alert she will bond more readily with the baby.

Checking For Tears

Once the placenta is out and bleeding is stable, the mother will want to know if she has torn, and you'll be anxious to resolve this question for yourself. Reglove, wash the mother with warm water and Betadine and discard the bloodied underpads beneath her, replacing them with several fresh ones. You must use fresh gloves (sterile technique) to check for tears because the cervix is still open and the uterus is susceptible to infection. Arrange good lighting (a high intensity lamp works well) then open some gauze, put on your gloves, take gauze in hand and part the labia, and see what you can see. You should check for abrasions, obvious tears around the urethra and perineum, and internal muscle splits which are best discovered by feeling gently and carefully around the vaginal walls (see Chapter 5 for further instructions).

If the mother needs no stitching, her uterus is firm, her placenta is complete, and her baby has good color and responsiveness, you can finally settle back a bit. You can also facilitate family integration with some heartfelt comments about the birth and the baby. This will help with any self-conscious feelings the mother or father might have about their behavior during labor. As the new family relaxes and draws closer together, give them their privacy and go out to the kitchen for a break of your own. Take the placenta along for closer examination, and tell the mother to call if she feels herself bleeding or feels weak or dizzy.

Check in on her every ten minutes, and bring her some juice or something to eat if she wants it. When the band of observers begins to disperse and she is ready to get up and around, be sure someone goes with her. Then attend to cleaning up, changing the bed linens, etc.

Newborn Exam

Because of the AIDS risk, wear gloves for this. Be sure the mother has breastfed and that both parents have had a chance to fondle and bond with the baby. Do the exam right on the bed so the parents can watch, and explain each step as you move along (refer to Newborn Exam form, Appendix H).

Begin by listening to the baby's **heart beat**. Take a close listen for any abnormal or unusual rhythm pattern, and then time it carefully. The heart rate often drops a bit after delivery; this is normal. Normal rate is about 110–150.

Then check the **lungs**, listening carefully

from the baby's backside. Position your stethoscope up near the shoulders, and then again down at mid-back level (listening twice on each side). The lungs should sound clear, air resonating as if in a hollow chamber without any rattling or scratchy noises. This is particularly important if there has been any meconium at delivery; if such is the case and the baby's lungs sound obstructed, take the baby to the pediatrician right away.

Next (beginning at the top of the list), observe the baby's **overall condition** and activity level. Give a brief description, e.g. "pink, vigorous, strong cry," or "good color and reflexes but quiet, didn't nurse for one and a half hours." Thus you set the tone for the rest of the appraisal.

Then check the **skin**. Note the color; a bright red tone is associated with prematurity and a condition known as *polycythemia* (excess red cells), which necessitates medical attention. *Desquamation* (peeling skin) is associated with postmaturity and is no cause for alarm. Babies of Black, Mediterranean or Hispanic parentage may have *Mongolian Spots* (patches of dark tone) at the base of the spine, which are normal and will usually vanish in time. Note any birth marks, or hairy moles. If vernix is present, be sure to rub in any collected in skin folds or it can cause inflammation.

It's important to check the **head** carefully for any excessive molding, bruising or swelling. All of these indicate some trauma with delivery. *Caput* is a normal, generalized, top-of-the-head swelling, whereas *cephalhematoma* is an abnormal, lump-like swelling confined to a particular area; it does not cross suture lines and is associated with internal bleeding. This is a serious sign of trauma, necessitating a pediatrician's attention and vitamin K injection to prevent further hemorrhage. Sometimes cephalhematoma subsides all by itself, but it does require close surveillance. If combined with bruising or excessive molding, the baby should definitely be seen as soon as possible.

Check the **eyes** for red spots (conjunctival hemorrhages from the pressure during birth) and instill medication. I prefer tetracycline drops or erythromycin ointment. Both have antibiotic properties; neither causes irritation. Either will be effective against gonorrhea or chlamydia.

ENT means **ear, nose and throat.** Check the lips, and check the palate by placing your little finger (soft side up) in the baby's mouth and feeling carefully all around and way to the back to be sure it's intact. Take a look at the ears, check for skin tags and note the general ear placement. The top of the crest should be at the eye level; low lying ears are often associated with kidney problems. Such a baby should be seen immediately.

To check the **thorax** for *retractions*, observe the chest and stomach action when the baby breathes. Ribs and belly should inflate smoothly together; if baby struggles and skin pulls tight against ribs, the baby has retractions which can indicate immature lungs, lung damage or obstruction. A pediatrician should see the baby at once.

Next check the **abdomen.** Occasionally you will note *umbilical hernia*, which appears as a bulging at the base of the cord stump. This is not caused by any particular method of handling or tying the cord, but is a congenital defect which can be remedied by surgery when the child is around two years old. Also feel the belly for masses, lumps, swellings; all should feel smooth and even.

Check **genitals** carefully to be sure that all the essential parts and openings are present. Boys should be checked to see that both testes are descended. This is not difficult; simply place your finger at the top of one side of the scrotum to close off the inguinal canal and feel carefully for the testis, then repeat on the other side. This is especially important in breech births as trauma may cause torsion and swelling, and one testis may be lost unless the problem is detected within several hours of delivery. Girl babies frequently have some vaginal mucus.

The **back** of the baby should be closely examined along the spine. This area can be easily overlooked. Check for incomplete fusion and look for sinuses (appearing as deep dimples), especially in the sacral area.

Now check the **extremities.** Count fingers and toes, and check for webbing. Check the arms for symmetry and good muscle tone. This is especially important if there has been a tight squeeze with the shoulders, as shoulder dystocia can cause fracture of the clavicle and/or nerve damage. Also check the hips by doing the "click test," rotating the legs firmly in their sockets and listening for any clicking sound that might indicate dislocation. If you hear something, make a note of it and then turn the baby over to check hip creases from the backside. These should be even and symmetrical; if not, have the baby seen by a physician.

Reflexes have usually been demonstrated by now, at least sucking and swallowing. The baby should be able to grasp your fingers so tightly that you can lift its head slightly off the bed. The startle (moro) reflex is observed when the baby is tipped back suddenly; the arms and hands should extend evenly. These reflexes are important as their presence is a sign of maturity and neurological health.

Check the **anus** by observation; it is not necessary to insert a thermometer to check for patency. If the baby has not passed meconium it will often have a mec plug visible at the opening; this is also proof of patency.

Last, but definitely most interesting to parents and friends, is the **weighing and measuring.** Measure the head circumference first, in centimeters (average measurements are 34–37cms.). Then measure the chest; the difference between head and chest should be no more than a few centimeters. If the head is much larger, there may be an abnormal amount of fluid in the cranial cavity which should be checked immediately by the pediatrician. Measure the baby's length by setting the tape alongside the baby's body with top edge at a level with the tip of the head, then stretch the leg out and measure at the heel. Chart both centimeters and inches (inches for parents). To weigh, use either a standard baby scale or the more convenient hanging scale, which has a hook from which the baby is temporarily suspended in a stork-style bundle. Whatever you use, don't forget to subtract the weight of the blankets. Chart in both pounds and grams.

Wrap the baby in dry blankets. If it is content, this may be a good time for the father to hold it while the mother takes a shower or stretches her legs a bit.

Postpartum Watch

Your postpartum watch should last for at least two hours, longer if there has been repeated or recent bleeding or if anything unusual is hap-

pening with the baby. The mother should have something to eat and drink, should urinate and nurse successfully before you go. Be sure to leave copies of the Birth Record and Newborn Exam for the parents to take to their pediatrician. Go over your postpartum instructions carefully (see Appendix K), making sure that parents understand everything. Encourage them to call you anytime, about anything, at any hour. And don't leave until *they* seem to feel comfortable about your going.

You should also be sure that *you* are in a stable condition before leaving. Particularly after a grueling labor or difficult delivery, you may be absolutely exhausted and should rest, eat something and relax with your partner before getting back on the road. Those first few hours after the birth fly by; make a habit of getting something to drink or a bite to eat immediately

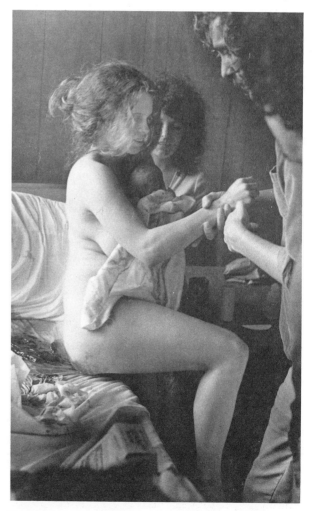

Triumphant and tender, the new mother gets up with her baby for the first time.

after delivery so that you're in shape to go when it's time to leave.

* * *

Talk about getting on the road—I once had very unusual circumstances getting to and from a birthing. I was seeing a woman who had quite a bit of edema in her legs and ankles, so I decided to take my kids and go over midweek to check her blood pressure and urine. Catherine was fine, and I was heading down the stairs carrying a big bag of clothes she had given me for the kids, when I slipped and fell and twisted my ankle! Wow, I knew it was the *real* thing; I called for ice, did some deep breathing, etc. My kids gathered around me, concerned, and helped me to make it out to the car. I crawled up my three flights of stairs, got my son to bring me a bucket of ice water to soak my foot and settled in for a rest.

Then Catherine called to announce that her water bag had broken and she was having regular contractions! After several moments of pure panic, I called Linda (my apprentice) who said she'd come over and make dinner while we waited to see what Catherine would do. Not long after the kids were asleep my friend George showed up, and then "the call" came from Catherine saying that her labor was really moving and feeling intense. So was the pain in my ankle about this time, so Linda volunteered to go over while I waited and rested some more.

Then Linda called and said, "she's only three centimeters but she says she can't stand it and wants to go to the hospital."

"Are you sure she's only three?" I asked.

"Yep," said Linda. "What should I do?"

"Talk to her, get her in the shower on a stool, rub her back, and help her with her breathing," was my reply, and I relaxed, figuring on a good long rest (and time for my ice to work) before running off.

One hour later Linda's voice came ringing, "Liz, she's complete, she feels like pushing!"

"Oh my god," I said. "Alright, I'll be right over." Luckily George is a muscle-

---

Golden Tips for Fathers

Here are some special ways to assist your partner during labor:

1. If labor begins at night and is light, help her back to sleep with a massage.
2. If labor begins during the day, take her to a place you both love where you can get used to labor together.
3. Help her to eat as long as possible; prepare (or buy) her favorite foods.
4. Wear something she likes, and keep in close, relaxed physical contact with her.
5. As labor progresses, help her relax by encouraging her to let her body "go limp," and stroke her gently to reassure her.
6. Breathe with her if she starts to panic.
7. Don't be embarrassed to use common endearments with your midwives around; she *needs* to hear them from you!
8. In transition, speak tenderly to her between contractions, and maintain eye contact during contractions.
9. Once she is pushing, get your body close to her somehow so she feels your reinforcement.
10. Let her know when you can see the baby's head, and help her reach down and touch it.
11. Tell her you love her, especially after the baby comes out.

man, so we made it in style. Down three flights of stairs, into his car and up Catherine's steps he carried me, until moments later he deposited me on a well-placed chair right at the edge of the bed. I felt like an obstetrician on her little black stool just waiting for the catch! Luckily there was an end table nearby, on which I propped my throbbing foot.

And Linda and I immediately clicked into action; I directed while she got Catherine comfortable, checked vitals and set up for delivery all in a flash.

After a marvelous, tear-free birthing of a beautiful girl, I had the supreme pleasure of being escorted home in the same glorious fashion. A hilarious and wonderful night for everyone!

CHAPTER 5

Complications in Labor

Complications arising during labor present the midwife with both challenge and test. Prenatal problems are not so crucial as there is usually time to consider, consult and re-evaluate from visit to visit. But labor is so condensed that decisions must be made both carefully *and* quickly. Close and vigilant attention throughout will alert the midwife to the first sign of trouble. Beyond that, sensitivity and objectivity must be combined to evaluate whether a chosen course of management is proving effective. Labor is so intensive that feedback is fairly immediate, as long as you stay open to it.

One of the midwife's most essential skills is the ability to consider the total picture, while pinpointing the area on which to focus the remedy. In the midst of every difficult labor it is *essential to keep the overview*, to keep an eye on loose ends which may require attention later on in labor or postpartum. And be sure that belief in the principle of non-intervention never becomes an excuse for laziness or indifference. There is a delicate balance between the parents' right to give birth undisturbed, to proceed at their own pace and learn their lessons, and the need for the midwife to use her knowledge in such a way that strength, stamina and safety are maintained to the end.

The effect of maternal emotions on labor should never be underestimated. There are definitely instances when emotional problems portend physical danger, and still there is safe leeway for turning the tide and getting labor back on course again. The miraculous changes that occur with emotional breakthrough are as critical to positive outcome as physical care and treatment.

Handling complications means *facilitating*

change. This is part art, part logic. Take it step-by-step, like this:

1. determine the possible cause or causes of the complication;
2. test your diagnosis through further observation plus discussion with your partner and the parents;
3. modify your diagnosis if need be and then implement your remedy by gaining an agreement with parents to give your suggestions a try;
4. follow up with close and careful checks on vital signs and progress to determine effects and results; and
5. watch carefully for any side effects which might be arising and re-evaluate if indicated.

It helps tremendously if the entire birthing team is dedicated to working together. If you sense a non-committal attitude from the parents, you've done your best to counsel hope and courage and still the response is tentative, it may be that the birth is not meant to happen at home. Wasting time in limbo is dissipating, particularly when labor forces are struggling to move ahead. If the parents agree to go to the hospital, the move should be made as quickly as possible.

Sometimes parents request transport, not out of fear or desperation but because they sense that something is really wrong. Always honor this decision and never try to dissuade parents from it.

Transport is a complication and trauma in itself, especially if labor has been long and everyone is tired. Parents usually need help with preparations for leaving: getting dressed, packing a bag, making childcare arrangements and calling a few relatives. Some men are moved to tears at this point out of sympathy for their partner, out of sadness for the loss of their home-birth dream, and out of sheer frustration and exhaustion. Some get angry and accusing. Meanwhile, you must contact the obstetrician and call the hospital to arrange for admission. Trying to be lucid and medically articulate while suffering from sleep deprivation can be quite a challenge. It helps to have a Transport Form filled out with the most vital information, so questions from hospital personnel can be kept to a minimum when you do arrive (see Appendix). And be sure your chart is totally up to date; work on it in the car if necessary.

Life threatening emergencies seldom arise, but when they do, the focus is on survival and there's no time for integrating the unexpected. But with the majority of hospital transports there is time en route to give reassurance, support and hope to the parents. Being a source of strength in either case is one of the greatest services you can render.

Prolonged First Stage and Maternal Exhaustion

Prolonged first stage has many causes, some emotional and some physiologic. Often the two are interwoven and it's up to you to sort through and get down to the primary problem. For example, say you're working with a woman with a large baby that never engaged before labor; it's common to see an arrest of progress at around six centimeters due to lack of descent and insufficient cervical stimulation. Quite possibly the mother will become frustrated and impatient, but no amount of counsel or encouragement can override an inadequate pelvis if that is the principal cause of arrest.

In itself, a long latent phase is no cause for concern as long as the woman is handling her contractions with relative ease and is able to eat, exercise and rest in good measure. Latent labor should not interfere with normal life; encourage the woman to go for a walk, to a movie or to visit friends. The midwife can gauge her own involvement by the way the mother is reacting to her contractions. If she is only one or two centimeters dilated and is panting, groaning and plugging away, she needs a hand at winding down in order to conserve energy and maintain her sense of humor.

But occasionally you have the confusing case of a woman who seems to be in *active* labor, with contractions coming every five minutes, lasting a minute or more, moderately strong by palpation and yet no dilation past two or three centimeters over a period of hours. To interpret such a case as "long latent phase" would be a mistake: you must go by the length and strength of contractions. Dilatation measurement aside, this is actually an arrest of very early, *active* labor.

There is a stereotype that tends to this problem; it's the woman with a strong athletic or intellectual component who is unable to surrender control. Uterine fatigue and inertia are not long in coming and at this point, a complete break for everyone is the best solution. If the uterus has made its first attempt at labor and for one reason or another has become exhausted, it will start up again after a period of rest (and dilation may take place quite quickly). In the meantime, you may find yourself feeling rather foolish, having gotten so involved in coaching and carefully listening to the baby, only to end up with a woman at two centimeters with no more contractions. It's natural to wonder, "What was I doing here, anyway . . . maybe I just should have waited at home!" But strong contractions do necessitate surveillance of mother and baby, so involvement is no mistake. Best thing now is to go home and have a meal and rest; suggest that the parents do likewise, taking a glass of wine for relaxation before they get some sleep. Often the chance to be completely alone, with a taste of true labor behind them, will set a couple to talking about any unresolved conflicts or their immediate need to be close to each other. This sets the stage for rapid progress in the next round.

The confusing thing in such cases is determining just how much energy should be put into stimulating labor. On one hand, you don't want the mother to resist or minimize active forces (by ineffectual positioning, for example) but neither do you want her running around at a time when rest would conserve her strength. I attended a birth that was classic in this

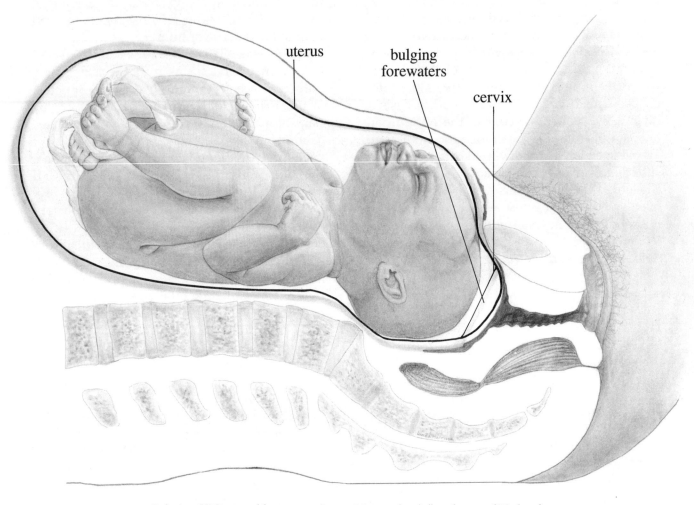

uterus

bulging
forewaters

cervix

Relative CPD caused by a posterior position and a deflexed, asynclitic head.

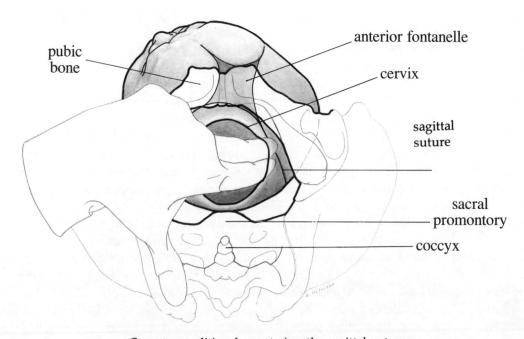

pubic
bone

anterior fontanelle

cervix

sagittal
suture

sacral
promontory

coccyx

Correct asynclitism by centering the sagittal suture.

pattern; for 12 hours (a good part of the night) we had the mother walking, squatting, in and out of hot baths, drinking stimulating teas, etc. It felt rather ironic but liberating to be sitting around the following afternoon with labor halted, sharing a glass of champagne (we went ahead and opened it) and simply relaxing together. With no sign of maternal or fetal exhaustion, why worry? We went home, and after a six hour break were called back to find her dilated to seven centimeters, handling her labor well, and birthing shortly thereafter. When we asked what had happened she replied, "Well, after you left we got in bed and talked a lot, fell asleep and then it just started up again really strong."

Once a woman has passed six centimeters, an arrest of progress is a more serious matter because the uterus is now hard at work and tends to keep it up, regardless of maternal tension. This means that if a woman resists her sensations and works against her body, she may reach a state of clinical exhaustion before her uterus takes a break. The symptoms of clinical exhaustion include ketones in the urine, elevated pulse and temperature. This condition is also known as ketoacidosis, because the mother's blood pH becomes increasingly acidic. If the fetus in turn becomes acidotic, cardiac output goes down and the blood carries less oxygen. In other words, unless this condition is reversed, *maternal exhaustion can lead to fetal distress.*

In order to prevent this, the mother should be carefully monitored throughout an arrest phase and if signs of ketoacidosis manifest, remedial measures should be undertaken immediately (see page 71). The baby must also be monitored more closely for any signs of distress. It must be understood, however, that merely treating the symptoms of arrest (or complications thereof) will not rectify the situation. You must do your utmost to *determine the cause.*

Begin by doing a thorough vaginal exam to ascertain any impediments. Check carefully the position of the head and how it's presenting. Posterior babies often present deflexed and if they are also large, **asynclitism** may be noted. This means that the suture line can be felt running either high or low in the pelvis, rather than

directly across the cervical opening (see illustration, opposite page). This finding may indicate cephalo-pelvic disproportion (CPD), particularly if other factors such as size of baby, size of the mother's pelvis and the condition of cervix, tend to concur. Both disproportion and posterior presentation (covered in detail later in this chapter) can cause arrest, and must be ruled out before considering other possibilities.

Another cause for delay may be **cervical edema.** If swelling of the cervix occurs early (at 5 or 6 cms.) and the woman has been favoring prone positions, chances are the cervix will thin out if the mother is more upright. This is because increased pelvic space will decrease the pressure of the head on vaginal tissues adjacent to the cervix, so that venous return will improve and swelling reduce. The cervix may also swell if the head is ill-fitting, so be sure to rule out malpresentation or CPD. Cervical edema most commonly occurs around 8 or 9 cms., due to the mother's involuntary bearing down efforts. Squatting can increase pelvic space so dramatically that improved tissue circulation will resolve the swelling in no time.

Sometimes a **cervical lip** will be the last obstacle to complete dilation. This is a swelling of the anterior portion of the cervix (the rest being fully retracted), due to pressure from the descending head against the pubic bone. For a persistent lip, one midwife recommends the application of ice, placed in the finger of a sterile glove and held against the cervix. Once the swelling is reduced you can try pushing the lip back. As the mother prepares to bear down, press the lip back over the baby's head as it descends. Hold the lip up behind the pubic bone as the contraction recedes; if it stays back, you've succeeded. If not, try again. This may be moderately painful for the mother, but don't force the cervix if it won't give. It helps if the mother is in a squatting position while you do this.

Sometimes tense membranes (water bag) will retard descent and dilation. This is most common at eight centimeters. You have the option of **artificially rupturing the membranes (AROM)** but first you must be certain the head is low enough in the pelvis to prevent cord prolapse. The standard rule is that the head must be at 0 station, but it's quite common for a larger head (particularly in a deflexed, posterior position) to fill the pelvic cavity snugly at −1 station. If the head is too high for the procedure to be safe, the mother must walk, squat, relax and wait until it descends. Be forewarned, this may take hours, so be sure the mother drinks plenty of water, takes honey, eats if possible, and keeps her bladder empty.

You may occasionally be tempted to intervene by artificially rupturing the membranes early in labor. I once made the mistake of doing so at four centimeters, in hopes that descent would result and that the additional pressure on the cervix would stimulate progress. This decision was made after 38 hours of erratic contractions and another 12 hours of regular, moderately strong ones. A tense bag of waters was forming, and the baby's head (which was small and engaged) was not well applied to the cervix. The mother had a generous pelvis with no abnormalities, so I reasoned the water bag was holding the baby up. Surprisingly enough, rupturing the membranes did not bring descent. The real problem was that the mother was still early enough in labor to have active control; she used her excellent abdominal and vaginal muscles to hold the baby up inside her so she'd feel less pressure on her back. And as a result of my intervention I created a new complication, prolonged ruptured membranes, which eventually necessitated pitocin induction as more time elapsed and infection became a concern.

To perform AROM don a sterile glove, squirt a bit of sterile gel over your fingers and splint the amni-hook between them. Insert your fingers **between** contractions and then, as the next one begins, push upward and pull back so the hook snags the membranes. Remove your fingers slowly and carefully, keeping the hook guarded. It's best to do this with the mother fairly upright. Be sure to take heart tones immediately after, and record your findings in the chart.

Once you've determined that there are no physical obstacles impeding progress, you have to consider both psychological and environmental dynamics. There are many different reasons why a woman or couple might resist the process of opening up. Usually emotional problems revealed at prenatal visits will have given specific clues as to what might go awry, but here is a general list of possibilities:

1. woman not feeling enough love, communication, or authority coming from partner;
2. partner feeling unable or unwilling to let go and give, due to inhibitions with self, or inhibitions in the woman;
3. worries about becoming parents; for the woman, loss of personal attention she enjoyed during pregnancy; for the man, moving from limbo to responsibility;
4. an awareness of sexual dysfunction awakening with the physical-emotional intensity of labor; or
5. disharmony in the environment—too many people, too many comings and goings, no feeling of privacy.

Most of these problems can be solved by facilitating intimacy. As has been said before, it's very easy for the midwife to take over and use her well-seasoned skills to provide warmth and comfort, but it's better for her to stay neutral and exemplify techniques, while subtly enlisting the mate's energy and attention. Breathing guidance during contractions, with massage and touching in between, is a good way to begin. Once the couple is working well together, take vital signs and then leave them alone.

As for the environment, the labor room can get rather stale after a while, so change of scene should be made frequently. If the couple feels that a veritable party is impinging on their privacy, hanging outside their bedroom door, how free can they be with expression? Clear out friends and family kindly, by explaining that it will probably be a while and now is the best time for a break. At any rate, get the woman up and moving out in the backyard, to a nearby quiet park or through the woods (if you're lucky). Touch with nature and open space works wonders. If you go along, see that someone else straightens up the birth room, remaking the bed, bringing in fresh tea and water, etc., so that when you return it's a new beginning, another round.

Characteristic arrest points, emotionally based, occur at four centimeters, seven to eight centimeters, and sometimes at nine centimeters. The four centimeter point is the connecting phase of labor, the time when a woman must humble herself to her need for assistance and find support from her partner and/or friends. (Otherwise, she'll need you to help her through this reckoning.) Seven to eight centimeters is early transitional labor when new sensations enter in, strong vaginal pressure surges which a woman may resist for fear of "splitting open" and losing the last remnants of her identity. Sexual surrender issues arise here, and it's alright to tell a woman how flushed and warm and sensational she looks, or to suggest the same to her mate. Showering together can be great fun for a couple that needs to regain their sense of humor. The nine centimeter arrest can be a last minute holdout for pregnancy versus parenting, but this fear generally comes into focus in second stage (see Prolonged Second Stage).

Keep in mind that release of emotional tension is necessary for complete relaxation, and is the key to opening up. When a woman completely surrenders and has no physical obstacles to progress, she can dilate *very* quickly. I've seen a number of women go from five centimeters to complete in an hour or less, spilling out fear and anxiety one minute, easing into sensation the next, and suddenly feeling like

pushing. *Never* leave a labor or take the woman for a walk outside if you sense this kind of release is about to happen.

In the event of an emotional arrest be sure the mother keeps her bladder empty, because a full bladder can hinder relaxation and descent. And listen frequently to the FHT for signs of distress, as maternal tension may affect oxygen flow to the baby.

It's important to understand that psychological delays at a point when a woman has no physical reserves can rapidly deteriorate into pathology. You've got to be a guardian of the baby's welfare, sometimes shaking sense and perspective into parents by being very frank about immature behavior. At the *first sign* of physiological effects of emotional stress, discuss the possibility of transport. This may elicit either determination or despair, but regardless, the decision must be made. Give parents a bit of time to consider their alternatives, keep tabs on vitals during the decision-making period, be encouraging but firm, and the course of action will soon become evident.

Cephalo-Pelvic Disproportion (CPD)

CPD is a condition in which the baby's head cannot engage or pass through the mother's pelvis. As Myles' *Textbook for Midwives* states, disproportion can be pelvic or cephalic in

Obstructed labor is often more painful; the sooner you let go of easy birth fantasies and ask for help, the better your chances for progress.

origin, due to small pelvis, large baby or a combination. However, these factors are modified by the molding of the fetal skull, the degree of flexion, the amount of flexibility in the mother's pelvic joints and the strength of her contractions. Strong coordinate contractions in combination with upright positioning and the active participation of the mother have been known to override a marginal case of CPD. It's been said repeatedly that, "The best pelvimeter is the baby's head," and this is absolutely true.

CPD can seldom be diagnosed before labor unless the pelvic inlet is small and the baby large, with head floating/bulging over the pubic bone. You can check for **overlap** in the last few weeks of pregnancy by seeing if the head can negotiate the inlet: grasp the head firmly just above the pubic bone and attempt to press it against the spine and down into the pelvis slightly. If you feel "give" front to back and a bit of descent, then there should be no problem. But if there seems to be little space, you'll have to monitor labor very closely.

Failure to engage cannot be considered diagnostic, because large babies (particularly in posterior position) may stay at –2 or –3 station until strong contractions bring them down. Women with very strong or tense abdominal muscles may also hold the baby high until active labor begins. Extremely poor abdominal tone may also prevent engagement because the fetus is not aligned for descent.

It is essential to do careful pelvic assessment, once early in pregnancy and then again at the end, checking for increased flexibility of cartilage and re-checking for any bony peculiarities. A pelvis diagnosed small early in pregnancy may be medium sized at term. Pay attention to any odd characteristic of the pelvis, as it may cause a minor degree of CPD which in turn may cause an arrest in progress.

For example, if you find a pelvis to be basically gynecoid (roomy inlet, deep, rounded sacral curve and ample pubic arch) but notice rather close-set, prominent spines, you can anticipate some delay or struggle with descent due to midpelvic contraction. The pregnancy should not go much past term, as the baby's head must mold well to adapt. The mother should understand that sometimes it is neces-

sary to push *hard* in second stage, and over an extended period of time. She will need to be in top shape.

Another example is the pelvis which is gynecoid at the inlet but with a heavy, flat sacrum. In this case, be prepared for some difficulty with descent and engagement. Be certain that the head is well flexed in the last few weeks of pregnancy, and encourage the mother to practice squatting daily so as to stretch the cartilage as much as possible.

Be prepared, but don't be paranoid. It's quite miraculous sometimes to see borderline CPD suddenly overcome by fetal rotation, or by some subtle re-positioning of the head. Even if progress does halt at home, pitocin augmentation might effect just enough extra strength in uterine activity to avert a Cesarean. So even if you must transport, don't be pessimistic about the possibilities of vaginal delivery but give hope to the parents as honestly as you can.

How does one diagnose CPD during labor? First, it must seem a reasonable suspicion based on foreknowledge of the baby's size, gestational age and the mother's dimensions. A typical pattern indicating **inlet contraction** includes lack of descent (–3 or –2 station), some asynclitism and cervix not well applied to the head. Particularly ominous is the cervix hanging "like an empty sleeve" with membranes loose inside it; sometimes it's even possible to slip fingers *inside* the cervix and up along its interior surface two or three centimeters. Usually dilation arrests at 6 cms; it is possible for a woman to progress to eight or nine centimeters with her baby held high, but generally the last centimeters can only be dilated by the head descending and moving through the cervix. Another oddity of the cervix which is not well applied to the head is its tendency to re-close. I've seen several cases in which the cervix, loosely dilated during a contraction, spastically closed up as the contraction ended. This happens when the cervix has nothing to hold it open, neither the head nor adequate strength in the lower uterine segment, as is evidenced by weakening, incoordinate contractions. The mother's symptoms are sharp, isolated, spastic pains.

Midpelvic disproportion presents a bit differently. Usually the head engages without

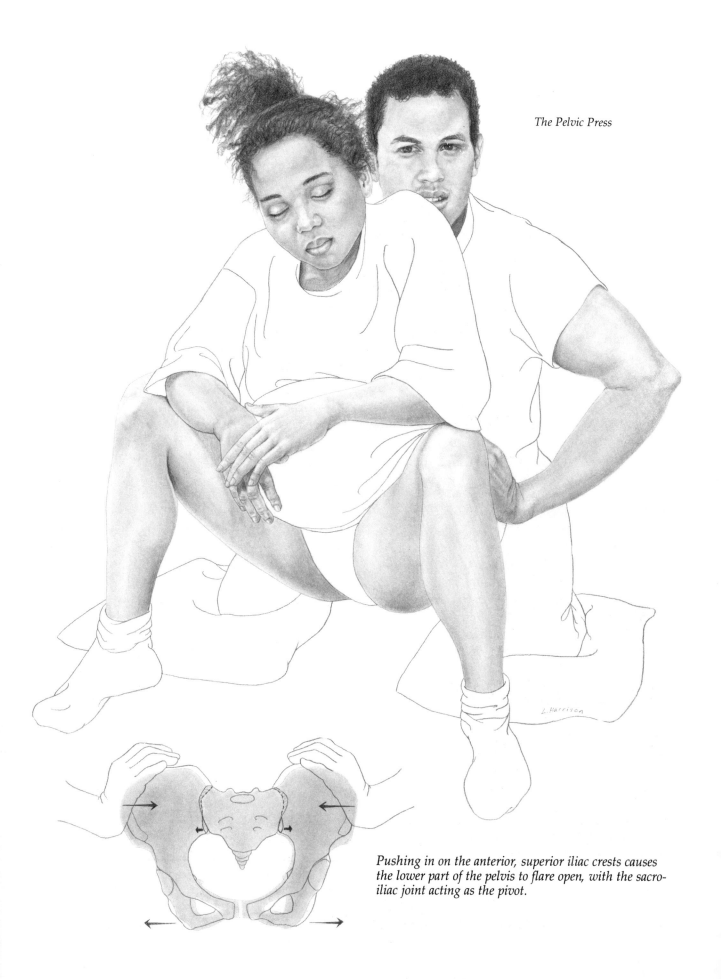

Pushing in on the anterior, superior iliac crests causes the lower part of the pelvis to flare open, with the sacro-iliac joint acting as the pivot.

trouble, dilatation may proceed normally but second stage is prolonged. Sometimes the baby gets stuck in *deep transverse arrest*, meaning that the head is wedged behind the ischial spines and cannot rotate to the antero-posterior position.

Any tricks you can try for CPD? Well, if the cause appears to be malpresentation, (deflexion or asynclitism) you can try internal maneuvering to reposition the head. This works best with the mother in knees-chest position (to lessen the force of gravity) and with membranes intact (to serve as a cushion for internal manipulation). To secure flexion, follow the directions and diagrams on page 102. To correct asynclitism, attempt to center the suture line by pressing firmly inward on the protruding side of the head. In cases of deep transverse arrest, secure flexion and attempt to rotate the head to the anterior position.

Another possibility is the **pelvic press** (popularized by Nan Koehler, author of *Artemis Speaks* and authority on VBAC). This must be done with the mother in a squatting position, and will require a bit of physical strength. *Kneeling behind the mother, place your hands firmly on the iliac crests (hip bones) and press them together as hard as possible, or until you feel some motion* (see illustration, previous page). Pressure on the iliac crests allows the symphysis and sacral joints to flex, opening the midpelvis and outlet so the head can descend. This procedure should be done during a contraction. Since you are trying to effect descent you should have the mother bear down, even if she is not fully dilated. Check heart tones immediately after the attempt. You can try this several times consecutively, and may need to repeat the process later in labor. Results are often remarkable; effecting dilation of several centimeters in less than half an hour and enough descent to keep labor moving ahead.

In terms of time, there are some limits. There is a definite danger of uterine rupture if one waits endlessly for descent to occur, and the uterus proceeds to thin its lower segment away to nothing. However, maternal exhaustion and/or fetal distress will usually arise first, necessitating transport. Once CPD is suspected and all reasonable efforts to correct the situation have failed, the mother should be taken to the hospital *before* she has frittered away all her energy in strong but ineffectual labor. Pitocin, forceps or Cesarean birth; all are relatively traumatic procedures handled best by mother and baby still in good condition.

If pitocin is given slowly and results are carefully monitored, it can work wonders in borderline cases. Another possibility is pain relief, epidural anesthesia being first choice because of its strong, *local* effect plus the fact that it does not reach the baby. Particularly in the presence of strong contractions, complete pelvic relaxation may allow the bones to stretch just enough to let the head pass through.

Even if neither of these is successful, at least the attempts give the parents a chance to feel that they've really tried, and a chance to work through the stages of hope, frustration, despair and final resignation. Seeing a woman through a rough labor that eventually ends in Cesarean birth is difficult at best, but fortunately more and more hospitals are giving women the option of local anesthetic with the father present during the surgery, so that the moments of birth and bonding are shared as a family. Nevertheless, the mother will need extra care and support postpartum (see Appendix for resources). Be sure you or your partner visit the hospital daily, and do what you can to pave the way for the return home. Encourage the mother to *nurse and get plenty of rest*, and to get up and walk (with staff recommendation and assistance) as soon as possible. This helps eliminate painful gas and speeds the healing process.

Years ago, I coached a woman who had a nine-pound baby in breech position, arrested progress, and an eventual need for Cesarean. Both her mate and I were present in the operating room. She had been given a spinal but was unable to tolerate the sensations of total numbness around her lungs; she felt as if she wasn't breathing. So she asked for a general anesthesia and was put under.

Her mate got to hold the baby immediately, she was taken to recovery, and the baby went to the nursery to be checked out, where the father and I took turns rocking and holding it. During the next few days, the mother went through some periods of very intense depression and paranoia; even though she had her baby with her, she felt so incapacitated, so vulnerable to hospital impressions, so worried about her two year old son and husband at home, and so overall disappointed. One night it got so difficult for her that she called and asked me to come and spend the night at the hospital. We did a lot of talking in the weeks and months that followed; she had many questions about the moment of birth which she asked repeatedly, and needed not just simple reassurance but specific observations, fine nuances, and every little detail that I could give her. A year later I received a picture of myself holding her baby girl in the nursery, along with this letter:

> Dear Elizabeth,
>
> It is a year on the 11th. Thank you so much for all that you gave me. What words can I use to tell you that without you my birth experience would have been really cold, my hospital stay a nightmare, but most of all, I would not have had a true witness to the birth, and how beautifully and perfectly you filled these needs. How I counted on you!
>
> I hope that I am able to give something so wonderful into the great supply of love in the Universe.

Posterior Arrest

Posterior arrest occurs when the baby gets stuck in either LOP or ROP position during active, first stage labor, so that descent is inhibited and dilation slows or stops. When the head enters the pelvis posteriorly the occiput tends to get snagged on the sacrum, which forces the sinciput downward first and causes deflexion. Thus a large circumference hinders descent, and prevents a firm, smooth fit of the head against the cervix. Lack of pressure on the cervix causes contractions to become irregular and to lose intensity and coordination. Posterior arrest occurs most frequently at about six centimeters, with station of −3 or −2. Occasionally cervical edema develops to compound the problem.

The clinical picture is very similar to the big-baby, small-pelvis condition, CPD. But by now you should know mother's and baby's dimensions well enough to set this possibility aside.

Assuming there *is* adequate room and that baby's position is the cause of arrest, it's obviously necessary to do something to effect rotation. What are your options?

In the past, my only solution for this problem was hospital transport for pitocin augmentation, in hopes that stronger contractions might force descent and rotation. Of course we would try everything possible at home before coming to this decision—positioning on hands and knees, squatting, tea to stimulate labor (cohosh), nipple stimulation, etc. It was frustrating to encounter this posterior pattern repeatedly, and to fairly well know in advance that home efforts would be for naught and we'd probably end up in the hospital.

Then I discovered a technique of manual rotation advocated by an Australian obstetrician named Hamlin, in his out-of-print work *Stepping Stones to Labour Ward Diagnosis*. He claims having had success in over 1000 attempts. With practice I've modified his techniques somewhat, but the basic principles remain the same. It is definitely worth trying, but requires two skilled midwives to make it work (see diagrams, page 102).

First of all, you must make certain of your posterior diagnosis. You may not be able to find the posterior fontanelle, particularly if the head is deflexed, but you should be able to feel the anterior fontanelle running along the upper margin of cervix. When you find the anterior fontanelle, exert steady, even pressure on the *bony edge only* to effect flexion of the head, aiming slightly downward and inward. Often flexion occurs quite suddenly, and as extra space is created the baby may begin to rotate spontaneously. Once you've moved the anterior fontanelle to a transverse position and have flexed it almost out of range of feeling, the posterior fontanelle should move within reach. Now you are ready to begin rotation to the anterior.

Have the mother lie back, with ample bedspace to fling her leg over her body as she rolls to a right or left side position. Which way she will turn depends on which way you want the baby to turn—it will be one and the same. Your assistant should sit on the opposite side facing toward you, and ready to assist rotation by grasping the baby's shoulder and backside,

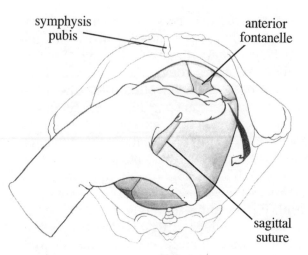

symphysis pubis

anterior fontanelle

sagittal suture

ROP to ROT

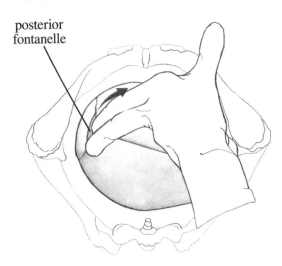

posterior fontanelle

ROT to ROA

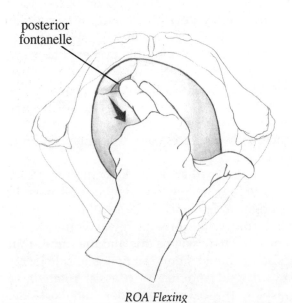

posterior fontanelle

ROA Flexing

lifting and pushing it to the anterior position while you are rotating the head internally. While you and your assistant are coordinating your efforts, the mother should roll over slowly, her shift in movement encouraging the pelvic bones to open up and make room for rotation. Once she has flipped over, gravity helps the baby to stay put.

How much force do you need to use? Well, Hamlin uses the image of "dialing a telephone" to describe, but actually this is a bit misleading, considering the effort involved in maintaining flexion during the actual rotation. If you feel *strong* resistance with no response, you shouldn't attempt any further.

However, you might try the internal maneuvers alone, with the mother in knees-chest position. (Of course, with the mother upside down you must reverse your manipulations.) Knees-chest has the advantage of zero gravity and increased pelvic space, plus the technique can be done without assistance. It is especially good if membranes are ruptured.

Yet another technique employs two fingers placed on the suture line, spread apart, then rotated. Sometimes if rotation to the transverse or anterior seems impossible, try turning the baby to OP. This may loosen the fit, and allow for rotation to the anterior. Even if the baby stays OP, at least it can descend and birth in that position.

If you do succeed in turning the baby, check the heart tones immediately, then have the mother assume an upright position. After a few contractions, check once again to see if the baby is still in place. Sometimes the first rotation attempt appears to be a failure, as the baby rotates and deflexes almost back to original position. But don't be discouraged; if rotation were to be accomplished easily, it probably would have occurred by itself. It may take you two or three attempts, and with each the baby will gain a bit more flexion and a bit more descent, which will help to hold it in place.

Here's an example. We once assisted a woman who was several weeks post due, with a large, ROP baby. She had a long latent phase, about twelve hours to four centimeters of dilation. In three more hours, she was at six centimeters, but the head was still high (–2 station) and sharply asynclitic, with the right parietal presenting. We couldn't even feel the sutures as they were way up behind the pubic bone. The cervix was not well applied to the head, and after a few more hours it started to swell and close up, although the head had come down a bit and sutures could be palpated.

So we did our first rotation, bringing the baby to ROA. It promptly rotated back again to ROP, but gained a centimeter of descent. An hour later, in the presence of good contractions, we tried again and this time the baby settled at ROT, station –1. Half an hour later, we rotated the baby again to ROA and it sharply flexed itself and came down to 0 station, at which point we artificially ruptured the membranes to secure engagement. The FHT was fine throughout, and the baby was born two hours later in good condition.

In retrospect, the mother said the procedure was definitely uncomfortable but given the choice between it and the hospital, there was no question in her mind. Along the lines of minimizing trauma, you should attempt rotation earlier rather than later, with mother and baby still in good condition and with plenty of energy to handle it.

Prolonged Second Stage

After the cervix is fully dilated, delay may be caused by one or both of the following: 1) some degree of CPD, or; 2) poor management of second stage contractions by the birthing team.

As stated before, one can seldom be certain prenatally that CPD exists but upon finding close-set, prominent ischial spines or a narrow, reduced pubic arch, you might anticipate delays in second stage. Midpelvic contraction will often cause the formation of a considerable caput, which can be felt as a soft bulge atop the baby's head (not to be confused with bulging membranes). Caput may reach a thickness of an inch or more. This indicates considerable fetal head compression within a particular pelvic dimension, causing impaired venous return and swelling. If you discover caput and note lack of descent, especially in the presence of strong contractions, check for any vaginal resistance which might be diminishing available space. Even if the head is at a high station, you can start internal massage on tense areas.

Squatting is a tremendous aid, though tiring for the mother. Have her alternate squatting with periods of semi-reclining. This gives you a chance to auscultate fetal heart tones, which will tell you how well the baby is handling head compression. You can consider early decelerations normal as long as they go no lower than 100 BPM, *and* as long as the recovery is immediate with the end of the contraction.

Style of breathing is crucial to progress. With midpelvic arrest a woman needs to focus and concentrate her force, and really *bear down* with

A look of anguish on the laboring woman's face can be frightening, but is often just a stress reaction to great exertion.

the urge. She should also breathe deeply between contractions ("breathe to the baby").

How long is too long for second stage? It all depends on the nature of the obstacle; your fingers can tell you if it is a bony problem or a muscular one. One thing for certain, it is *not* wise to let a woman flounder along with no progress for more than an hour, hoping she'll find her way or get the knack. Instead, you should check and encourage, check and advise, and consistently update your management. An average second stage for a first birth is probably about an hour, although two hours is fairly common. It really should take no more than an hour and a half to bring the baby down to the perineum.

If this is not happening and you feel that the mother is doing her best, then you can assume it's CPD. In a case like this, with FHT pattern of early decelerations (to confirm diagnosis) and good recovery (to assure you that the baby is still doing well), you might consider using pelvic presses to effect descent. These are described on page 100, in the section on CPD. You may wish to combine these with a bit of **fundal pressure** during a contraction and with the mother's pushing efforts. This is not advisable if more than a minor degree of disproportion is noted; the head should be moldable, the woman still strong and doing well. *You should not attempt to apply fundal pressure unless you've had enough experience to be sure of all these factors.* Be sure to monitor the FHT closely during these maneuvers.

Suppose a vaginal exam reveals plenty of room for descent, but the baby remains high? Then it's probably a matter of maternal tension, so help the mother loosen up and relax. Massage her shoulders and back, and tell her to move her focus downward. Sometimes massaging the inner thighs seems to help. Try hot compresses to the perineum, or have her sit on a heating pad, or push on the toilet.

But if you pick up variable decelerations with this finding (roomy pelvis, head high), the cord may be around the neck, hindering further descent. Listen to the baby with every contraction; you may need to transport.

Delay at the outlet is yet another problem, most frequently caused by muscular tension or rigidity. If this is the case and the baby is in dis-

tress, episiotomy and rapid delivery may be necessary; otherwise, use massage and hot compresses. But if delay is due to bony contraction it's another matter. A reduced pubic arch mechanically forces the baby's head down onto (and often right through) the perineum. It's unrealistic to expect a tear-free delivery; you should be prepared to do an episiotomy and should discuss the reasons with the mother beforehand. Mediolateral is probably best; if it extends it won't go through the anal sphincter. If you don't do an episiotomy you're almost certain to get a jagged, third-degree tear.

There are also emotional reservations that can cause a second stage arrest. The fear of becoming a parent can definitely cause a holdup right after dilation is complete, but usually it's enough to say, "You've got a strong, healthy baby, and I think it's time for your baby to come out." Especially if the father makes some comment like "Come on out baby," the mother can release an orgasm of energy and bring delivery on. Fear of sensory overload and loss of body image may also be a hindrance, but this can be worked out gradually by encouraging the mother to move, make sounds, and hold on to her mate.

Last minute fears of tearing or "splitting open" can sometimes be alleviated by having the woman feel the baby's head, or best of all, take a look in the mirror. One glance will remind her that she is still present in her body, and that her outlet is stretched no more than what she has seen in pictures. Objectifying herself can aid her concentration.

Fetal Distress

Fetal distress has been covered in many separate sections of the book, Chapter 4 having many references to both normal and unusual FHT patterns, as well as suggested management. In the event that you do transport for fetal distress, the baby will almost certainly be monitored by internal monitor. This is an electrode attached to the baby's head; it gives a more accurate reading than the ultrasound used in the external monitor.

Many hospitals now have facilities for *fetal scalp sampling*. This test involves taking a bit of blood from the baby's head, which is then

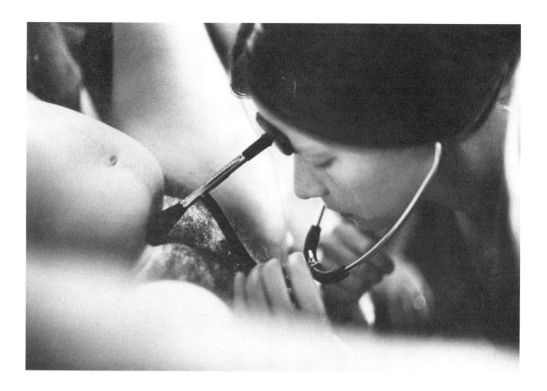

Using The Fetascope

tested for pH to determine whether or not the baby is acidotic. This test is more accurate in determining fetal well-being than the monitor; the heart rate pattern may look terrible but a good scalp sample shows that despite the stress the baby is undergoing, it is holding up just fine. Any reading over 7.26 is normal.

Some obstetricians are now switching from fetal scalp sampling to *fetal scalp massage.* If after ten seconds or so of massage the fetal heart rate accelerates, the baby is determined to have good reserves for continuing through a stressful labor. Either test can avert a Cesarean that might otherwise occur if following monitor readings alone.

Cord Problems

There are several types of cord problems which can affect the blood flow to the baby, thus causing fetal distress. **Cord nipping** means the cord is being pinched between the head and pelvic bones, a situation which causes variable decelerations in the FHT. During first stage, repositioning the mother sometimes eases the pressure and brings the FHT back to normal, but in second stage, nipping may progress to cord compression, depending on how low the cord is lying.

Cord compression usually indicates an oc-

cult prolapse, meaning that the cord is low in the pelvis and the head is pressing on it firmly with force of the contractions. If compression is severe, late decelerations may develop. It is also possible that the head may move past the point of maximum pressure and the FHT may gradually return to normal. You need to listen assiduously, as late decelerations constitute a crisis with very little leeway. Place the mother on her left side to assure as little pressure on the vena cava as possible, then give oxygen by mask. Check the FHT with each contraction. If there is no improvement after four or five contractions, transport.

If it's a case of **cord entanglement,** such as cord around the neck, descent will probably be inhibited and you may actually hear cord sounds over the FHT. Tight cord will also tend to deflex the baby's head, as it puts pressure on the back of the neck. Regardless, the bottom line is persistent lates, which means it's time to transport.

Complete cord prolapse is an altogether different problem, an obstetric disaster which tends to occur if the head or presenting part is high when the membranes rupture. Occasionally it can be diagnosed in the last weeks of pregnancy, if the cord is felt pulsating through the effaced cervix or lower uterine segment, synchronous with the FHT. This finding necessitates immediate hospitalization and Cesarean to save the baby. Should the membranes rupture during labor and the cord prolapse, you must transport the mother in a knees-chest position with your fingers inside her cervix, holding the head up and away from the cord. Should the cord prolapse all the way outside, replace it in the vagina as cold air can cause spasm and constriction. Knees-chest position works on a stretcher (if you can get an ambulance quickly) or else ease the mother into a chair on the floor, then lift and tip her backwards until her head is lower than her hips and carry her thus to the car. *Keep fingers inside and pressure off the cord throughout.*

Complete cord prolapse occurs very rarely, but be on guard whenever the head is high in the pelvis near term. If this mother calls to report that labor has begun with her membranes rupturing, go over immediately to check the FHT.

Maternal Hypertension

Hypertension in labor is a danger to both mother and baby because it may progress to pre-eclampsia, even if there have been no prior signs. For this reason it is critical to monitor the mother carefully. Urinalysis is somewhat unreliable as cells in the amniotic fluid may wash down and give a false positive for protein. So check for hyperreflexia and clonus, and transport at the first sign. There is also an increased risk of placental abruption.

Herbal remedies may help to stabilize or lower blood pressure; the best tea is hops, scullcap and valerian blend. Probably best is tincture of hops, as hops is one of the strongest sedative herbs known. Tincture form insures potency (much stronger than tea) and quick assimilation (dissolved in alcohol and easier to keep down if vomiting is a problem).

Sometimes labor is therapeutic for high BP. And remember that blood pressure often rises with second stage exertion, as high as 140/90. It's the *steady rise in early active labor* that signals the need for transport.

If blood pressure does climb as labor becomes more intense, place the mother on her left side and push fluids, as dehydration can increase blood pressure. Transport only if this does no good.

Standard procedure in the hospital is a mag-sulphate IV for the mother and fetal monitoring for the baby. Magnesium sulphate slightly lowers blood pressure, but mainly prevents changes in brain activity which can lead to convulsions. Other than the nuisance of the IV and monitor hookups, the mother can still have a normal and beautiful birthing if the hospital staff is amenable. This probable course of events should be discussed with parents as soon as the problem emerges so they will be prepared.

A woman with borderline hypertension prenatally or during labor may show an even greater rise *after* delivery. There is a type of eclampsia which can develop in the immediate postpartum, so be on the lookout for this.

Prolonged Rupture Of The Membranes

Prolonged rupture of the membranes (PROM) is a *potential* (not actual) labor complication. It's quite normal for the water bag to break at the beginning of labor; the concern is that the time lapse between rupture and delivery will put the baby at risk for infection because the uterus is no longer closed to germs in the vagina or coming from outside. Conventional procedure is to wait no more than 24 hours before inducing labor, and some physicians will start even earlier so the baby is delivered before 24 hours have elapsed.

The trouble is that neither the research nor this standard of care takes into account an individual's health, personal cleanliness or environment. Women planning home birth are usually in excellent health, and believe in the power of the healthy body to ward off infection. And it is a proven fact that danger of infection is much greater in the hospital than at home, as patients are exposed to alien (and virulent) strains of micro-organisms to which they have no resistance.

Infection due to prolonged ruptured membranes is a *theoretical* complication. Who wants hospitalization and probable pitocin induction for a problem which may not exist? In effect, the issue is political; it's the pathological medical approach against the holistic perspective of the midwife and her clients.

In my experience, it's not unusual for a mother to go 24 hours after the waters break without even starting labor. But in order to minimize the risk of infection (chorioamnionitis), she should follow these simple guidelines and commonsense measures (also listed in Chapter 6):

1. no tub baths until the woman is in advanced, active labor, but showers are fine and encouraged;
2. no hand-mouth-genital contact;
3. utmost care when using the toilet, wiping backwards, and washing hands both before and after;
4. no underwear, just clean loose clothing, and preferably no sanitary pad unless flow is really considerable, in which case pad should be changed often;
5. plenty to drink in order to replenish amniotic fluid and keep system clean;
6. increased dosages of vitamin C, up to 2 grams per 24 hours (250 mg every few hours);
7. good quality, unconstipating foods, to keep energy high; and
8. temperature readings every three or four hours, any increase reported at once.

Beyond these basics there are environmental factors; if the home is less than clean, you might be more conservative with your time limit. Or, make an effort to stimulate labor. There are several means to this end; one is castor-oil induction, the other is blue cohosh tea or tincture, and then there is the standard walking and activity pattern. Breast stimulation may be helpful too as it triggers the release of oxytocin, the hormone which causes contractions. These measures can be used in combination: castor oil first, then a long walk with a jug of strong tea, plus periodic nipple stimulation en route.

Basic management of ruptured membranes includes close phone contact during the immediate post-rupture period, checking the woman's morale and making sure she is following your basic guidelines for avoiding infection. If the wait is longer than 24 hours, you should also take heart tones periodically (or train the father to do so) as fetal tachycardia is one of the first signs of infection. As soon as a contraction pattern is established, go over and do your best job of facilitating labor, allowing no turning points to slip into arrest. Vaginal exams should

be limited, in fact avoided as long as possible. *Research has shown that the risk of infection increases dramatically after the first exam.* Rely on observation and intuition as much as you can. If you must check, be sure to use antiseptic solution with a sterile glove and check gently and slowly, to avoid pushing vaginal material into the os.

One more thing: it's a good idea to have the baby seen within 48 hours, and to leave parents with a clear idea of *normal* newborn behavior. A baby which shows evidence of dehydration, acts listless or irritable should be checked at once. It's wise to call the pediatrician to alert him/her to the circumstances of the birth and possible repercussions.

Now for some birthing tale examples.

This first labor was that of a woman with large baby in posterior position. Her labor began with ruptured membranes, a few sporadic contractions and light meconium in the waters. Because of the mec I went over immediately, but the baby sounded fine and meconium was *very* light. After a few hours we tried the walk-tea-nipple stimulation routine, but the baby was so high up (−3 station) that this did little good. Mother remained in prodromal labor throughout the night and was still in early labor at 24 hours.

In the morning she tried castor oil and an enema, and about six hours later we checked to find her at five centimeters, meconium still light and baby still fine. Pulse and temperature normal, but moderate ketones in her urine, so we gave her extra fluids with honey.

By seven centimeters forewaters had formed (original rupture was a hind-leak) then the forewaters broke with a gush. Still light mec, but descent and rotation were effected and complete dilation came shortly after. Two hours of pushing, De Lee suction with birth of head, and a baby boy 9/9 Apgar, no postpartum problems. Mom had internal tear, few stitches. Total time since rupture, 40 hours.

Another woman went into labor just under 37 weeks but I palpated her baby to be over six pounds, and near term by its recent, consistent growth pattern. Also, she had always felt intuitively that she would go early. At her last prenatal she was already 85 percent effaced, and one to two centimeters dilated.

Few contractions for 16 hours, then she took castor oil, and had consistent contractions by 24 hours. All vitals OK.

Baby delivered at 40 hours since ROM, 7/10 Apgar, no postpartum problems. Gestational age by exam, 37+ weeks.

This third example was compounded by confusion over dates; the woman was supposedly term by menstrual history but 35 weeks by sonogram. Baby felt very small, about five pounds.

Labor began with membranes rupturing (clear) and the mother spent the day walking around. We arrived in afternoon. An inadvertent check on the refrigerator gave us an uneasy feeling, as did the unclean condition of the house. All vitals were fine but we felt the birth should take place in the hospital, mostly because the baby felt so small. However, we decided to try to get labor going at home and transfer towards delivery time.

We spent 12 hours on the walk-tea-nipple stimulation routine, but labor never became established. Higher doses of cohosh caused frequent contractions, but also caused fetal tachycardia. At 24 hours with absolutely nothing happening, mom said, "I feel like I'm just waiting to go to the hospital," so that's what happened next. Then pitocin induction, more tachycardia (but not severe) and baby born at 42 hours. Five pounds, 8/9 Apgar, 38 weeks gestational age and in fine condition. Because the baby was healthy and term, it stayed with the parents and was released to their care despite its small size.

Last comes the most complex; a woman with reduced midpelvis, palpated at 38 weeks to have possible fetal head overlap. This was also a woman who had often come to clinic in a state of physical and emotional disarray. Due to her unresolved personal problems, we decided to do the birth at the alternative birth center. When her water broke one morning we advised her to go in immediately, but the obstetrician said she could wait at home if she would keep track of her temperature and report any rise. She was admitted to the hospital at 24 hours with no contractions and was given pitocin IV.

Her labor was so very difficult for her that all our energies were focused on emotional support. Eventually she requested an epidural. After many hours of labor (including pushing) it became clear that the CPD could not be overcome. She had a Cesarean birth with general anesthesia at 37 hours; the amniotic fluid was found to be both stained and infected so the baby was given a complete septic workup. According to our prenatal assessments, this woman was at risk in many ways so the outcome was no surprise. Anyway, the baby had to spend time in isolation, the mother's recovery was slow (her incision became infected), and she had many emotional problems postpartum.

This last example shows the danger of prolonged ruptured membranes, but the other cases show how common sense measures of self care can make a difference. If PROM is treated on an individual basis with intelligence and intuition, fetal and maternal well being can be maintained to the end.

Unusual Presentations

Face Presentation This is quite rare, occuring once in every 250 deliveries. You should notice a marked degree of deflexion (by palpation) some weeks before term. If you discover this before the head is down in the pelvis, make an attempt at securing flexion. This is a simple procedure (see Chapter 2, page 32). The only exception to using this technique could occur with the posterior baby, in which case the occiput would be tucked so far to the rear that it might be impossible to reach. Keep in mind that face presentation is sometimes caused by tight cord around the neck (which pulls the head backward as it descends), so it's wise to have an assistant listen to the FHT continuously as you slowly attempt to flex the head.

Another cause of face presentation may be pelvic inlet contraction, so be relatively sure at the onset of labor that there is no CPD; otherwise you are wasting time and energy at home.

The mechanics of delivering the face presentation are such that the baby *must be born face upward*, with the body in a posterior position. Although labor may begin with the baby anterior, descent in this position is impossible because the crown of the head impinges on the symphysis. Once the baby is facing upwards

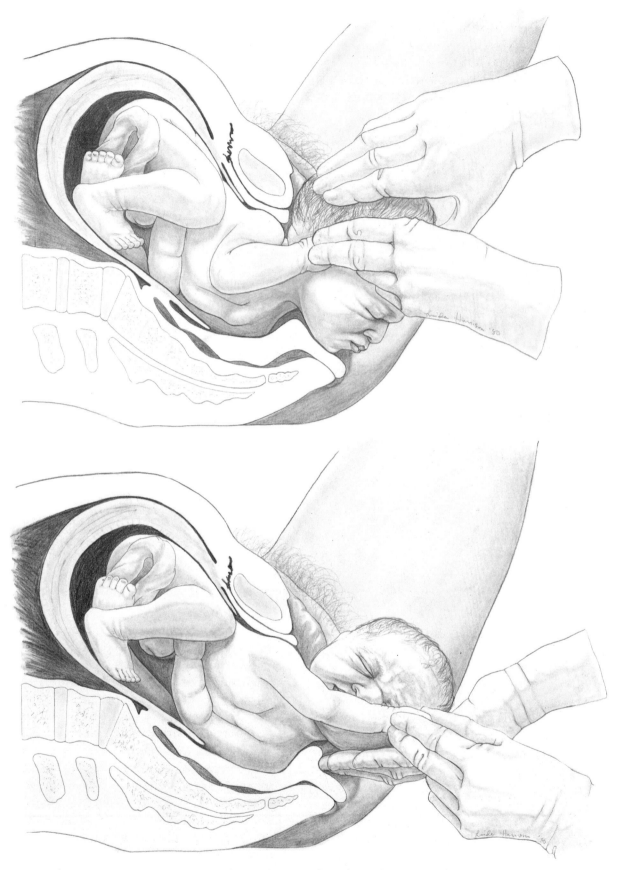

Extracting the Nuchal Arm

and ready to deliver, the midwife must hold back the forehead (by applying pressure to the perineum) until the chin escapes, or the chin may get caught behind the pubic bone. Obviously, the occiput will put extra pressure and burden on the perineum. Tearing is common in these deliveries; you may not be able to prevent it. Suction is usually necessary because the baby is facing upward and likely to get a nose full of fluids as the head is birthed.

The baby probably will be born with considerable bruising and swelling, and for this reason a vitamin K shot is a good idea. This will insure proper coagulation should there be any internal bleeding due to delivery trauma. Also watch for breathing difficulties due to tracheal edema.

Brow and Military Presentation These deflexed positions of the head can be remedied prenatally during the last few weeks of care. If they are discovered in labor by internal exam (via location of the fontanelles) you may be able to flex the head by internal maneuvering. See the section on Posterior Arrest for instructions.

Compound Presentation Most frequently this means a little hand and arm coming down alongside the head. Sometimes it is not discovered until the head is birthing; it all depends on how far down the hand is extending.

The biggest problem associated with "nuchal arm" is the increased circumference extending the perineum; tearing is likely. You may be able to avoid this by gently pinching the baby's finger, which may cause it to retract its hand. If not, you must be ready to extract the arm so the shoulders can be born. The easiest way to do this is to grasp the hand and rotate the head (aiding restitution), while bringing the arm across the chest and outward.

This maneuvering comes naturally in times of crisis; it's mechanical logic that flows of necessity. Still it's wise to think it through once or twice so the sense of it is imprinted and ready when you need it.

Membranes Presenting at Delivery This is not strictly a presentation problem, but it is a quirk of delivery that is somewhat out of the ordinary. When the membranes present and are bulging (full of water) from the vagina, they will usually break as the head distends the perineum, though sometimes the break occurs farther up and away from the baby's head. This leads to a condition known as *delivery in the caul*, which means the membranes will envelop the baby's face after it is birthed and will obstruct breathing unless removed.

Some midwives automatically break a presenting water bag so the baby can be born through the rent, with membranes pushed aside and out of the way. But some mothers resent this interference, especially because there is some superstition that birth in the caul brings good luck. Once thing is for certain, the sensation of pushing a full water bag plus the baby is quite intense. If the mother shows signs of overwhelming discomfort or asks you to pop the bag, then go ahead, but be sure to warn her in advance as the release of pressure can come as a shock.

If the bag is left intact and the baby is born in the caul, you must immediately hook a fingernail into the membrane below the chin and peel it back over the face so the baby can breathe. My daughter was born in the caul and my midwife used a clean cloth to catch and lift the membrane edge, which adhered to it. The most important thing, whatever you do, is to be sure and quick.

Shoulder Dystocia

Shoulder dystocia is a serious delivery complication, which becomes fully evident once the head has birthed and the shoulders fail to appear. Shoulder dystocia occurs when the baby's anterior (top) shoulder is impacted behind the mother's pubic bone: the shoulder girdle is simply too broad to pass through the anteroposterior (front to back) dimension of the pelvis. There is also considerable chest compression for the baby because it is squeezed so tightly in the birth canal, which can cause impaired venous return from the head and lead to intercranial bleeding, brain damage and death.

It is easy to panic with this complication, but less likely if the problem has been anticipated beforehand. The mother with either a big baby or very small, abnormal pelvis is a prime candidate for shoulder dystocia. Nevertheless, it's

*C*are that is provided by another woman can be special. A midwife is a birthing woman's equal, not her authority. She is a confidante. She understands the importance of being respectful and gentle with another person's most intimate parts of herself. She knows that safety in childbirth is more a matter of prevention than treatment, of learning to listen closely, helping a woman have a healthy attitude, and promoting normalcy. She sees the need for young girls to be brought into adulthood with understanding and support for their womanliness. She protects both the privacy of the woman and the integrity of the family.

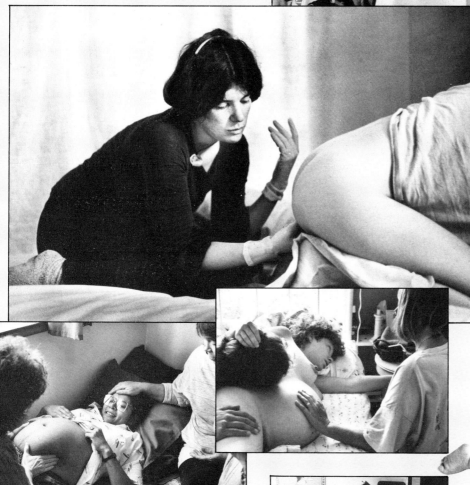

A Midwife's Guide to Pregnancy & Birth

*B*irth demands that we let go and surrender to the forces of creation. This is not always an easy thing to do. But the signs of letting go are easy to see—limp wrists and ankles, loose jaw and an unfurrowed brow. Support of the right kind can be the critical factor for progress in labor. Family and friends can actually help a woman lose her self-consciousness, by giving her permission to let go into the process.

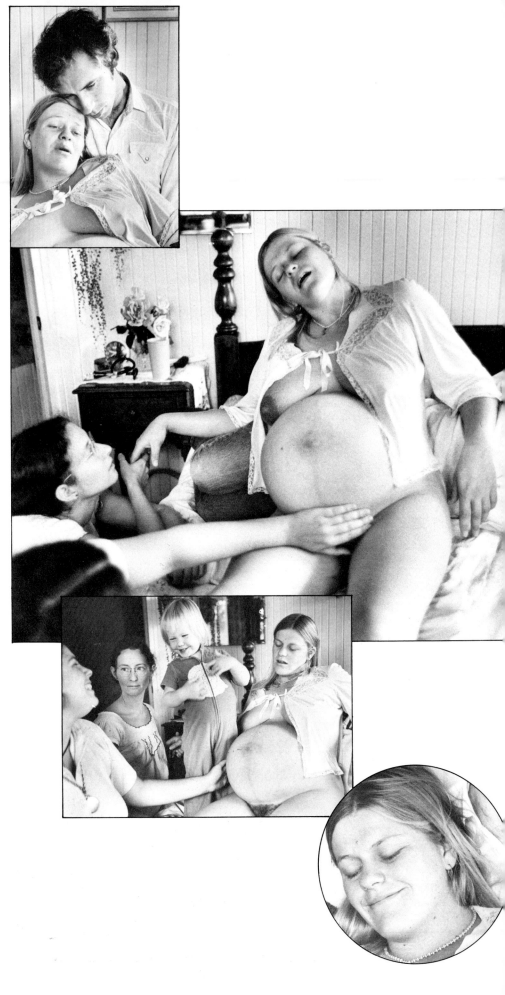

*T*here are times in many a woman's labor when a change of position, moving around, being on her feet, can make all the difference. The woman herself may not feel like moving; yet she can find no comfortable position. That is when assistance is needed to provide both inspiration and physical support. Making sounds, with an open, loose throat and jaw, can release some of the tension that builds up and allow a laboring woman to sink deeper into herself. Losing control may actually speed the process of birth.

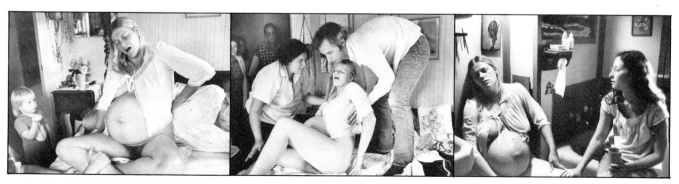

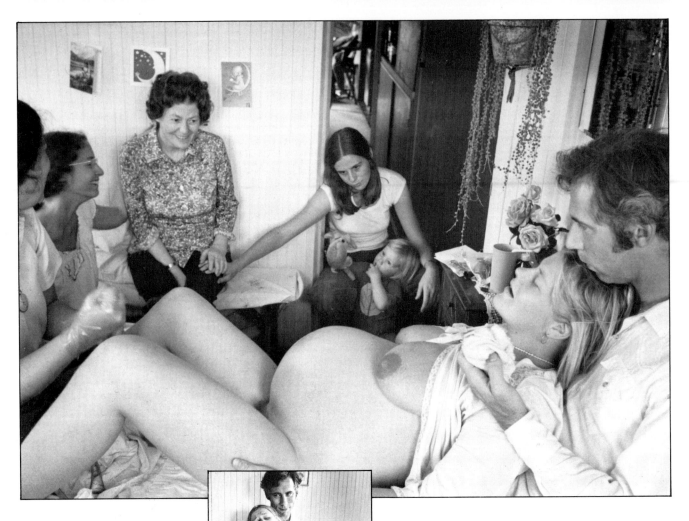

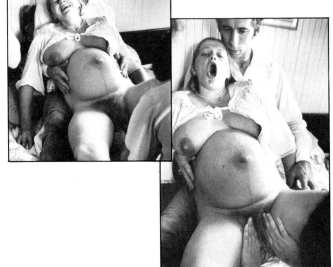

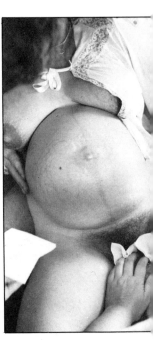

*A*s the intensity of labor builds to its climax, women draw even more heavily on the support of those around them. The woman in these photographs wanted her mother, sister and 2½ year old daughter with her, along with her husband and midwives. Because her child was free to wander in and out and was herself supported, and because there was no fear in the room, the experience was positive.

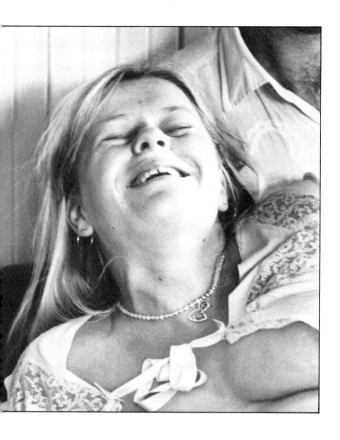

Often no technique is required for the pushing phase. Nothing except a further letting go, allowing the uterus to do the work. Even a large baby, like this one of 10 pounds, can often be born with no drawing up of the legs, no forcible bearing down, no holding of breath, and no tearing of the woman's tissues.

The line between pleasure and pain is blurred in birth. The body secretes its own pain relief, endorphines, that put a woman into an altered state of consciousness. But with the birth itself comes the rush of ecstatic release, that it is over, that all you have dreamed and worked for is here at last. That a baby has come.

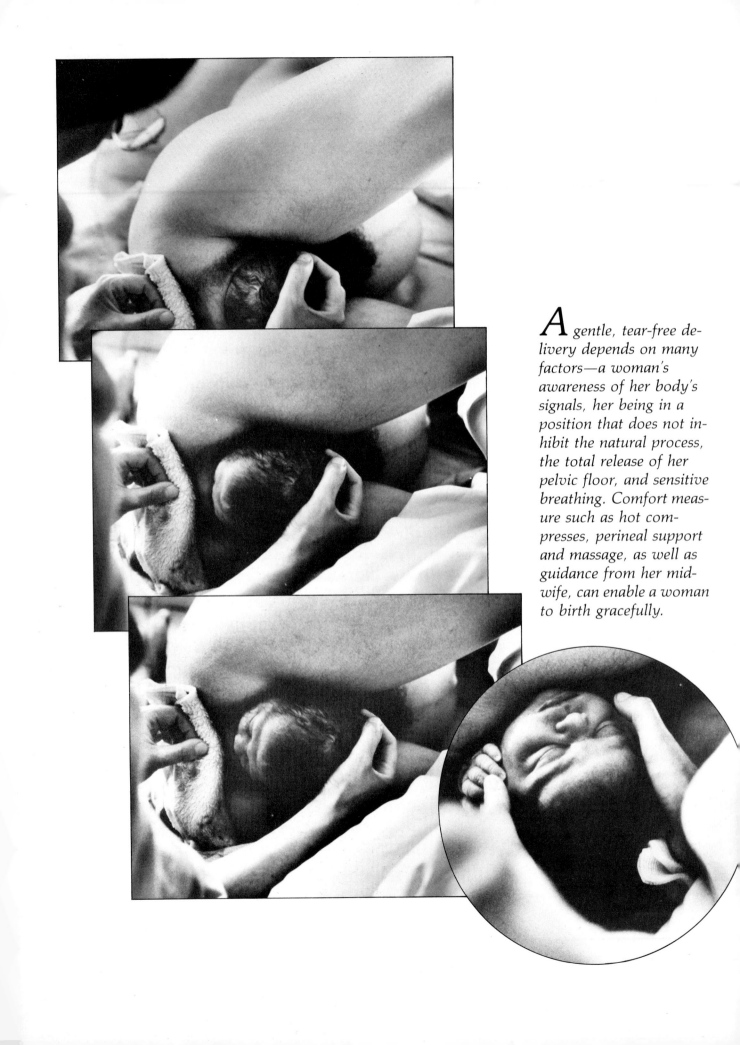

A gentle, tear-free delivery depends on many factors—a woman's awareness of her body's signals, her being in a position that does not inhibit the natural process, the total release of her pelvic floor, and sensitive breathing. Comfort measure such as hot compresses, perineal support and massage, as well as guidance from her midwife, can enable a woman to birth gracefully.

*W*hen a baby's hand presents along with its head there is often a tendency for the mother to tear. But in this case a deliberately slow and controlled delivery kept the perineum intact. The art of gentle birth is as much for the well-being of the baby as for that of the mother, because babies are conscious at birth.

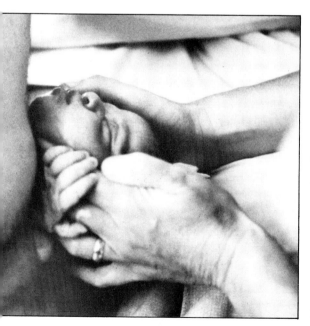

*T*hroughout history, in the most trying and adverse situations, midwives have always uniquely provided the security and support women need to birth safely. Today, even in places like war-torn Nicaragua, the role of the midwife is critical to the health of the nation. Here, where women still birth in the privacy of their own homes, it is the local midwives to whom they turn. In these photographs, Dona Irma, midwife for 45 years, humbly performs the simple and essential tasks that are the hallmarks of true midwifery.

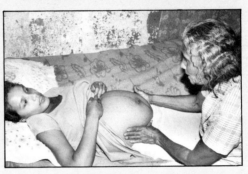

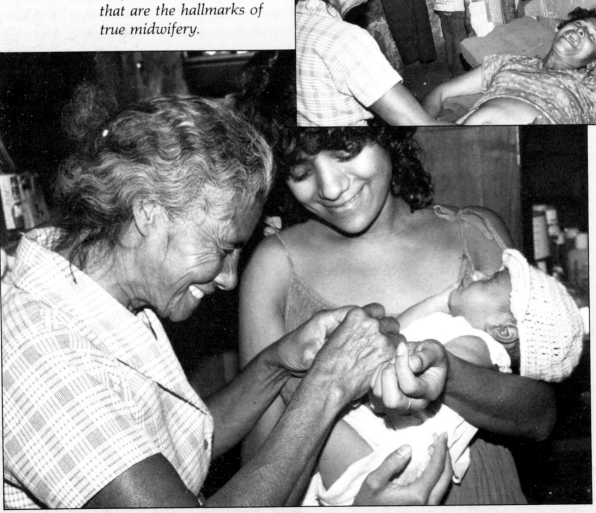

important to remember that if the head can pass through *so can the shoulders,* although you may need to do a bit of fancy maneuvering to make it happen.

Here is the usual course of events. Most commonly an unusually large head passes over the perineum then pulls back (retracts) against it. Restitution occurs slowly, haltingly, sometimes requiring manual assistance. Both of these occurrences indicate that the shoulders have not moved low enough in the pelvis to allow the head freedom of movement. Checking for cord is difficult because no neck is exposed, and then you realize that no shoulder is presenting. The baby's mouth is probably tightly clenched, and by this time its color is rapidly darkening. As you urge the mother to push with her next contraction, you exert as much downward traction on the head as you dare, but nothing changes and your diagnosis is made.

Immediately have the mother flip over to hands-and-knees. This position allows the pelvis to open fully, and enhances your ability to maneuver. The next step is to try the **screw maneuver.** Start by finding the posterior shoulder, then place two fingers in front of it, against the juncture of chest and armpit. Rotate backwards, pulling the baby outwards at the same time (like the grooves of a screw). This should dislodge the anterior shoulder, collapse the shoulder girdle and bring the baby out. Usually a 180° turn is enough to free the baby, though occasionally you may need to repeat this process in reverse for the other shoulder. And if you have trouble turning the posterior shoulder, use the fingers of the other hand to push the anterior shoulder forward (see below).

Or, with the mother reclining and her knees hyperflexed, lift the head upwards (or have an assistant help), while you hook a finger be-

Managing Shoulder Dystocia

hind the shoulder and move it to an oblique position. Often just rotating the bottom shoulder will birth the baby, but bringing the arm out will further reduce the diameter if necessary. To do this safely, you must splint the arm with two fingers and then move it across the chest. This maneuver will bring the hand within reach so you can grasp it and extract the arm.

Some books recommend cutting a large episiotomy as soon as dystocia becomes evident, but the need depends on the condition of the perineum. If it is loose and stretchy, episiotomy is just a waste of time and additional trauma.

It sometimes helps to have your assistant apply **suprapubic pressure** if the mother is reclining, in order to dislodge the anterior shoulder. Don't confuse this with fundal pressure, which will only impact the shoulder further *unless* it is used concurrently with suprapubic effort.

The worst case of shoulder dystocia I ever had was forewarned by another midwife. She visited me just a few days before, and told me she had had a very severe dystocia and that *nothing*, not even the screw maneuver had worked. "Well, what *did* you do?" I asked, and she said, "We pushed, pulled and prayed I guess until finally the baby came out." Sounded like a panic scene I'd just as soon avoid, but sure enough, a few days later . . .

This mother was small, and nothing was known about the father as she had been artificially inseminated. At her last prenatal, fundal height was 40 cms. The head delivered smoothly and without a tear, but I had to push the perineum back over the chin and there was no restitution. As the face rapidly turned purple, we had her move to hands-and-knees and my apprentice (who was doing the delivery) tried the screw maneuver, but couldn't reach enough shoulder to get traction. She called for suprapubic pressure and tried once more, but no change. By this time we were all yelling at the mother to push and I tried the screw maneuver myself, asked someone to do fundal pressure in addition to suprapubic and *at last*, blessings be, I could reach the shoulder and complete the maneuver. The baby was quite depressed, needed mouth-to-mouth and blow-by oxygen to get started but was fine after-

wards (Apgars 2 and 8). The mother had a fourth-degree tear (all the way through her rectum); I had done an episiotomy to create more room and it extended badly.

My youngest apprentice (I had two with me) said she had "seen the angel of death" and it certainly felt to me for a time like we might lose the baby. Then that super-human burst of strength passed through me to help me complete the maneuver. And yes, I guess I prayed, or at least offered up my total concentration.

On another occasion, I was co-managing a planned hospital birth with one of my favorite obstetricians. This mother had attempted a home birth with her first but had a horrendous posterior arrest; she came to me interested in trying for home again but decided later in the pregnancy that she'd prefer to be in the hospital, in case she wanted pain relief. She started out in the ABC and progressed to about 6 cms, then opted for an epidural and so was moved up to labor and delivery to be monitored. She dilated rapidly from this point but slowed down in second stage, and the physician offered to leave the room because he noticed she did much better when he was gone. She was all hooked up to the monitor but I had her squat, and the head immediately crowned.

I called for the instruments as the head delivered but soon it was apparent that the shoulders were stuck. Both the physician and I were quite disoriented; he was used to having the mother in lithotomy position (on her back, with stirrups) and I was used to having her flip to hands-and-knees, which the tangle of monitor tubes and wires prevented. Since I was hands-on he directed me to "pull down, down, down" on the head, until fearing I'd damage the neck I said, "No, you do this, you know what you're doing." Apparently he did not because he began twisting the head this way and that, and I realized he was panicking. Suddenly my mind cleared; I pushed his hands aside and gave suprapubic pressure as I directed him to go for the posterior shoulder, and the baby promptly delivered.

Later as he was filling out the chart he asked me, "What would you call that delivery position?" The mother had actually been sitting on the lap of my partner who had been kneeling, so I suggested the term "supported squat."

"Hmm," he responded, "sounds good . . . and that was suprapubic pressure with rotation to the oblique, was it not?" A nice gesture of acknowledgement, to top off a most challenging co-management experience.

Check the baby who's had shoulder dystocia carefully for any bruising injuries to the clavicle bone, or possible Erb's paralysis due to nerve trauma. Severe dystocia is an automatic indication for vitamin K. Consult with a pediatrician immediately.

Surprise Breech

Even if you have decided not to handle breech births at home, it is wise to practice this routine until you have it memorized and flowing automatically. There may come a day when firm abdominal tone, extra belly fat, or excess amniotic fluid confuses your evaluation of position, and suddenly you have a surprise breech on your hands! Be ready for it.

1. The mother *must not push* until she is completely dilated, and the breech is down to the perineum. This is bound to be stressful for the mom, but she must pant-blow while waiting.
2. If the breech is frank or complete (feet above buttocks), and there seems to be a delay with delivering the body, it may be necessary to "break down the breech" by extracting the legs. To do this, reach up, splint the legs one at a time, then bring them across the body and down.
3. Once the legs are out and the baby has birthed to the umbilicus, pull down a loop of cord to create some slack for delivery.
4. Wrap the baby's body in a towel or two blankets to keep it warm and to prevent stimulation of respiratory efforts.
5. Grasp the baby at the hip bones and gently rotate the body to the anteroposterior position (shoulders vertical), then assist delivery of the shoulders one at a time.
6. Rotate the body again so the baby is *face down*, and reach a finger inside to create an airway. If you let the baby's body hang down (with support) it's weight will cause the occiput to clear the outlet first, thus keeping birthing diameters the smallest possible.
7. Once the occiput has cleared (hairline visible), have an assistant apply suprapubic pressure as you lift the baby up and over the perineum. You may need to hook your airway finger inside the baby's mouth to maintain flexion of the head; do so *gently*.
8. Bring the baby all the way out, place it on the mom's belly, and then assess the need for suction, stimulation, etc.

Hemorrhage

No one wants a heavy bleed to happen at home! This is why it's crucial to take a complete medical history and give thorough prenatal care (including appropriate lab tests), so the woman who seems likely to bleed is either screened out or anticipated with emergency measures in readiness. A routine hematocrit should be done early in pregnancy and again at seven months. A high reading will at least insure maximum resilience if bleeding does occur. A history of previous hemorrhage doesn't necessarily contraindicate home birth; it depends on the cause of the bleeding, particularly if there is some question regarding third stage management. For example, a story like this, ". . . I was fine right after my last birth, but then the doctor pulled hard on the cord . . . it really hurt, and then I really started to bleed a lot," should lead you to deduce that the bleed was probably caused by over-zealous attendants.

However, additional questions about subsequent measures required to stabilize the mother (such as transfusion), and questions regarding excessive postpartum flow will give you a more accurate picture of the woman's tendency to bleed and her ability to recuperate. Any history of excessive bleeding following injury, surgery or dental work should be investigated via lab tests for clotting factors. These tests are numerous and require complex interpretation, so get some medical consultation on this.

If there is no general propensity to bleed and previous third stage hemorrhage seems unrelated to management, consider poor health as a possible cause. Take a good look at the woman; observe her energy level, vitality, appearance and muscular condition, and then suggest appropriate nutritional changes, herbal remedies or exercise. A woman who has several children already, who feels fatigued and looks dragged-out, needs lots of B-vitamins (100 mg daily), plenty of good quality protein, and a good balance of minerals, including adequate iron. Recommend exercise for toning up the abdominal muscles, and suggest brisk walking or swimming for stimulating the circulation. Cayenne pepper (three to six capsules daily) helps revitalize the system. The woman might also take alfalfa tablets regularly during her last weeks, as alfalfa is rich in vitamin K (known to facilitate the clotting process).

Of course, you must be realistic regarding a woman's chances for improvement. What can you expect from a worn down mother with previous history of bleeding, who's just weeks from her due date? She'd be better off in the hospital.

Bleeding During Labor There are two main causes of bleeding during labor; one is placenta praevia and the other is placental abruption.

Placenta praevia means that the placenta is implanted low in the uterine wall, either over the cervix or at its edge, so that separation and bleeding occur with effacement and dilatation. Generally it is diagnosed in the last weeks of pregnancy by painless spotting or bleeding (see Chapter 3 for more information).

Placental abruption means premature separation of the placenta, i.e., separation before delivery. This poses grave dangers to both mother and baby; the mother bleeds uncontrollably, while the baby's oxygen supply is severely reduced or cut off completely. The only way to stop the bleeding is to effect immediate delivery and this of course means Cesarean section, unless the mother is in second stage and about to give birth.

What causes placental abruption? Sometimes the placenta is pulled away from the uterine wall by tension on the umbilical cord, due to extreme entanglement which has left no slack for the baby to move or descend. Another cause is maternal hypertension. At any rate, since the situation demands *immediate action*, it's important to know the symptoms:

1. severe, persistent abdominal pain, different from the ebb and flow sensation of contractions;
2. abdominal tenderness;
3. fetal distress, with FHT pattern indicating definite hypoxia and;
4. blood appearing at the outlet (may or may not occur). Sometimes it's a case of concealed abruption, meaning that the blood is completely trapped between the placenta and the uterine lining. At other times the blood begins to trickle down, which makes diagnosis easier.

Any woman with sudden excruciating abdominal pain must be transported at once, and should be given oxygen en route to the hospital. You should also treat the woman for shock, being certain that her head is down and that she is covered and warm.

If a woman complains of severe *but sporadic* pain, keep a close check on the FHT and apply heat to the area of the uterus that is affected. It may be a case of incoordinate uterine action (due to prolonged labor or CPD) but if the pain worsens, you must transport immediately.

Vasa praevia is an exceedingly rare complication in which vessels running through the membranes present over the cervical opening. They may be running to an accessory lobe, or may be suspended in membranes at the juncture of cord and placenta (velamentous insertion). If the membranes rupture at that spot the mother will hemorrhage, and the baby may die. Occasionally this complication is detected in the last few weeks of pregnancy by internal exam, particularly if the cervix is effaced or dilated (the membranes feel peculiar, and disturbance of the fetal heart may be noted during exam). If not, chances are it will be noticed in early labor. Otherwise, rupture of membranes may be combined with hemorrhage. If so, give the mother oxygen and rush to the hospital.

If there is a velamentous insertion of the cord but labor has proceeded normally, you may note an unusual "give" with cord traction. Stop traction immediately, or the cord may pull away from the placenta completely. Instead give pitocin and have the mother squat and push.

Third/Fourth Stage Hemorrhage Postpartum hemorrhage is generally defined as blood loss exceeding 2 cups, or 500 ccs. Estimating blood loss is not easy for beginners; try pouring a measured amount of liquid on an underpad to get the idea. Don't forget that clots must be added into the measurement.

There are three major causes of postpartum hemorrhage: 1) partial separation of the placenta, 2) cervical or vaginal tissue trauma, and 3) uterine atony (relaxation) after the placenta has delivered. Partial separation is the most dangerous because as long as part of the placenta remains attached, the uterus will be distended and the muscle fibers will be unable to contract and close off bleeding vessels.

Partial separation has several causes. One is incoordinate contracting, often caused by "fundus fiddling" attendants. Left to itself, the uterus will clamp down uniformly and will shear off the placenta in one smooth sweep. But if poked and prodded it may only release certain sections. Another cause is morbidly adherent areas of placenta which resist the retracting of uterine muscle, no matter how strong and coordinate contractions may be. If the labor has been of moderate length with second stage not over-extended, bleeding is probably due to adherent areas as the uterus that is not over-tired should have ample strength and momentum to separate the placenta all at once.

Signs of partial separation include bleeding that does not stop, with no apparent lengthening of the umbilical cord. To make certain of your diagnosis, put on a clean glove and *follow the cord up to the cervix*; if the placenta is right there in the os you have separation after all and can use controlled cord traction to remove it. If not, pitocin (10 units IM) should be administered immediately in order to stimulate strong contractions. (There is no reason to fear this procedure as pitocin *does not* close the cervix; it works on the longitudinal fibers of the uterus only, not the circular ones at the cervix as methergine does.) After giving pitocin, have the mother squat and push while you do con-

trolled cord traction, carefully guarding the uterus to prevent prolapse or inversion. This procedure should definitely bring the placenta unless it is truly adherent. If there is any doubt in your mind, follow the cord up again and check to see if you can feel margins still attached. If so, repeat pitocin injection (there should be at least a five-minute interval) and transport immediately, treating the mother for potential shock and giving oxygen en route.

Usually the pitocin will control the bleeding and stabilize the mother's condition somewhat. But if this doesn't work and she is pouring blood, your only option is to manually remove the placenta then and there. Someone should call the ambulance and notify the hospital as you come to this decision. Manual removal is traumatic and painful, and thus it should only be done in dire necessity. The procedure is not too difficult. Reglove, pour a squirt of Betadine over your gloved hand and insert into the uterus, then find the nearest margin and begin prying the placenta away (using your hand like a spatula). Once you have the placenta removed, go over the uterine wall *quickly* to remove any adherent fragments. An assistant should give methergine and/or pitocin as soon as the placenta is out, and vigorous uterine massage should be started at once. The placenta itself should be examined carefully to be sure it is complete: if there is any question, the mother should be taken to the hospital immediately for a D and C.

If attempts at manual removal should fail, i.e., sections of the placenta are impossible to remove and the mother continues to bleed, methergine can be given as a last resort. This will cause very strong contractions and *may* close the cervix, but in this case the priority is to save the mother's life by stopping blood loss during transport. This is certainly wise if the way to the hospital is long.

I once had an uncanny experience with partial separation. Before going to this birth, I lay down to clear my mind and focus my energies on my upcoming task when an inner voice said clearly, "There's going to be a partial separation."

"Well," I thought, "that's reasonable, she had bleeding in the first trimester. No problem, I'll just go up inside the cervix like I've done before and grab it."

"No," the voice insisted, "this time it's different, this time you'll have to go all the way up and really pry it off."

Oh boy, was I frightened! But I put it out of my mind, dismissed it as a logical fear based on the mother's history and went on to the birth.

But it paid to be prepared. The baby delivered beautifully and then torrential bleeding began. I followed the cord up and felt it meet the placenta just inside the cervix and thought, "Oh good, it's right here," but as I attempted to remove it, I realized there was a battledore insertion with the upper margins still adherent, and soon I was doing a complete manual separation. I had my assistant give 20 units of pitocin IM (which I'd drawn up in advance), meanwhile the blood was *pouring* down my

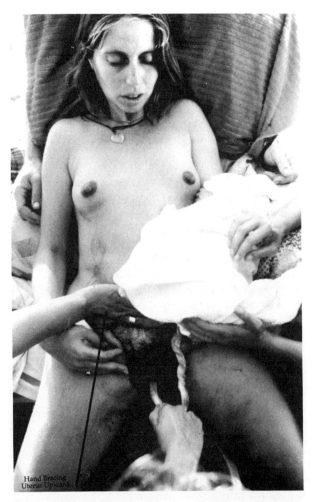

Hand Bracing
Uterus Upward

Controlled Cord Traction

arm. But the process was quickly completed and the uterus firmed up right away. Mother was stable, with total estimated blood loss (EBL) at 800 ccs.

One cardinal rule in dealing with a woman who is hemorrhaging is to keep her attention focused on the here and now. This means commanding her to stay with you, to look you or her mate in the eyes, or to touch and speak to her baby. In essence, this is the mustering of her vital force and participation, especially critical if she is drifting or fading out. Delivery is such an enormous release of tension that it takes a real effort of the will (both yours and the mother's) to hold on and stay present. This is one reason why prenatal communication has to be authentic: you must have channels open and ready to be activated in case of emergency.

Cervical tearing is highly unlikely if you've determined the woman to be complete before she begins her pushing. **Vaginal tissue trauma** is a possibility whenever there is a large baby, compound presentation or unusual tension in the muscles. Sometimes a small artery may split if a vaginal tear runs deep enough, in which case the bleed can be controlled by an artery forceps at each torn end, with subsequent tie-off suturing (see Suturing, this chapter).

Whenever there is postpartum bleeding it is essential to eliminate vaginal tears as a possible cause. Partial separation is usually characterized by gushes and spurts of blood in such amounts that there can be no other explanation, but tissue trauma bleeding and bleeding due to uterine atony can be confused. Check the vaginal vault carefully with sterile gauze, dabbing at any torn areas and examining closely. A torn artery is distinguished by spurting or running bleeding, rather than the slow seeping characteristic of normal tears.

Uterine atony can result in considerable bleeding following the delivery of the placenta. There are several causes; one is a long, drawn-out labor which leaves the uterus too exhausted to clamp down efficiently; another is precipitous labor, wherein contractions have come so hard and fast up to delivery that the uterus is unable to shift gears and make a smooth muscular adjustment to its reduced volume. Both of these are usually controlled with fundal massage and oxytoxic drugs unless there is a pathological condition of the blood which inhibits coagulation.

If you are faced with a seemingly uncontrollable bleed following the placenta, and massage and medications won't work, you must immediately call for help while giving the mother oxygen and **bimanual compression.** In addition to the method pictured in the illustration on the next page, you can also perform this maneuver externally by grasping the uterus firmly with both hands, lifting it up from the belly then pressing your hands together as hard as possible.

The mother should be treated for shock and given fluids (by mouth or IV). And like the mother who is bleeding from partial separation, this woman needs to be focused on summoning her vital forces and staying present.

Sometimes you'll have a case of slow trickle bleeding, a sort of lazy, sporadic flow, which may reflect the mother's emotional state. Particularly if the birth has been difficult, and especially if for some reason the mother isn't glad to see her baby, she may become passively withdrawn (emotionally shocky) and may literally "let it bleed." Here's where you take a strong stance, reprimanding her to stop and pull herself together for her beautiful baby. Herbal tinctures may help, particularly if given along with warm, sweetened tea. Blue cohosh and shepherd's purse are the most effective; give a large dose, 2 droppers full under the tongue, then follow with tea.

Another possibility is **sequestered clots.** These are blood clots in the uterus, which prevent it from clamping down completely. Massage will often expel them, but if the uterus feels somewhat enlarged and bleeding continues, do a gentle, sterile exploration to be sure all clots are out. And be certain her bladder is empty.

Watch the slow trickle bleed very carefully. It can start and stop again, and may not respond to breast stimulation, massage, or tinctures, although all of these should be tried repeatedly. Sometimes it is necessary to give pitocin or methergine as much as 45 minutes after delivery if the blood loss is accumulating to a debilitating level, and if the woman shows no signs of stabilizing. You must *continually reassess blood*

Giving an Injection

1. Take a moment to steady yourself.
2. Locate the outer, upper quadrant of one hip.
3. Flick the ampule to get all the medication into the base and break off the tip, being careful not to touch the edges.
4. Remove the syringe from package.
5. Unscrew the bottom of the needle package, remove tip from syringe, and screw needle onto syringe. (Do not touch hub of needle or end of syringe.)
6. Remove needle cover, place needle into ampule and pull back plunger to draw up solution.
7. Pointing syringe upward, tap sides and press plunger to remove air bubbles.
8. Use left hand to cleanse injection site with alcohol, then hold area firmly, skin spread flat.
9. Plunge needle in about three-quarters of the way (one quick movement).
10. Draw back on the plunger to see if a vein has been entered. If blood comes up, push needle in a bit more and check again.
11. If clear, inject *slowly*, pushing plunger all the way down to the base.
12. Draw needle out quickly (one smooth movement) and put pressure on site with alcohol pad until the bleeding stops.
13. Dispose of needles and syringes properly, i.e., caps back on, etc., with other hazardous waste.

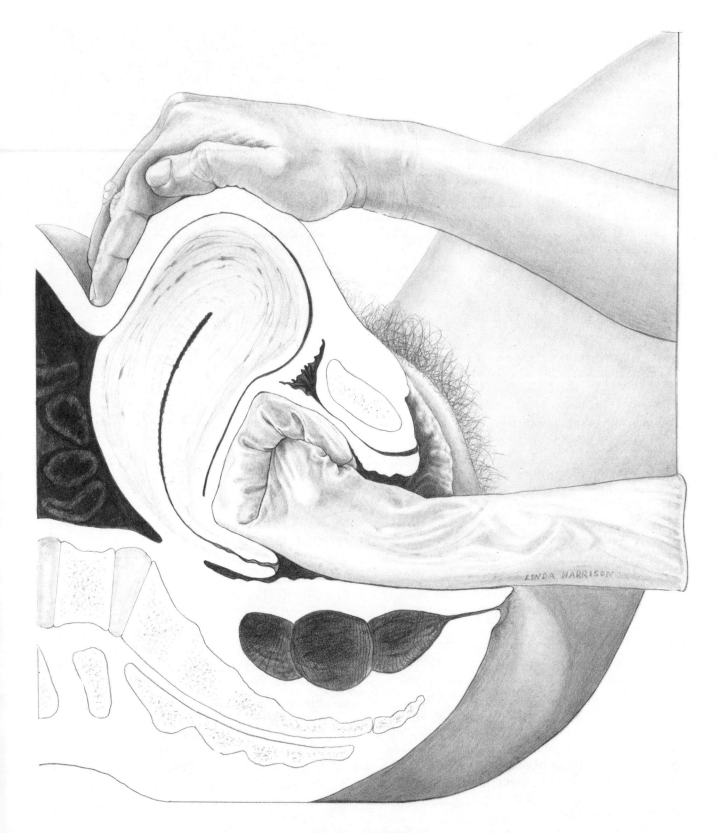

Bimanual Compression

HEART & HANDS

loss; if it exceeds 750 ccs. (3 cups) you must transport, even though the situation does not appear critical.

Retained Placenta

The placenta usually comes away from the uterine wall with the first few contractions following delivery. Generally there is a delay of ten to twenty minutes, while the uterus recovers its strength and reduces in size sufficiently to shear the placenta away. If the uterine contour is round, chances are the placenta is not yet separated. And absence of the characteristic "separation gush" is a definite sign to wait and see.

Nevertheless, it's wise to encourage the mother to concentrate and bear down as soon as you notice the uterus contracting again, even though the mother may barely feel anything. Have her squat over a bowl to add gravity's force, and you can help with controlled traction. If you stick to this routine, you'll find the placenta usually delivers within 20 minutes.

There are several situations which may cause exceptions. One is the long, drawn out labor which leaves the uterus so exhausted that it can't finish the job. If the mother is tired and baby not yet nursing, you might try nipple stimulation, or tincture of cohosh. Another solution is to give an injection of pitocin to stimulate contractions and get the placenta out. However, if none of these work there may be a problem with unusual implantation.

A rare condition known as **placenta accreta** describes the placenta which is actually imbedded in the uterine muscle. This is rare indeed, but the slim possibility of this argues against putting undue traction on the cord. There is an unforgettable picture in *Williams Obstetrics* showing a fatal case of inverted uterus, pulled completely out of the vagina with placenta still attached. Placenta accreta may necessitate hysterectomy if there is no other way for the placenta to be removed, although hysterotomy (opening the uterus for surgical removal) is usually tried first.

More commonly it's a matter of maternal inertia which stalls delivery of the placenta. I recall one birthing which went quite quickly; we arrived when the mother was nine centi-

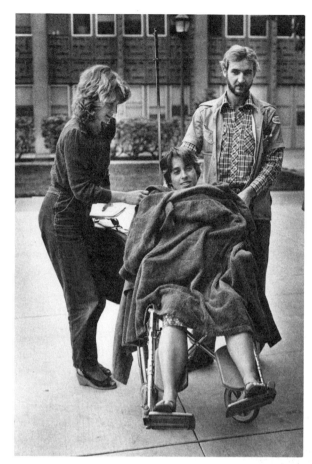

Don't lose faith in yourself if you have to transport!

meters. She had established a routine and intimacy with her mate, and regardless of our closeness prenatally we felt a bit like intruders. She delivered very much on her own, and then we began our wait for the placenta. Two hours later after squatting, cord traction, teas, baby-nursing, etc. she went into the bathroom to pee and delivered the placenta herself (in private). She came out and handed it to us, saying good-naturedly, "Here's what you wanted!"

Sometimes women resist letting go of the placenta because it represents the last remnant of pregnancy, the last obstacle to full-fledged motherhood. Focusing the new mother on the beauty of her baby or the pleasure of nursing will often bring the placenta. Sometimes a bit of encouragement, "Let's just get the placenta out now and you'll feel so relieved!" will provide the stimulus for letting go.

How long is it safe to wait? Try an injection of pitocin at 45 minutes and wait another hour or so (or as long as the uterus remains firm, there is no bleeding and fundal height is stable). Beyond that, it becomes a problem of extended watch causing fatigue and anxiety for the mother (and her attendants). Also, the cervix tends to close after several hours, presenting an obstacle to easy delivery. Infection is another potential danger, as the cord is now extending from the vagina and germs may travel up into the uterus. After two hours you should "talk hospital" and after another 20 minutes, go ahead and transport.

Assessment and Repair of Lacerations/Episiotomy

One of the most interesting facets of my apprenticeship was observing the unique ways in which various midwives did their suturing. Also interesting were the decisions on when, and when not to repair. After observing the healing time and relative discomfort caused by various techniques, I developed a personal preference. This is presented in the following section, along with many other critical elements of technique, by my friend and mentor, John Walsh.

Always remember that episiotomy is rarely justified, except in cases of fetal distress necessitating emergency delivery, or with perineum persistently thick and resistant. An episiotomy may be easier to suture than a tear but one is obliged to cut through muscle, whereas the tear tends to be more superficial. Episiotomy weakens the musculature unless perfectly repaired, and causes much greater discomfort and slower recovery for the new mother.

With most deliveries, the mother sustains a few, very minor tears. These are usually simple abrasions (my midwife friend Tina called them "skid marks") and none may actually require stitches. Generous use of olive oil with sensitive massage helps to prevent these skin splits, or at least minimize them. A few small scrapes and one small, first degree tear to the perineum (skin and a bit of tissue only) are preferable to a deep episiotomy wound.

Here is a typical post-delivery picture. Labial skin splits are noted on each side of the introitus (no deep tissue tearing), a minor internal muscle split (bulbocavernosus muscle) can be seen and felt, but the perineum is found to be intact. If bleeding from the internal tear can be controlled with a bit of pressure (using sterile gauze), I usually do no suturing at all. Labial skin splits, unless they are really deep, are much more uncomfortable and slower to mend when sutured. Internal tear edges will usually meet and join together as long as the split is no more than halfway through the muscle and the mother is careful about keeping her legs together when she sits. Superficial, first degree perineal tears will also heal by themselves if the woman is careful.

But be sure to make a thorough and honest assessment of each and every laceration. Unfortunately, there is a strange status quest among midwives regarding ability to do tear-free deliveries; do not let this prevent you from suturing when it is clearly necessary. Sometimes the mother will be *more* comfortable if sutured, especially if tear edges do not approximate (fit together) by themselves. Suturing is a valuable and necessary skill for midwives!

Suturing Technique, by John Walsh, PA/Midwife

Unlike most obstetricians who prefer to make an episiotomy for a variety of rationalizations, midwives take great pride in delivering the placenta (and the baby) over an intact perineum. This is the hallmark of a real midwife and is genuine proof of her patience and loving touch. Nevertheless, tears occur commonly and sometimes surprisingly. A nine-pounder slides out without a nick, while a five-pounder creates a third degree laceration unexpectedly. Often the head is guided out exquisitely, only to have the shoulders do damage because of some urgency. And what does it gain a woman to have a wonderful delivery at home only to have to pack up, drive to the hospital, and be sutured by strangers who may receive her with rudeness or even pointed hostility?

After the first fifteen or twenty deliveries, every midwife has had to reckon with a few serious tears. They are simply going to happen, no matter how ideal things are. In fact, she may even decide to do an episiotomy on rare occasions, and this requires a repair job.

Every midwife should learn to suture and do it without recoiling. It is one of those skills that has a great aura of mystery about it. This is probably because suturing is usually considered part of the province of surgery, with firsthand experience not easy to come by. Although it is a skill acquired by seeing and doing under the guidance of a teacher, it requires understanding and rehearsal before actual practice.

It is essential to set up properly for the procedure, or you won't be able to do a good job. The mother should be made comfortable on the bed's edge. She should have a clean, dry underpad beneath her. You must have excellent lighting; carry your own tensor lamp and extension cord to eliminate this worry. Also, you must get in a comfortable position as you begin—your back will definitely begin to ache, and sweat will pour down your nose. This is really hard work.

The first step in repair is careful examination. Wear a sterile glove for this. It is helpful to place several gauze sponges in the vagina to aid exposure and sop up the oozing which obscures the landmarks. Roll up the gauze and insert like a tampon. Just don't forget to *remove it when you are done*—it will be practically invisible because it will be blood-soaked.

Take your time to be sure you see the full extent of any tears or bleeding sites. Don't assume that everything is OK. You must look. If the mother is uncomfortable during the exam, it may be best to give the local anesthetic (2% lidocaine) now and continue the exam as it takes effect. It will help if she is arranged comfortably and is holding her new baby, not paying much attention to what you are doing. However, it is important to warn her gently whenever you begin something painful like injecting.

Lidocaine does not completely anesthetize tissue. Usually women can feel moderate pressure or pulling sensations, although these shouldn't be painful. This worries some women, as they are afraid your next movement will hurt alot. Don't do anything sud-

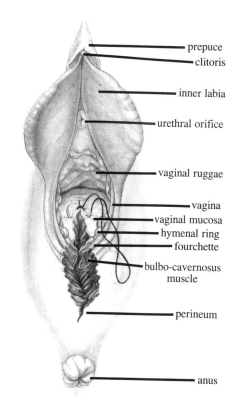

prepuce
clitoris
inner labia
urethral orifice
vaginal ruggae
vagina
vaginal mucosa
hymenal ring
fourchette
bulbo-cavernosus muscle
perineum
anus

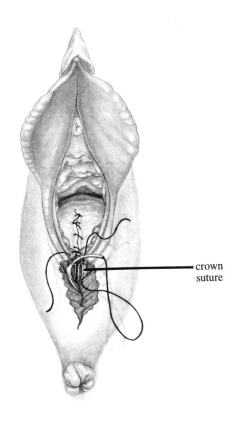

crown suture

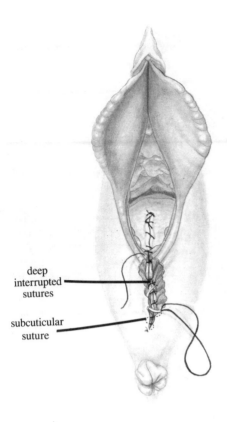

deep
interrupted
sutures

subcuticular
suture

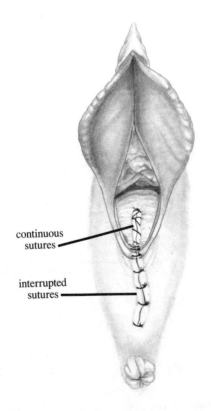

continuous
sutures

interrupted
sutures

denly, and the mother will begin to relax and stop anticipating pain.

The basic suture kit needs to contain:

1. A needle holder. The six inch Baumgartner is probably the best. The tips are small and serrated to hold the needle tightly without slipping. A hemostat should not be substituted, because the balance and the grip as the needle is driven through tissue makes a subtle but important difference in doing a good job;

2. A tissue forceps. These look somewhat like tweezers but are called forceps. A very delicate kind called Semkin-Taylor or Adsons are a good choice. They have tiny, interlocking "rats teeth" at their tips and with them you can hold and lift tissue very nicely without pinching or destroying membranes. Thumb forceps or dressing forceps are not suitable for handling skin, and the usual tissue forceps found in medical supply houses are too large and clumsy to do precise and careful work;

3. Two or three mosquito hemostats. As their name implies, these are hemostats with small tips used for clamping small "bleeders." They should never be used for anything else;

4. Scissors. A pair with sharp/sharp tips is used for trimming tissue and cutting suture material precisely. It should not be the scissors used in the delivery or for cutting the cord;

5. 4 x 4 sterile gauze pads or sponges;

6. Betadine solution;

7. Suture material. Generally 3-0 or 4-0 chromic gut on a round needle half-circle is the most useful. The half-circle needle is sturdier and penetrates deeper. Sometimes a 4-0, three-eighths circle with a cutting edge is best for more superficial tears. It pops through the skin easier but would bend if used for deep muscle sewing. By the way, "cat-gut" really comes from the submucous connective tissue of sheep intestine. It dissolves in about five to seven

days, unless it is impregnated with chromic oxide which prevents the suture material from decomposing so readily. The designation 3-0 refers to the diameter and tensile strength of the suture. 5-0 is smaller, weaker; 1-0 is thicker and stronger. 3-0 has a pulling strength of approximately two and a half pounds. 4-0 has about one and a half pound knot-pull tensile strength. Sooner or later you will break a suture just as you tie an important knot. It is exasperating (but you will learn a finer touch). The needle itself is swaged onto the suture material so there is no "eye" or bump of thread to go through.

The repair instruments should be kept wrapped up and sterile until the local anesthesia has been given. Suturing must be done by *sterile technique*. This step-by-step procedure seems complicated and difficult to organize at first but practice makes perfect. It is essential to have an assistant help you; you both must know exactly what to do. For the purpose of making the following explanation clear, the one doing the suturing will be called "A" and the assistant will be called "B."

1. A opens her pair of sterile gloves and puts them on, then places the sterile inner wrapper down to serve as the sterile field.

2. B opens outer suture wrapper and drops sterile suture packet on sterile field, then does the same with 5cc syringe and sterile gauze pads.
3. A takes the sterile instruments (needle holder, scissors, mosquito hemostats and tissue forceps) and places them on the sterile field.
4. B wipes the lidocaine top with an alcohol pad and opens the packet of a 21 gauge needle (1 1/2 inch), being careful not to touch the base of needle.
5. A holds up the syringe, and B screws the needle onto the tip.
6. A draws back the plunger of the syringe and injects 5–10 ccs of air into the bottle of lidocaine which B holds up, then A draws up the same amount of lidocaine (use the larger amount for bigger lacerations). A and B must be careful not to touch each other's hands or tools; this requires a delicate choreography between them.
7. B holds up the needle cover for the 21 gauge needle, and unscrews the needle from the tip of A's syringe.
8. B holds up the smaller, 23 gauge needle (1/2 inch) and screws it onto the tip of A's syringe.
9. A now begins injecting lidocaine around the edges of the wound and prepares to suture.
10. B puts on a pair of sterile gloves, and assists by holding the labia open while

A does the suturing. She can also reach for gauze and dab while A is stitching.

A word now about injections. You should read the package literature that comes with lidocaine—especially the part about side effects. If a woman says she feels peculiar after you have injected, stop everything and assess the situation carefully. Every now and then, a woman may have a reaction which is simply one of distaste for shots and needles. Make sure that's all it is. If she is feeling faint or suddenly says she feels hot and shaky, watch for signs of shock. Take blood pressure and pulse, monitor skin color, check the uterus for firmness, etc. True drug reactions are rare but emotional reactions common.

It will be easiest to inject if you start at the top of the tear and work down. Inject directly into the sides of the laceration. It takes a surprising amount of force to squirt it into the tissue. If you try to do it fast it will sting the mother a lot, as you blow a bubble of lidocaine under the skin. Work slowly. As you inject, you will notice that you change and distort the tissue as it distends with anesthetic. Try not to plunge the needle all the way to the hilt, as that is its weakest point. Inject no more than one cc at a time, pulling back the plunger to make sure that a vein hasn't been entered.

Now you are ready to begin suturing. The repair of a second degree midline laceration goes something like this (there are many variations). After the anesthesia has taken effect, use the tissue forceps to examine the edges of the internal vaginal tear. Continuous sutures are begun at the apex of the tear. The tissue forceps (or pickups) grasp the edge of one side, the needleholder directs the needle in a curving motion and a good, deep bite of tissue is taken. The needle pops through the other side to be clamped by the holder again, and is re-inserted about a quarter of an inch below the first stitch. By pulling slightly on the strand as it is placed, the edges to be closed next will come into view easily. It is also a good idea to re-approximate edges (hold them together) every stitch or two, to make sure they are matching up correctly. The continuous suturing is continued until the hymenal ring is reached. This first suture string is sometimes left dangling there to be tied to a second strand used to repair the perineum.

The next step is to join the deeper perineal muscle tissue with a series of three or four interrupted sutures. These will bring the edges of the skin closer together, distributing tension and eliminating dead space. It is not necessary to go deeply here as with the stitches inside the vagina. In fact, you must be careful not to prick the rectal wall.

Next the superficial layer of outer perineal skin is closed with a subcuticular stitch, starting at the bottom and working up to the junction of the vaginal suture. Then the two ends are tied together. Alternately, interrupted sutures could be used to close the skin layer.

Here are some basic principles to keep in mind for any type of suture job:

1. Close lacerations (no matter where they are) in layers—muscle, fascia, skin. The basic idea is to eliminate tension in any one spot. You use interrupted, "buried," sutures to bring deep muscle layers together. This is especially important in mediolateral lacerations (those starting at the fourchette and going off to one side) or otherwise they will heal in a distorted manner. This is particularly true if they haven't had the pull on the deep layers distributed evenly. Things may look alright on the surface skin, but as the deeper tissue heals it will contract in the direction of the unbalanced tension and create a puckering.

2. Eliminate all dead spaces between layers. If you don't, oozing can occur and a small (or large) hematoma can form. These are terribly painful swellings which can be serious enough to cause the repair to fail. Also the integrity of the entire pelvic floor depends on the quality of your repair. Dead, empty spaces are weak and prone to infection.

3. Don't suture too tightly as it may impair the circulation. Anticipate slight suture swelling as you sew, and compensate so that tissues will not be choked. Fortunately, vaginal tissue is highly vascular and it is difficult to make serious mistakes.

4. Check your landmarks very carefully and repeatedly. If you have waited several hours to do a repair, significant edema may confuse the picture. Double check what goes with what. Go slowly. It is sometimes helpful to tack the middle of a laceration together, instead of working from both ends only to find that things don't quite match up. The bulbocavernosus muscle at the mouth of the vagina is an important landmark; it should be united very meticulously. A deep double stitch should be used to join both sides so that the skin goes to meet exactly. Take care not to pull too tightly. Also, you must be certain that the levator ani muscle round the anus has not been torn either partially or completely. This is a job strictly for the experienced! Don't attempt it if you don't know how, and more importantly, don't neglect it, hoping that since it's only a "little tear" it will be OK. Anal incontinence is very difficult to remedy later.

5. Sutures should be placed so that the depth is greater than the width. This is the best way to produce a closure where the edges meet correctly. This is a fundamental principle of suturing and it is important to reason out why this is so.

6. The curved needle is best grasped at about two-thirds of its length. If it is held at the end, it frequently bends or worse, breaks. The needleholder should be held firmly and the piercing motion is made with the entire hand and wrist in a twisting motion. It is sometimes very difficult to pop the needle through the skin; use the tissue forceps to grasp the area firmly with your other hand.

7. Every suture should have three alternating knots. The first should be a friction knot (put end through loop *twice* before pulling snug) and the other two should be alternating slip knots. This three-knot process creates a very strong, true square knot. Be careful never to clamp the suture with the needleholder, as it will tend to break at that site. Suturing is easier if you wet the suture with Betadine before beginning. This keeps the string from sticking to itself and your gloves as you are working.

8. Your assistant can be very helpful by cutting sutures as they are placed. This saves you the movements of laying down the needleholder and forceps to pick up the scissors. You should hold both strands up rather tautly as your assistant prepares to cut. She takes the scissors and then, with the index finger pointing down the blades, the scissors tops are opened just slightly and placed slowly on the strands at just the right place and the strands are quickly snipped. The tails on interrupted sutures are usually made about a half centimeter in length—some people feel that if they are too short they may slip, whereas long ends may cause irritation by poking adjacent tissue.

If there is swelling after the repair, apply an ice pack (crushed ice in a sterile glove will work just fine). Make sure to tell the mother to rinse off with peri-bottle or jar of water, with a squirt of Betadine added, each time she uses the toilet. After the first 24 hours, it is perfectly OK for the mother to soak in the bath tub. It will not dissolve the sutures. It is also a good idea to expose the perineum to a light bulb or sunlight to dry it. The mother should avoid applying vitamin E or other oils to the wound as these retard the healing process. If you have done a good job, the majority of the healing will take place in a few days.

—*John Walsh*

* * *

Infant Resuscitation

Here is a topic you need to discuss with parents before the birth. Many will pose the ultimate question, "Have you ever had a baby born that wasn't breathing?" In order to explain your procedures for resuscitation, you must explain the various causes of fetal depression. It's important that parents realize that some occurrences, such as cord accidents (prolapse, true knot) or placental problems (abruption, vasa praevia) can lead to fetal demise regardless of your best efforts, and that the presence of resuscitation equipment is no guarantee of absolute safety or security. Beyond that, the basics of detection and management should be discussed so that if resuscitation is necessary, parents will have a sense of what is taking place and birth team efforts can be concerted.

Much has been said already about interpreting FHT patterns and scalp tone so that fetal distress is not allowed to persist and deepen into depression. By far the most common type of fetal depression is the last-minute variety which occurs with ultimate head compression and molding, just before the baby is released. Length of labor, relative proportions of mom and baby, and maternal stability all have a bearing on the baby's tolerance. Keep in mind that the baby of a clinically exhausted mother can react suddenly and severely to last-minute stress. As has been said before, any prolonged drop in the FHT is definite reason for effecting immediate delivery via squatting, hard pushing, or episiotomy and sacrifice of the perineum.

Whenever a baby is born in a compromised condition, your top priorities are *clearing the airway* and *providing warmth*. Regarding the latter, it is critical to appreciate the folly of trying to bring a baby around if it is chilled. Babies come out naked and dripping wet and can therefore lose body heat very rapidly. Cover the baby closely with three flannel blankets (preferably warmed in the oven) and make sure to cover the head. Suction according to need, being careful not to stimulate the gag reflex by placing the bulb syringe too far back in the throat.

Unless at risk due to stressful labor, postmaturity, prematurity or intrauterine growth retardation, a baby with a hypoxic phase of less than ten minutes will generally come around fairly quickly if given *sensitive stimulation* and kept warm. Minor last-minute depression causes no major change in the baby's pH (acidosis) which could hinder spontaneous recovery. Remember that the baby will receive oxygen as long as the cord is left pulsing, which allows the baby to make a natural transi-

tion to respiration without undue stress. This transition takes some babies a bit of time; it is not abnormal for 20 seconds to elapse before significant respiratory efforts are made.

More serious neonatal depression is termed apnea, literally meaning "without breath." There are two catagories: primary and secondary. The first denotes the baby who has probably been depressed for less than ten minutes and should respond well to stimulation and a few breaths mouth-to-mouth. But the baby born in the secondary apnea has suffered such severe depression that its spontaneous respiratory reflex has already been stimulated in utero or in the birth canal. It will not attempt to breathe on its own again so *waste no time* with stimulation; this baby needs sufficient oxygen, via mouth-to-mouth or bag-mask, to reverse the acidosis that results from severe distress.

Determine the appropriate resuscitation techniques by taking your cues from the baby's

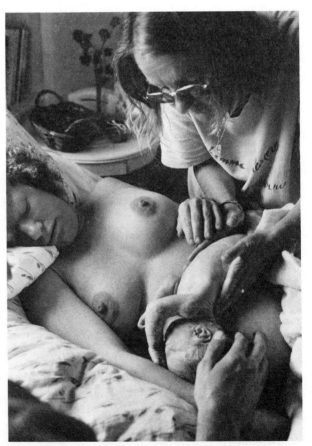

The midwife stimulates a baby making a slow transition, keeping the baby warm against the mother.

skin color, muscle tone and general in-the-body quality. A baby who delivers blue-pink, without much flexion of the limbs but with definite emanating presence, needs immediate, firm but gentle massage at the base of the spine, working up the back. This action should be understood for what it is: an outpouring of positive energy through the hands and stimulation of vagal response. The baby should be against the mother's skin for warmth and contact; you can slip your hand under the blankets to massage. Concerted verbal encouragement like "Come on, baby!" helps to maintain everyone's focus and commitment. Get the mother to talk to her baby! An interesting study was done in which neonatal intensive care nurses noted how babies' oxygen levels would jump upon hearing the sound of mother's voice. Try all the above and response should occur within ten or fifteen seconds; if not, a further step is to lift the baby and see-saw its body up and down. This affects diaphragmatic pressure and can stimulate respiration. And get fresh, dry blankets on the baby as soon as possible.

Long labor can cause a minor type of depression in which the tired baby makes a rather slow transition. Sometimes the parents themselves are so exhausted that they cannot muster welcome and attention for the baby. I have seen several babies deliver in fine condition and then proceed to go pale and flaccid due to lack of warm and enthusiastic reception from the parents. Sometimes this is due to the undesired or unexpected sex of the baby. You use your heart in moments like these: "What a gorgeous girl (or boy) you have!" or to the sibling standing by, "You have a sister (or brother)!" There is a tangible quality of energy that kindles life and response, pure, strong and loving, and it's the midwife's job to work with everything she's got in order to initiate this at the given moment.

Standard hospital treatment for the slightly depressed or tentative baby is quite different. Duties are sharply divided between obstetrician and pediatrician due to legal liability. It's simply out of the OB's jurisdiction to make any efforts at neonatal stimulation or resuscitation. When confronted with an unstable baby, his first priority is to pass it on to the pediatric team. This means premature cord clamping and further compromise of the baby's condition, so that the marginal baby is rapidly on the way to needing real resuscitation. The pediatrician then places the baby on its back in a resuscitation unit, applies mechanical suction with nose and throat tubing, and then oxygen by face mask. Time and again I've seen babies worsen with this treatment or else struggle awkwardly to get their own rhythms established. I usually find myself saying, "Somebody touch the baby!" or I move over and do it myself. Observation and participation has taught me that touch usually brings swift and dramatic improvement.

The baby born in secondary apnea, easily recognizable by its shocking white and completely limp appearance, is another story. As soon as suction is complete, this baby needs immediate mouth-to-mouth resuscitation until the oxygen system is set up. An assistant should take heart tones, as the absence of FHTs indicates the need for cardiac massage. A friend or the father should call for the ambulance.

Mouth-to-mouth resuscitation is often sufficient for all but the most severe cases. Mouth-to-mouth, known as the "kiss of life," is a very sensitive technique. There is a smooth interrelation between giving the breath and feeling the baby's response through your hands, which gives a clear and accurate sense of revival. Often the baby will open its eyes as if signaling awareness and willingness to respond, which aids your concentration. The Red Cross offers special courses on infant resuscitation (CPR). It is best to take a class, and to practice carefully until you can maintain a safe pressure level with each and every breath.

Sometimes babies make rattly noises while you are breathing for them; this may mean that more suctioning is in order (using a DeLee). But as long as the throat passage is clear enough to secure ventilation, this is your top priority. Sometimes there are thick globs of mucus in the throat which can be quickly removed with a fingertip. You'll get a sense of this with practice.

I had an experience with resuscitation recently that bears repeating. The baby was born after an hour-long second stage (first baby) and trouble-free labor. The heart tones were good throughout crowning, and the scalp tone was pink. No meconium in the waters, but the baby was born with a tight cord around the neck and I had to clamp and cut immediately. However, the shoulders came quickly so there was no reason to expect what happened next.

The baby failed to make any respiratory efforts and lost the little muscle tone it had at delivery. Apgar at one minute was about a four. Stimulation helped somewhat, the baby began to pink up a bit and when extra suction was given by DeLee, it began to suck. I thought the baby had made it then, but instead it proceeded to pale and become flaccid. More stimulation, gentle suction and then mouth-to-mouth to which the baby responded mildly, although it had never really stopped breathing! It seemed to need more stimulation, so I tried that once more and got a fairly good response but when I stopped, the baby began to fade away again.

Minutes had gone by, so I decided that I would take the baby and give it all the attention and energy I could muster (I also had my apprentice call the ambulance). As I took the baby in my hands and started to do the diaphragmatic see-saw, someone in the room observed that the baby had not opened its eyes yet. At that, it winked its lids and I began to swing its body slowly from side to side, hoping to stimulate it to take a peek. Not much of anything, so I stopped and remembered how its strongest response had been sucking on the DeLee tubing, and put my little finger tip in its mouth. It began to suck, opened its eyes and looked right at me, and then turned nice and pink. The ambulance team walked in but realized that nothing but observation was needed, and so left shortly thereafter.

How to explain the baby's in-and-out behavior? The probable causes, such as prematurity,

---

Principles of Infant Resuscitation

If the baby is born limp and floppy, with white body:

1. *Provide warmth:* wrap the baby with blankets and cover the head.
2. *Clear the airway:* suction mouth with bulb syringe or DeLee if necessary.
3. *Position the baby so head is not overextended,* or airway will be occluded.
4. *Begin mouth-to-mouth:* puff your cheeks full of air, place your mouth over the baby's nose *and* mouth, and give four short puffs to the baby. Do not use your lungs! If this does not institute breathing, continue at the rate of 30 breaths per minute.
5. *Have your assistant take heart tones:* if pulse rate is found to be absent, begin cardiac massage. Apply pressure on the sternum bone midway between the nipples, pressing two fingers in about ½ inch. Continue at the rate of 80–100 times per minute.
6. *Every fifth beat, as you release pressure, blow air into the baby without interrupting the rhythm of your heart massage. This is full CPR.*
7. *After one full minute, briefly stop and recheck pulse. If absent or still below 60, carefully reposition your fingers and continue CPR.*
8. *Periodically re-check pulse,* but never stop for more than one minute maximum. Continue on as necessary.

infection or maternal drug use did not apply. There were, however, definite and extreme psychological tensions between the parents regarding each other and the baby. Moments after the birth, the father moved away to the other side of the room, and the mother froze up completely. I think the baby felt rather unwanted and was plain reluctant. This was my intuition when I gave it my finger to suck and said, "It's not so bad here . . . come on in."

In any marginal situation like this, be sure to maintain an extra long postpartum watch and check the baby very carefully (especially the reflexes). You shouldn't leave until the parents are warmly attentive and the baby is glowing. And have them see the pediatrician as soon as possible.

Fetal Anomalies

Fetal anomalies may be caused by genetics or by certain viruses; most commonly though, defects are caused by synthetic drugs and environmental pollutants. Every midwife should have a list of common pharmaceuticals and their effects on pregnancy.

Extreme abnormalities are often signaled by polyhydramnios or conversely, by a lack of amniotic fluid (oligohydramnios). Careful palpation may disclose hydrocephalus (enlarged cranium) or anencephalus (little or no cranial vault, with extremely large, long limbs). Minor defects like cleft palate are undetectable until birth, whereas more serious ones like spina bifida (exposed spinal meninges) can only be detected by early pregnancy testing (see Chapter 2) or ultrasound.

The most important thing to remember when assisting delivery of the abnormal baby is that the parents need to bond, see, feel and touch, regardless. It's illuminating to know that most mothers, when confronted with a baby with a defect, will still touch and fondle their babies, often emphasizing the beauty of other features. This is as it should be; here is a spirit in vital relation to its parents and minor defects are unimportant in those first moments.

Be sure to stay with the parents (in the same room) until you are certain they have noticed the defect. On the other hand, it's not appropriate to point out defects unless parents are clearly avoiding acknowledgement. Then it should be done simply and gently, and without long discourses on treatment, cause, possible outcome, etc. All of this information will surely be requested later; let the parents set the tone for dealing with it.

Some midwives feel an odd sense of shame when first assisting delivery of a defective baby. This is probably a carry-over from the medieval days when midwives were accused of practicing witchcraft and causing deformity. You'll definitely need to make your adjustment along with the parents.

Most defects require no immediate treatment, except for spina bifida which should be covered with sterile gauze soaked in warm sterile saline. However, babies with anomalies should be seen by a sympathetic pediatrician as soon as possible, as there may be additional or internal defects which are not so easily detected.

If the defect is so severe as to be life-threatening and you sense that parents and baby have very little time together, that's all the more reason to let be. Occasionally a mother may totally reject a severly deformed infant upon its delivery, as an instinctive protection of her emotional sanctity and her future desire to reproduce. In this case, it would be wise to give a verbal confirmation of the many perfect features of the baby. This is a way of providing the mother with essential information for bonding without forcing her to confront the negative aspects.

The traditional model for dealing with anomalies has been cover-up and evasion. Often defective babies are whisked away by hospital personnel before the mother even has a chance to see. If the baby dies in the nursery, the mother is truly robbed of the experience of giving life, no matter how imperfect. Psychological scars of unexperienced loss run deep, and take longer to heal.

I once heard a story of a couple whose baby was born with Down's Syndrome. Their obstetrician was a personal friend who could not bear to tell them. His way of resolving this problem was to drop a book on Down's Syndrome in their mail slot, ring the doorbell and then slip away. By lack of communication his kind intent clearly became an act of violence.

These problems have to be dealt with personally, with comfort and support.

Infant Death

Often death is caused by severe deformity, and it's clear at delivery that there are only moments of time for greeting, acknowledging and letting go. It's a blessing that birth energy is generally so pure that these transitions can be made within a positive, open framework. Once again, if you sense deep denial in the parents and you know the baby is departing, you should tell them simply that their baby has such serious problems that it is going to die. Your emotional support will help them to experience loving and sharing in the remaining moments.

Many women considering midwifery practice stop at the thought of losing a baby. Is it the personal fear of accusation that frightens, or is it confrontation with death itself? It helps to remember that birth and death are both high energy, transitional stages, and the guidelines for handling the intensity are the same. Sure it's tragic and incomprehensible to lose a baby, but it's easier if everyone stays present, open and feeling.

It's different when a baby is stillborn; perfect, beautiful and lifeless. Then there is genuine shock and sense of loss, a reality warp in which the mind struggles to grasp, explain, control. The best thing to do is clear your mind and make a space from whence to simply feel and experience. Do this in yourself and you can pass it on to the others. Help the mom get hold of the baby, encourage both parents by example to touch and see. Keep your sense of rites of passage. Don't give consolation or suggestion; there will come a time for that later on.

It is very hard for the mother in the first few days postpartum, with hormone changes and milk coming in. (Lactation can be suppressed with sage tea, or by binding the breasts.) Grieving is a slow process, but can be dignified if parents are given support for all the phases of feeling. Just your *being there* in the first weeks, as a witness and friend, is all that's needed.

Some believe that naming the baby is important, and I agree. The mother should be encouraged (the father too) to write a chronicle of the event, an expression of impressions and emotion. They may want to save a lock of hair, or take a photograph. The hardest thing for both friends and acquaintances to accept is that grieving is a non-rational and sometimes drawn-out process. Life is the antidote, and love and friendship provide the energy for moving through it.

In Case of Transport

1. For the mother: don't panic! It is easy to feel despair and to lose control upon arriving at the hospital. But you have a better chance for a normal outcome if you *stay relaxed.*
2. For the father: if your partner is exhausted or nearly so, *don't expect her to make complex decisions about hospital routine or physician recommendations.* Here is where all your study and questioning during the pregnancy pays off: the better you know your stuff, the easier it is to respond to suggested procedures with either agreement or alternative solutions.
3. For both of you: *ask for what you want,* or enlist your midwives' assistance in doing so. You have only one birth of this baby; don't hold back! The hospital is an intimidating place, but just because the routine runs a certain way doesn't mean it can't be altered. For example, you can definitely refuse: to wear a hospital gown; people running in and out

The machinery is intimidating, but your baby desperately needs your touch, the sound of your voice and your reassuring presence.

continually; attendants talking during contractions; bright lights in the labor or delivery room; routine IV; routine episiotomy; stirrups for delivery; or baby not given to mother immediately (barring breathing difficulties).

4. In the event the baby is temporarily stable but requires care in the nursery, *keep the baby with you as long as possible.* The father should go with the baby to the nursery until the mother can join them. Once in the nursery, maintain physical and verbal contact with the baby (the isolettes have holes you can put your hand through).

5. If you are unsure about any recommended test for your newborn, ask your midwives or pediatrician. Don't be railroaded into a package treatment; *let them convince you that each test is truly necessary for the baby's welfare* and not just malpractice protection.

6. If you must stay in the hospital, be sure that you *activate your postpartum support system immediately.* Don't wait till you get home—you need it now! Have fresh food brought in at least twice daily, as hospital fare is inadequate in quality and quantity for a breastfeeding mother.

7. Don't hesitate to *ask for privacy, or to be left alone for a time.* Routine checks on mother and baby occur on a regular schedule, but unless they are truly necessary because of something irregular, refuse the constant monitoring or you will never get any rest! You may also find that as shifts change and new nurses appear, each will have some suggestion about wrapping, feeding, or caring for the baby. Cheerfully thank them, but explain that you'd rather figure things out for yourself. (If they press you, just say you'll be fine and not to worry). Otherwise, you'll go crazy with input and will lose confidence in your natural mothering abilities.

8. If you've been in the hospital for a few days due to some complication, *be*

prepared to be absolutely exhausted when you get home. You don't get much sleep in the hospital anyway, but combine this with the stress of worry and adjustment of becoming a parent and you can imagine how tired you'll be. Arrange it so no one is there when you first get home, except other children and their caretaker.

9. *Take it easy on the processing;* it may take some time before the whys and the wherefores become evident. If you start to feel emotionally overwhelmed, call on your midwives.

"SCHOOL OF MIDWIFERY",

East Glamorgan General Hospital,

Church Village,

NR. PONTYPRIDD,

Mid. Glam.

CHAPTER 6

Postpartum Care

The postpartum period is the last frontier for midwives and those associated with maternity care. For so long this phase of birthing was simply ignored, and the woman and her family were left to their own devices. Now midwives refer to the first three months after the birth as the fourth trimester, with the understanding that pregnancy and birth are such intense experiences that naturally there must be a reintegration phase afterwards. This period has been studied in terms of physical changes and emotional flux and much new information has emerged.

Preparation for this fourth trimester should begin prenatally. There is nothing more important you can do than connect pregnant women with one another, or better still with others who have recently given birth. Exercise classes or support groups can serve to accomplish this. Women who are used to being independent and spend most of their time alone may be overwhelmed by the pressure and intensity of routine mothering, with nothing to break the monotony. For women who choose their friends carefully, insisting on intellectual common ground, you might suggest a more tribal approach to the universal in motherhood. Mothering in the early months is made up of many mundane questions and concerns, and contacts with others in the same phase, even if not the deepest friendships, will serve a great purpose.

Sometimes pregnant women do not want to face the prospect of caring for a baby, in which case you should tune them in to what's impending by suggesting books on breastfeeding, mothering, etc. Give out La Leche League information and encourage women to attend meetings. Part of the reason for doing this is simple practicality; you just can't continue to give your attention to every new mother with problems or you'll have no time for those in the process of becoming. Besides, when a woman has a baby she enters a new phase of her life, plays a different social role. Better for her to launch herself with a feeling of self-reliance and self-support than dependence or uncertainty. Remember that midwifery is an art of facilitating passage! The midwife plays the guiding role for a while, but after the birth has happened and mothering begun, the woman must be encouraged to move on.

Recently a new mother approached me with an idea for a postpartum outreach program, one which might serve as a model for midwifery practices everywhere. Her idea was to connect the prospective mother with another who had already birthed and would help with baby care and light chores in the early weeks following delivery. The greatest advantage to this arrangement is the natural interest and pertinent information the mother's helper will have concerning parenting, nursing, etc. Both women can benefit from time to talk, relax and observe their babies together. This also allows the midwife to concentrate on physical caregiving and relieves her from having to address the myriad emotional and physical concerns which are so common in the beginning.

Postpartum care should include home visits on days one, three and seven, with phone calls in between. The final checkup should be given at four to six weeks postpartum.

Day One Visit

When you come back the day after the birth, begin by checking the environment for order and cleanliness and then lend a hand if necessary.

Some women haven't even gotten around to showering; assist the mother with this if need be. Check to see what she's had to eat and drink and see that there is a jug of water at her bedside. Ask her how she's been feeling; any dizzy spells, extreme fatigue or emotional upsets? Much of this depends on what her labor was like and on what kind of help she is receiving from her mate or friends.

It is *extremely important* to stress her need to take it easy for the first ten days or so, following body signals for rest and nourishment the same way she did while pregnant. Explain that the hormones for involuting the uterus are at their greatest potency now and she will have herself much more quickly back together if she rests and allows her body to recover. Overactivity and stress cause the release of adrenaline, which inhibits the action of oxytocin. This message *bears repeating* as it is critical to her recuperation.

The main purpose of the day one check is to see that she's off to a good start; relaxed,

happy, comfy with her baby and well taken care of. Wash your hands thoroughly before examinations, and use gloves when in contact with secretions. Things to check include:

1. **the nipples,** for soreness or cracking. If there are cracks suggest vitamin E or a lanolin-E preparation. If soreness is just developing, a solution of 1 part salt to 8 parts water is a good astringent and toughening agent when used between nursings and rinsed off before the baby sucks. And be sure the mother is lifting the baby to the breast, i.e., that it is not hanging from the nipple;
2. **the uterus,** for normal involution. It should be just below the umbilicus, and should feel firm and not too tender. Squeeze it firmly to expel any clots, then have the woman sit up for a few minutes before checking her pad for flow;
3. **the flow,** for color, amount and odor. The flow should be red-brown and not

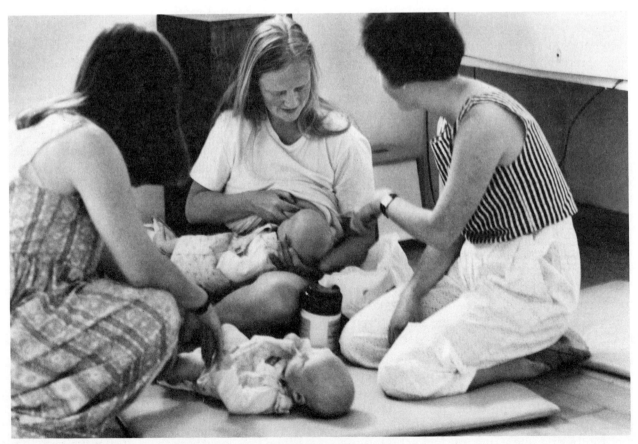

There is just no substitute for sharing concerns and insights with other new mothers.

too excessive, although some clotting is normal. Odor should be fleshy, like menstrual flow;

4. **the perineum,** while the pad is off, especially if there has been tearing and/or suturing. The swelling should be gone; if not, suggest more ice. If swelling has increased and mother complains of pain, she may have a *hematoma* (see page 144).

Also check the stitches to be sure they've held; the flesh should be pulling together, with wound edges dry and clean. Signs of infection include inflammation, pain and discharge; refer the mother to a physician if these occur. If the mother complains of tenderness but the area looks healthy, recommend Sitz baths three or four times daily. Fresh ginger simmered in water relieves burning and itching and stimulates circulation. Even plain hot water works!

Also check to see if she's had any pain with urination (remind her to use the peri-bottle or to pour warm water over herself as she urinates). And check to see if she has had a bowel movement. Often women are afraid their stitches will come out if they bear down; suggest a bit of counterpressure with a folded tissue at the same time;

5. **the woman's temperature record.** If it is elevated she may be dehydrated, or she may have a *uterine infection* (see page 144);

6. **her blood pressure reading,** if it rose during or immediately after labor;

7. **her pulse,** to assess general well-being;

8. **the baby's cord stump.** It should look clean around the base, not red or swollen. Be sure that parents are folding diapers back so that urine won't irritate, and they are swabbing the cord regularly with alcohol or peroxide. Remove the clamp if stump is completely dry;

9. **the baby's skin color,** inspecting for jaundice by depressing flesh and noting undertone. Jaundice is unusual the first day and so should be referred to a pediatrician. Depending on the degree, the baby may need to go to the hospital for a bilirubin count (see page 140);

10. **the baby's skin consistency,** for dehydration. A baby who needs supplemental water has the cracked and wrinkly look of cellophane around the wrists and ankles. Check to see if the house is too warm, or if the baby is overdressed. Sometimes dehydration develops in very hot weather. It's more apt to be a problem with wiry, thin babies or postmature babies as they have less subcutaneous fat. They may also need a bit of molasses added to the water for extra energy; a teaspoon per cup is about right. Do caution parents against using honey, as research suggests that botulism spores can live in raw honey and may be responsible for crib deaths (SIDS);

11. **the baby's elimination** pattern. It should be urinating frequently and passing meconium. If it has not passed meconium by 24 hours, consult a pediatrician;

12. **the baby's nursing pattern** and behavior. Sleepiness (especially after a long labor) is fairly normal for the first day, but lethargy is something else again. It can be recognized by drowsiness, apathy, disinterest in nursing and lack of muscle tone. This condition should be checked by a pediatrician, particularly if jaundice is noted.

Also ask parents about the baby's cry; if they report a high-pitched tone, *hypoglycemia* (see page 139) is probably the problem. Water with a little molasses (1 tsp. per cup) should be given immediately, and again after each nursing. Refer to a pediatrician;

13. **any abnormality noted in the Newborn Exam** if parents have not yet seen a pediatrician.

Usually parents are in a state of bliss and happiness at this point; if they look frazzled try to find out why. It's most common for the father to be exhausted; if such is the case suggest they send out for dinner, spend time in bed with the baby and get rest together.

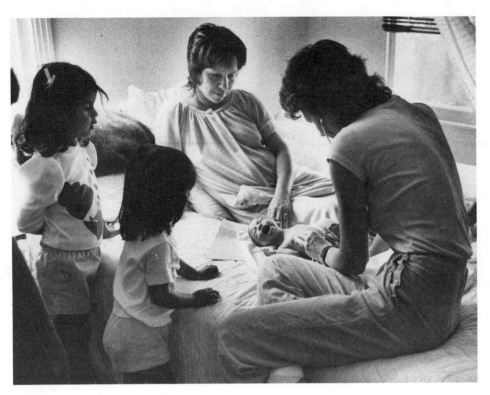

The midwife gives care to the entire family during the postpartum period.

Day Three

If anything unusual was noted on day one, call or visit on day two to follow up. For example, you may need to check the mom's stitches or the baby's hydration. Otherwise your day three checkup is sufficient.

By day three, the difficulties in integrating baby care with ordinary life have become evident and emotional outbursts are common. This coincides with the milk coming in; it is *very* common and appropriate for the mother's tears to flow at this time. And since the baby will be adjusting to breast milk, he/she will probably have some indigestion and crying spells. This will usually evoke some strong emotions from the parents, which you should be prepared to discuss. The father may be about ready to collapse in a heap, especially if he has been running around trying to do everything. This may leave the mother feeling stranded; if so, encourage her to ask for help from friends and relatives.

Things to be sure to check:

1. **the breasts** for any signs of engorgement, feeling for lumps along the sides under the arms and looking for any reddened areas. If engorgement is a problem, have the mother soak her breasts or her whole body in warm water; this will stimulate release of any backed-up milk. Show her how to massage lumps toward the nipple and how to express milk to get the flow started. Check carefully for cracks and ask her how it feels to nurse. If the nipples are cracked, it won't feel good! Recommend the healing measures mentioned in the previous section if need be;

2. **the uterus, the flow, the perineum,** etc. Recheck the perineum thoroughly using the guidelines from day one. Ask the mother if her flow has been consistent, check the odor on her pad and be sure she's having no pain which might indicate infection. Is she doing her Kegels?;

3. **her temperature.** Elevation to 101° is normal at this time because the milk is coming in. Nevertheless, rule out uterine infection by checking for symptoms (see page 144);

4. **the cord stump.** You can definitely remove the cord clamp by now;

5. **the baby, for jaundice.** A bit of a yellow tinge is normal in the face and to

the nipple line, but unusual in the extremeties. Generally when the milk comes in, the jaundice washes away. If the baby is very yellow you should refer to a pediatrician, or certainly check the next day (see section on Jaundice later in chapter);

6. **any dehydration** noted before;
7. **baby's behavior, nursing pattern, crying pattern,** etc;
8. **mom's management of nursing** (very important). Be sure she is not trying to impose a schedule or limit the amount of time the baby is nursing. Clear up any archaic notions and substitute orgasmic ones. The let-down reflex varies from mild tingling to a sexual sensation of release; try to promote a positive feeling around letting go with nursing;
9. **sleeping arrangements,** checking to see what has evolved. If the baby is in bed with the couple, how does the father feel about this? If not, how does the mother feel about getting up to nurse? Is she getting enough sleep? Is the father willing to get up and bring the baby to her?

There are often phone call ramifications of this visit, especially regarding the last three points. This is the time when beliefs about discipline start to come up, and conflicts may develop between partners. The whole notion of spoiling, amazing as it seems, often becomes an issue this soon! Many men truly worry that the baby will be spoiled by too much attention, too much contact, too much love. Some try to limit all of this, insisting that the baby be left to cry it out now and then . . . which generally leads to an increase in tension for both parents as the baby continues to cry. Whether due to cultural conditioning or simple jealousy, this masculine misconception should be discussed as openly and promptly as possible. It is crucial to point out that the baby has literally been enveloped by the mother for nine months with all its needs immediately met: it has no comprehension of waiting to be fed or held, cannot know that parents are close by in the next room, etc. Newborns need all the security they can get! There is *no such thing* as too much lov-

ing for a newborn. If the parents can surrender to love's sensitivity and vulnerability they will be stronger and wiser in the end, and the baby will grow to be a loving, secure child. Encourage parents to get to know the baby through touch, play and gentle massage.

Day Seven

By day seven many fathers are back at work, relatives have gone home and friends have found other interests. Day seven is a common time for the mother to feel depressed and forgotten, especially with her energy not yet up to par and her emotions so unpredictable. In fact, if she has been entertaining people and trying to do more around the house than she should, she may be absolutely exhausted. You may get a call (before you get over to see her) reporting an increase in bleeding, which is a definite sign that she's been over-active. This is prime time for the mother's helper to come over for cleanup and conversation, or the parents may want to hire someone to assist them.

Physical symptoms to monitor are now beginning to taper off. If there were any stitches they should be re-examined; skin should be drawn together by now. This visit is mainly for emotional support, so do your best to help the mother with any complaints or problems because you probably won't see her again for several weeks.

Three to Six Weeks Checkup

The timing for this final exam depends on the mother's rate of recuperation. If her flow stopped at least a week prior to contacting you, you can assume her uterus is well involuted, her cervix firmed up and that she is ready for the final checkup.

One important reason for this checkup is to give the mother the go-ahead on sex, along with suggestions to make the first time as comfortable as possible. Although women who have not torn with delivery may make love before this visit, it is often with some discomfort and the feeling that it's happening a little too soon. Advise the mother at her day seven visit to wait until her flow has *stopped completely.* Whenever intercourse is resumed plenty of lubrication should be used, as breastfeeding affects a woman's natural lubrication no matter how intense her desire. And some form of birth control is essential, as there is always a chance that conception might occur. This is very rare indeed but I've known a few nursing mothers who conceived as early as six weeks postpartum.

If the mother had stitches, the timing of this checkup is also determined by her report on the condition of her perineum. If the area is still highly sensitive to pressure, the woman is probably not ready for sex or contraceptive fittings. Nevertheless, every woman should be seen by six weeks because this should be adequate time for healing, and if not you must determine the reason. Sometimes deep second degree tears simply take longer to heal; as long as the flow has stopped already and the mother is feeling fine, you needn't worry. But the woman who reports continued bleeding, perineal pressure and general fatigue is cause for concern; these are symptoms of poor health and faulty nutrition which must be corrected if she is to recover. A woman in this condition at five weeks should be seen immediately, whereas a woman feeling great except for residual stitches pain can afford to wait six weeks or more before coming to be checked.

Sometimes you'll get a report of emotional conditions which will cause you to schedule the visit sooner than later. For example, a woman feeling blue and depressed at four weeks probably should be seen, even if you feel she needs several more weeks to recuperate physically.

Things to check out at the final exam include:

1. **the uterus.** It should be out of range of palpation, except by bimanual exam. If it is still high she is probably still bleeding and her cervix will be very soft; both are signs of poor recovery. Prescribe rest, long relaxed nursing sessions (so the oxytocin can do its work), better nutrition (plenty of iron and B-vitamins), and involuting tea of blue cohosh and shepherd's purse;

2. **the cervix.** It should feel firm and normally situated (like it was in the first pelvic exam). However, many women do not regain their pre-pregnant cervical tone until they stop breastfeeding;

3. **internal muscle tone.** It should be almost back to normal by now if the woman has been kegeling. If not, explain the importance of using the pelvic floor muscles for maintaining internal organs in their proper positions and for revitalizing sexual sensitivity. Check for tone high in the vaginal vault and just inside the opening; frequently a woman has one but not the other. Suggest appropriate exercise techniques. When discussing sex, be sure to explain how the hormones associated with breastfeeding may decrease desire, but urge her to be sensitive to her partner's needs;

4. **laceration or episiotomy, for complete healing.** If the woman had labial skin splits, they may still be somewhat tender because the newly formed skin layer takes time to toughen up. This may cause some discomfort with sex, but lubrication and positioning can help.

   If the perineum feels rigid with scar tissue, encourage the woman to do a bit of perineal massage (with oil) to soften the area and prepare for intercourse. This practice can be emotionally and physically reassuring for any woman nervous about having sex again;

5. **the abdominal muscle tone.** Have the woman lie down, then lift her head and shoulders forward as you place fingertips along the juncture of the abdominal muscles running from umbilicus to pubic bone. If you feel some gaping, suggest abdominal exercises, starting with single leg lifts and progressing slowly to full sit-ups (with knees bent). Most women have about a half inch separation, some very little. Refer women to postpartum exercise groups or yoga classes, if such are available, or suggest that groups of interested mothers get together informally for exercise interspersed with baby massage and conversation;

6. **the breasts, for tenderness or lumps.** It is said that the hormones of pregnancy tend to accelerate abnormal cell growth

if any is pre-existing. Even if a woman has seen a physician since the birth she may not have had a thorough exam, so do it yourself;

7. **the cervix, by Pap smear.** Even if the woman had a Pap done early in pregnancy, you should repeat it now (see reason given above);

8. **the hematocrit** if you have the equipment. This is especially important if the mother hemorrhaged or looks dragged-out and tired. In this case check her diet also;

9. **the diet.** It's very easy for a woman to neglect her own needs once pregnancy is over and she becomes completely focused on the baby. "No time for cooking, hardly time to eat," you'll hear, and frequently the father takes over food preparation though perhaps not as carefully as the mother has done before. Listen carefully to complaints of fatigue, nervous irritability, colds or infections and prescribe respectively more protein, more B vitamins, more vitamin C. If the hematocrit is under 40, prescribe 100–200 mgs. iron along with appropriate food sources;

10. **adjustment to parenting.** Broad category, but a few leading questions will help you get down to specifics. "How well are you sleeping these days?" or, "How are you and your mate getting along now?" or, "How's your frustration level with mothering?" If you don't get a confession on the last one, be certain there is not a repression pattern setting in; "mother martyr" role is hard on everyone, and ultimately an evasion of responsibility. It's nice to have the father present to discuss important issues unless you really feel that the mother must have privacy to express herself.

After the six weeks visit parents are basically on their own, hopefully with support from others doing the same thing. The above outline for care is cursory; following are some concerns that need to be considered in detail.

The Baby: Complications and Concerns

Hypoglycemia

Hypoglycemia refers to abnormally low blood sugar levels. 50–60 mg. glucose per 1 ml. blood is normal for a newborn; anything below 30 is a serious concern. Infants at risk include those large for gestational age, small for gestational age, premature and postmature, those who were hypoxic during labor or depressed at birth, and those born to diabetic mothers. Symptoms include apathy, irregular respirations, cold (hypothermia) and refusal to nurse.

If a baby at risk develops any of these signs, have the parents *immediately* give water with a little molasses (1 tsp. per cup) and repeat every few hours, preferably after a nursing. You should also have a dextrostix performed. This is done by heel stick; a drop of baby's blood is collected and tested on a special strip.

Central nervous system damage can occur when blood glucose is inadequate, so make certain to act on any signals immediately. Some babies need more aggressive treatment, such as IV therapy and hospital surveillance. If you do the dextrostix yourself, consult with a pediatrician if value is below 45.

Meconium Aspiration

Any infant with moderate to heavy meconium at delivery is at risk. If you are unsure that you suctioned adequately before the baby began to breathe, listen to the lungs in all quadrants for any sign of obstruction. If there is tachypnea (see next section) or the baby struggles for breath or shows signs of *respiratory distress syndrome* (grunting, nostrils flaring, see-saw of chest and abdomen) give oxygen blow-by (holding oxygen tube at baby's nose) and immediately contact a pediatrician. You can help the baby in the interim by providing steam; some midwives take the baby into the bathroom and turn the shower on full force to rapidly accomplish this. At the same time, place the baby across your lap and apply *percussion* to the back, tapping sharply with fingertips in each quadrant. If you position the baby with head downward, drainage will be more readily accomplished.

If the baby's respiratory difficulty seems resolved by this treatment, keep the baby under close surveillance for several hours and have parents see a pediatrician as soon as possible.

Transient Tachypnea

This is a temporary condition involving rapid respirations. The normal rate for a newborn is 40–60 per minute; with tachypnea the count may rise as high as 120.

This is a disturbing complication because tachypnea is a symptom of several very serious conditions: respiratory distress syndrome, meconium aspiration, and sepsis. If the baby is not at risk for any of these, the problem is probably temporary and will resolve spontaneously with time. But if there are any predisposing factors, or tachypnea is acccompanied by any sign of respiratory distress, you are obligated to take the baby promptly to the pediatrician.

The cause of transient tachypnea is delayed absorption of fetal lung fluid. Generally X-rays are performed on infants at risk and they are carefully monitored until the problem is resolved.

Neonatal Infection

If the mother had PROM and showed signs of infection such as fever, uterine tenderness or foul smelling fluid, the infant should be screened. Fluid drawn from the baby's stomach (gastric aspirate) should be tested and if there are signs of sepsis, blood cultures should be ordered. The problem is that the cultures take 72 hours to return, so antibiotics are often given prophylactically. This may seem very conservative, but consider that the first symptom of a strep B infection is apnea (cessation of breathing). This is why hospitalization is a good idea.

The baby with sepsis may show a variety of symptoms: lethargy, irritability, jitteriness and shakes. Tachypnea is a sign, as is cyanosis (blue coloration). If the baby displays any symptoms of infection, cultures of the spinal fluid may be recommended to rule out meningitis.

It is important to support parents in being with their baby as much as possible while all of this takes place. This will insure an adequate supply of breastmilk and continued bonding. It is very difficult for parents to face the fact that the baby may be ill, or to watch painful tests being administered repeatedly. They will need your ongoing support!

Jaundice

Neonatal jaundice is not the consuming issue it was a few years ago. It has become clear that normal physiologic jaundice is self-limiting and will not cause the dangerous rise of bilirubin associated with pathological types.

What is the cause of physiological jaundice? The baby has its oxygen needs met in utero by an abundant number of red blood cells, an amount which becomes excessive once the baby is born and taking oxygen directly. So the red cells break down until the level is appropriate for a breathing organism. A by-product of the breakdown is excess bilirubin, which deposits in the skin and is evident as yellow coloration. Thus a certain level of jaundice is quite normal, especially around the second or third day before the milk has come in to flush the baby's system clean.

Several other types of jaundice which are less common but seldom require special treatment include ABO incompatibility and breast

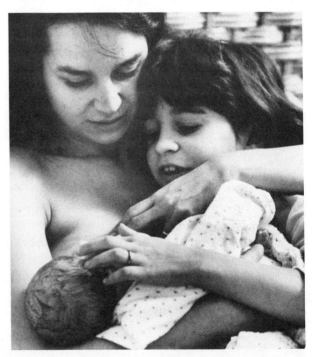

Nurse the baby frequently to help flush bilirubin from the system.

milk jaundice. ABO incompatibility is a phenomenon similar to RH sensitization: A or B type babies react to transfer of blood from an O type mother. Breast milk jaundice is caused by a hormone in the mother's milk which interferes with the baby's ability to break down bilirubin. The usual treatment for either of these is to have the mother continue nursing, while exposing the baby to sunlight (more on this in a moment).

Other pathological causes include obstructed bile duct, liver disease, infection or RH hemolytic disease. These generally manifest within the first 24 hours, a signal that something is seriously wrong (although ABO may also appear early). If the baby becomes extremely jaundiced, kernicterus may develop and cause brain damage unless the jaundice is quickly reversed.

How do you determine the degree of jaundice and appropriate treatment? Any jaundice noted on day one should be referred to the pediatrician. On day two or three, go by the location of bilirubin on the baby's body; if the baby is yellow on the face but not past the nipple line, encourage the mother to nurse frequently and expose the baby to sunshine (body naked, eyes protected, by a window) for 30 minutes twice daily. If the baby has jaundice on the extremities and the milk is not in, the mother should give fluids *after* nursing: a mix of molasses and water (1 tsp. per cup) given by bottle or eyedropper. As soon as the milk is flowing and the baby nursing regularly, the water should be discontinued.

The problem with using the sunlight method exclusively is that although the light will disperse bilirubin accumulated in the skin, levels may still remain high in the bloodstream. The baby with jaundice in the extremities should have periodic bili checks and frequent temperature readings to be sure no infection is developing. Jaundiced babies are more vulnerable to infection.

If the baby is lethargic or if the jaundice does not rapidly diminish once the milk is in, refer immediately to a pediatrician. Treatment under bili-lights is standard, but in many communities these can now be rented and brought to the home. There is some danger of side effects such as dehydration, burning, and possible genetic damage, so the lights should not be used unnecessarily or excessively, or without physician supervision.

It's been my observation that babies kept in darkened rooms for the first few days tend to have higher bilirubin levels than those liberally exposed to sunlight. Lack of light is probably a more significant factor in extreme physiological jaundice than the favorite theoretical cause, late cord clamping. I always clamp the cord after it ceases pulsing and after placing the baby on the mother's chest (above placental level). In eight years of practice I've seen only two homeborn babies become severely jaundiced, and in each of these cases lack of light seemed to be a determining factor.

Babies born to mothers who have had pitocin induction or augmentation must be watched carefully. Pitocin creates unnaturally strong contractions; those immediately following the birth (before the cord is cut) can cause an extra shunt of blood to the baby. Extra blood equals extra red cells to break down, which of course predisposes to jaundice. Pitocin also competes with bilirubin for binding sites, which compounds the problem of elimination.

Circumcision

Circumcision is a controversial procedure and no longer routine. In fact, the American Academy of Pediatrics issued a statement several years ago that circumcision cannot be considered medically necessary. There has recently been much research attempting to trace the origins of this practice and explain its popularity over the years. Circumcision goes back to the days of ancient Egypt; it is pictured in murals. For the Jews it is an important ritual, a "Covenant with God." It's noteworthy that circumcision has been most prevalent in hot, dry climates where water for bathing and cleansing has been limited. In order to make an informed decision parents must consider the pros and cons and potential side effects.

Circumcision is a surgical procedure. The skin adherent to the tip of the penis must be severed and cut back to completely expose the glans. Clamps are placed to control bleeding, and the procedure is completed. Sometimes a plastibell is used to clamp skin so that the blood supply to the foreskin is cut off and tissue necrosis occurs. This is done completely without anesthetic, so the baby must be strapped spread-eagled to restrain its movement in response to the pain. Possible side effects include infection (there have been several deaths documented) and penile sloughing, with subsequent need for reconstruction.

Knowledge of the procedure is enough to persuade many parents that circumcision is emotionally traumatic and potentially dangerous. But what about the alternative; the uncircumcised penis? What are the basics of care? What about the supposed dangers of infection?

The foreskin covers and adheres to the glans for the first year or two of life, at which point the little boy will begin to pull it back himself as he becomes aware of his genitals. Parents should not pull back the foreskin at first as this can cause bleeding and infection. But once the foreskin is moveable, cleaning beneath it is as simple as cleaning under the fingernails or cleaning secretions from the folds of the female labia.

There are various debates over the effects of circumcision on sexuality. The foreskin functions during sexual arousal to capture the first drops of moisture secreted, so that as the penis becomes erect and the foreskin pulls back, the head is automatically lubricated. The foreskin also preserves the sensitivity of the glans, which is somewhat lost on the circumcised penis due to constant friction with clothing.

Many circumcised fathers worry about their sons being different from the other boys or from themselves. But circumcision is diminishing; in my entire practice I've had only four sets of parents opt for the procedure. Actually the decision can be left up to the child; he can decide later in life if he wants to be circumcised. My own feeling is this: if nature had intended man to be without foreskin, baby boys would be born that way.

Nervous Irritability—Colic

Dealing with a nervous or colicky baby requires the same patience, concentration and endurance required in birthing. This can be particularly challenging after a long or difficult labor. Advise parents to recall tools they used for laboring like relaxation, deep breathing and touch release. Objectivity must be maintained at all costs; otherwise parents project guilt onto every anxious cry the baby utters and this makes things worse. It's a matter of learning to recognize the difference between new-in-the-body adjustment and an irritated response to overstimulation or some awkwardness in nursing, timing the bath, etc.

Suggest that parents begin by noting times of day that the crying spells seem to recur. Then have them check out their own maximum times of tension to see if there is any correlation. Often crying and fretting occurs around dinnertime; the father comes home

---

What To Do If The Baby Cries

1. Try nursing in peace and quiet, without jiggling the baby around.
2. Have the baby's bed in a quiet space that's still close to the center of activity.
3. If the baby wakes when set down, try nursing lying down, and then getting up quietly and moving away when the baby is asleep.
4. Let the baby spend lots of time in the baby carrier close to you in the front.
5. Establish a break ritual with the father taking over completely at a certain time of day (right after a nursing) for an hour or so.
6. Use that time to rest (take a shower, call a friend, etc.) and rejuvinate yourself.
7. If the baby seems to have gas (pulls legs up sharply, stomach rumbles), try giving warm anise tea by bottle or eyedropper.
8. If all else fails and the baby is crying hysterically, try running the shower or turning on the vacuum cleaner. High frequency sounds are calming if the baby is very upset.

from work emitting tension, the mother tries to make dinner despite the baby's fussing and may also try to talk with her partner and share the day's events. The baby feels the excitement, the stress, the confusion. If this is it, perhaps evening transitions can be made more gradually, with conversation between parents saved for later. The dinner hassle can be alleviated by relying on soups, stews, casseroles, etc. made while the baby naps and reheated later.

Sometimes parents try all of this and nothing seems to work, in which case they need to realize that it's the baby's style, they've done all they can and they have to let go. Chronic anxiety definitely retards a mother's recuperation and ability to pay attention. *Babies differ;* the feisty-wild ones simply are what they are, and there's not much to be done about it. With some it's a question of physical adjustments, with others a question of emotional make-up. My own experience has borne out that a baby's basic nature is evident at birth and tends to persist throughout life. If you feel sure that parents are doing their best job without any neurotic undertone, advise them to relax and learn to accept the reality of this, their child.

Minor Problems

1. **Diaper Rash:** A good natural oil should be applied with each diaper change, following a careful cleansing of the baby's bottom. Also effective are aloe vera gel (for wet, open sores) or calendula cream (for chafing or inflammation). Sometimes diaper rash is the result of improper laundering of the diapers; ammonia residue can build up and cause repeated episodes of rash unless the ammonia is removed by bleaching. Diapers can be bleached in a soak bucket, then washed with soap flakes and double rinsed. This last step removes any bleach residue, which also can be irritating.
2. **Cradle Cap:** Apply a natural oil to the scalp before bed and leave it on all night. The scales can then be removed with a soft toothbrush and natural shampoo.
3. **Heat Rash:** The obvious solution is to cool off the living space and have the baby cozily but loosely dressed. Teach mothers to check the baby's temperature by feeling its hands and feet, which should be slightly cool to the touch.
4. **Thrush:** this mild infection can be identified by the white coating visible on the baby's tongue. Since thrush is caused by the same organism that causes vaginal yeast, screen the mother and treat her if necessary. The baby can be treated with topical applications of acidophilus solution, three times a day by cotton swab. Sometimes it takes several weeks to go away; be patient. If it is severe enough to interfere with nursing, the baby should see a physician.

In general, try to avoid synthetic, artificial substances for bathing and toileting baby. Baby powder is blended with talc, a substance known to be dangerous to the lungs, and most baby oils are made with a base of mineral oil which leaches vitamins from the skin. Baby shampoos claim to be mild and gentle, but they are in fact complex chemical preparations rather than simple soaps. Many synthetic products also contain carcinogenic dyes which are absorbed through the skin. Suggest simple natural substances like cornstarch, olive or vitamin E oils and liquid castile soap, which can also be used as shampoo.

The Mother: Complications and Concerns

Minor Problems

1. **Constipation:** This is a common complaint immediately after delivery, particularly if the labor has been long and difficult. A daily serving of high-fiber bran cereal is probably the most effective and most pleasant remedy. Prune juice can be taken in moderation too, for its softening effect. Adequate fluid intake is critical: a nursing mother needs three quarts daily in order to meet her own needs and produce sufficient breast milk.

2. **Hemorrhoids:** Most common immediately after delivery, these respond well to ice packs and the application of witch hazel. Also healing if rupture occurs is aloe vera gel. Follow the above recommendations for constipation as a preventative measure.

3. **Afterpains:** These commonly occur with a second or third baby, generally while nursing or immediately after. Some women report that they hurt more than actual labor! This may be an exaggeration, but does indicate that afterpains can be very uncomfortable. The main cause is loss of uterine tone with successive childbearing; if the uterus is over-relaxed the normal involution contractions will hurt.

One solution is to try to stimulate overall contraction of the uterus, so that involution contractions are not felt as intensely. Herbs such as blue or black cohosh may be useful, and black haw has been found to be particularly effective. Tincture is most rapidly absorbed, and handy to use because it requires no preparation.

It is crucial that the woman keep her bladder empty, as otherwise it will prevent the uterus from fully contracting. It also helps if she lies down on her stomach with a pillow beneath her, to force the uterus firmly against the internal organs. Some women require pain medication; consult a physician if pain is severe and especially if she is avoiding nursing.

Hematoma

Hematoma is an asymmetrical and painful swelling of the perineal area. It is usually caused by soft tissue trauma in second stage, or by a faulty repair job wherein hemostasis has not been achieved, i.e., bleeding vessels continue to seep below the skin or mucosa surfaces.

Although the hemorrhage will almost always cease spontaneously, the swelling takes time to reabsorb. The primary danger with hematoma is infection, with resulting breakdown of the repair. The blood pooling around the wound serves as an excellent culture medium for bacteria; once sepsis develops surfaces will not adhere and the repair will not close. Traction on the sutures because of swelling is another factor in breakdown.

Immediately refer any woman with signs of hematoma to a physician; she should begin antibiotics as soon as possible. Measures to reduce swelling include alternating hot and cold soaks, which stimulate circulation and encourage reabsorption of the hemorrhage. Have the mother use a peri-bottle (with warm water and Betadine) *each time* she uses the toilet, and remind her to dry and air the perineum thoroughly afterwards. If the repair does break down, plastic surgery will be necessary. Do your best to prevent this!

Uterine and Pelvic Infections

Symptoms of uterine infection include fever (over 101°), pelvic pain, elevated pulse and subinvolution of the uterus. A woman is at risk if there have been intrauterine manipulations during the course of her birthing, such as manual removal of the placenta or exploration of the uterus for sequestered clots. PROM is another factor, as is delayed delivery of the placenta in which the protruding umbilical cord acts as a wick for vaginal bacteria. Improper perineal care is also implicated, and hemorrhage is definitely a factor because general debility makes the mother more vulnerable.

In my experience, a prime cause of uterine infection is over-activity and exhaustion in the first few days postpartum. I've had only two cases in my practice; both women had other children to care for and immediately resumed normal activity after the birth. And both had notably uncomplicated deliveries, with none of the precipitating factors cited above. One woman actually went out to a *swap meet* the day after delivery, walking around in the heat and dust with nothing to drink for many hours! Take care to warn mothers who have had easy deliveries that the reason for bedrest postpartum is not just to recover from the birth but from the *entire pregnancy,* and to allow the hormones which establish breastfeeding and involute the uterus to perform their necessary function.

Other potential infection sites in the pelvis include the pelvic ligaments, the connective tissue and the peritoneal cavity. These extensions of untreated uterine infection cause much more severe symptoms such as vomiting, chills and extreme pain. Very rarely the tubes and ovaries are infected, usually from a preexisting gonorrhea infection which has flared up again.

Thrombophlebitis and Pulmonary Embolism

Thrombophlebitis is the inflammation of a leg vein (either superficial or deep) which may cause the formation of blood clots. Women with varicosities are at greater risk. Symptoms of *superficial thrombophlebitis* include leg pain with heat, tenderness and redness at the site of the inflammation. *Deep thrombophlebitis* has symptoms of high fever plus severe pain, edema and tenderness along the entire length of the affected vein. Either of these conditions should be referred to a physician immediately, but in the interim the woman should be kept in bed with the leg elevated. *Never massage the leg*, because you may loosen blood clots and cause them to enter the circulation. If they lodge in the lungs, you have a life-threatening condition known as **pulmonary embolism.** This is characterized by chest pain, shortness of breath, rapid breathing and elevated pulse rate. Call the paramedics and administer oxygen.

Difficulties With Breastfeeding

A mother's problems with breastfeeding often spring from distraction, or the feeling that she should be somewhere else doing something different. This may either be free-floating anxiety or a definite desire to be back at work, out of the house, or out of the relationship with her partner.

It is nature's design that women learn by giving birth to let go and surrender to body rhythms and messages, in order to establish successful breastfeeding. But disapproval from relatives can conflict with instinct, as can extraneous information or over-activity. Breastfeeding is essentially an ongoing sexual experience which bonds, reveals and releases tension in a way that's wonderful, but it's also a demanding physical activity which can be draining and exhausting unless excellent health is maintained. If a woman is having problems with breastfeeding, try to get at the roots of disharmony and work from there.

Orgasmic breastfeeding is more than just an intriguing concept, it's actually a way of being in complete relationship. Orgasmic connotes the ability to respond and peak in high energy situations, and thus it is in nursing and caring for a baby. Daily patterns vary tremendously. Sometimes a nursing lasts only a few minutes, as friends enter the room and cause distraction. But then may come a full forty minutes of nursing, followed by a nap. Sometimes there is lots of eye contact, touching and playing. Sometimes it's public, sometimes private. Women definitely do experience physical orgasms while breastfeeding!

Breastfeeding has the same therapeutic value as sexual intercourse in that it offers a way to get down to basics, to be close and comforting

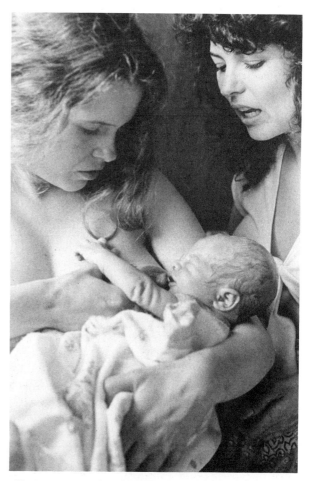

Alleviate sore nipples by lifting the baby to your breast, rather than letting him hang from the nipple.

to one another in times of change or upset. It is a gift of tenderness and vitality, with the mother's urge to nurse the perfect complement to her baby's desire. It provides opportunity for continuing bonding and imprinting.

Physical problems that sometimes arise include engorgement and mastitis. **Engorgement** generally results from changes in nursing rhythms; it is natural and normal for engorgement to occur when the milk first comes in or the baby gives up a feeding. The problem generally resolves itself as the milk supply adjusts to the baby's demand. To relieve engorgement, apply heat and express milk by hand to get it flowing, then have the baby nurse.

If milk is left pooled in the sacs, particularly if a residual amount is left time after time, it becomes a breeding ground for bacteria entering through the nipple. This is how **mastitis** occurs. Personal cleanliness is important in preventing mastitis, as is relaxed, unhurried, thorough nursing and adequate fluid intake for keeping the system flushed and clean. Mastitis can be diagnosed by fever (a sudden elevation to 103° or 104°) but is likely to develop wherever engorgement is allowed to persist, especially if lumpy areas begin to redden with inflammation. Sometimes borderline cases can be turned back with heat treatments and plenty of rest, but once fever has spiked, antibiotics are necessary. Erythromycin is best because it does not destroy intestinal flora and will not hurt the baby, although it can cause the mother gastrointestinal upset. But timely treatment is critical to prevent a breast abscess from developing, which can cause even greater pain and additional difficulties with breastfeeding.

Some women ask questions about weaning just days after having established breastfeeding, which may indicate some ambivalence about nursing or may simply signify curiosity concerning the scope of the experience. The best counsel for these mothers is to let the baby be their guide; the need for solid food will be indicated by interest (psychological readiness) and by teething (physiological readiness). Many pediatricians now believe that solid foods are not really necessary for the first nine months, as it takes that long for the baby's digestive system to mature. A relaxed approach saves parents a lot of trouble and allows the baby to develop naturally.

Postpartum Depression

Postpartum depression is most likely to occur in women who are not up to par physically, particularly those who have had difficult or debilitating births. For example, a mother who hemorrhaged at delivery might experience depression due to fatigue and exhaustion resulting from an anemic condition. Especially if this mother had no emotional problems during pregnancy, look to her nutrition, and need for the proper supplements.

If you've investigated physical causes and find nothing, rest assured that minor depressions are very common, and are apt to ebb and flow through the psyche of any sensitive, intelligent woman faced with a multiplicity of adjustments. Typical anxieties include loss of job-related identity, emotional dependence on family and friends, and changes in primary relationships.

Here's one mother's description of her postpartum experience:

> Postpartum blues? No, not me! The joy of long awaited motherhood and the emotional stability I had achieved over the years disqualified me, I thought, as a candidate for the postpartum syndrome. But I was not immune! My "blues," however, did not fit the picture of what I had expected. In fact, I came to feel that nothing I'd read or heard had adequately prepared me, since I was not depressed according to my usual definition.
>
> For me, the experience was one of drowning in a vacuum of mind—consumed with worry, anxiety and uncertainty. The responsibility seemed overwhelming. Doubts and questions plagued me . . . was my son becoming jaundiced? . . . was his cord healing properly? . . . why was his skin peeling? . . . how would I bathe and groom him? I longed for the recommended rest and would be famished yet could not seem to coordinate the time for my own needs between his care and the feedings every few hours. Trian was a good quiet baby, but I didn't have a handle on my end at all. I felt like I was failing miserably at my goal of being a perfect mother.
>
> Trian was several days old when I suddenly realized while nursing him

HEART & HANDS

One of the keys to a healthy postpartum adjustment is short outings, to break the monotony of routine.

shallow breathing—I would relax, do the deep breathing I had been taught for the birthing, and concentrate on how much I loved my baby. This allowed me to center myself and deal rationally with my fears, so that I could carry on.

Remedies for postpartum blues include outings, getting together with friends, and time away. Most babies will sleep contentedly during long car rides, out of mother's arms and in a car bed or car seat. What the exhausted mother really needs is to get the baby away from her body and being for a while. She should use her time alone to recuperate, fully relaxing into her own thoughts and feelings and letting her body *rest*.

Another more serious form of postpartum depression is the type based on problems or conflicts which remained unresolved at the time of birth, only to re-intensify with the stress of parenting. These may be problems with mate, with self esteem, etc. Here's where the extended counseling aspect of midwifery appears to be endless! Reiterating various alternatives and providing support for emotional catharsis is fine a couple times more, but if problems persist you'll have to refer the mother to general counseling.

One particular type of relationship tends to manifest postpartum woe. This is the unit wherein the father is little involved prenatally, but absolutely compulsive about proving himself in the birthing. This often leads to a marginal experience for both parents, with disrupted bonding and difficulty accepting the fact that the baby has really arrived. The woman in this setup is usually passive-dependent and the man authoritarian. He responds to fatherhood by making new rules concerning housework, expenditures, baby-rearing, discipline, breastfeeding, sexuality, etc. Sometimes this man is also a philosophical or spiritual fanatic, constantly evaluating the woman's behavior by abstract standards. No wonder she gets depressed! I've had a few heated discussions with these fathers and have found that it does little good; if the mother has chosen the situation and continues to stay, then what's an outsider to do? Of course she will keep asking for assistance or feigning helplessness, which is a part of her passive-

that I had not leisurely touched and explored his whole body. At this moment, I knew I had been in a vacuum for days, functioning but not fully aware.

To my amazement, I just couldn't "organize" my newborn. Fifteen years of pride at being a successful organizer in my career now proved totally useless. I had to learn to simply flow with Trian, emotionally and psychically, and let go of intellectual anticipation, expectations and planning.

My love for Trian was the grounding cord that held me together as I floundered with anxiety at the enormous task before me. When I learned to recognize my signs of postpartum syndrome—irrational fears overtaking me, heart racing, nausea, excessive perspiration and dependency play. You *must* extract yourself from this situation before you are emotionally (or even physically) abused.

Single mothers are prone to a special brand of depression that springs from sexual and emotional isolation. See to it that they have company and physical assistance.

Sometimes suspended sexuality is a source of depression, especially if a woman is made to feel that it's her job to get sex together again and that her mate is impatiently waiting (see next section for suggestions.)

The type of postpartum depression most difficult to clear is that resulting from a disappointing birth experience, particularly one in which pain medication affecting awareness was used, or one in which bonding was disrupted. A woman may carry the scars of this experience for life, and painful memories can be absolutely overwhelming during the first few weeks when sensitivities are heightened and fatigue causes distortion. Understand that she is grieving, and try to support her throughout the phases of this natural process of adjustment. You may also need to refer her for additional counseling.

Cesarean birth is in a class by itself. Women who have had Cesareans often feel they have failed their mates, their babies and themselves, particularly if they've had general anesthesia and missed the actual delivery. The mother who plans a home delivery is usually so well-schooled in the importance of immediate bonding that she may overreact to the outcome of her birth by feeling that her relationship with the baby is hopelessly and irretrievably lost. There are also certain psycho-physical side effects from Cesarean birth; the vaginal part of normal delivery is definitely a climax that has been missed. No matter how thrilled to have her baby this mother may be, she will still have subconscious yearnings and may dream vividly of vaginal delivery, especially in the first few weeks postpartum.

What can you say to a woman going through all this? Probably the unkindest thing to say is to forget it, or that she should be thankful for what she's got. Birth is not just the act of bringing forth a baby, it's a major event in the *woman's* life, one which she will review and try

to comprehend for a long time to come. Acknowledge her grief, and support her by sharing her feelings. There are also Cesarean support groups available in most areas (see Appendix A). Refer her to one of these for ongoing assistance.

For the mother who's had her homebirth plans disrupted by transport, you will need to go over the birth in detail. Allow her to air any misgivings or regrets. If she was fairly even-tempered before the birth, she probably just needs to talk things over. But the more fanatical type, sure her birth would be perfect and that she would never have to go to the hospital, may be embittered and irresponsible about caring for herself and the baby once back home. In fact, she may suffer postpartum depression bordering on psychosis, with overtones of violence. If you are concerned that this may be developing, refer her to counseling or secure the advice and support of a family agency. These basically immature women desperately need contact with other mothers whose style and confidence they can emulate. Do what you can along these lines.

Sexual Changes

Not enough has been written about postpartum sexuality, aside from the physiological aspects. Maintaining sexual communication after the birth is critical to a healthy relationship. But the couple formerly used to undisrupted intimacy, spontaneity and their own personal ritual of foreplay will probably find that a newborn upsets it all. And that's natural, because the relationship has definitely changed and must be expanded and adapted to include another person.

Time is the key to making this adjustment. If a man and woman are mature enough to recognize the extension of their love in its awkward beginnings (the baby!), their sexual relationship takes on new meaning and will eventually adapt and deepen. But in the meantime, fatigue, tension and occasional feelings of isolation make getting together difficult.

It's very easy for man and woman to become polarized at this point. No doubt the father is being heavily impressed with his responsibility and the mother distracted by her turbulent emotions, running contrary to the ideal of even-tempered madonna. If the man is out in the "real world" trying to take command and the woman is pulling at his feminine side with her need for companionship and reassurance, he's going to feel the stress of being torn in two different directions and she in turn will feel guilty and insecure. New baby care is physically exhausting and both parents are apt to reach the breaking point at unpredictable moments. Sex is a logical way to reunite diverging energies, but fatigue and distraction definitely interfere.

There seems to be a critical point at about six weeks postpartum when expectations and disappointments run high; this is the time when the woman is supposed to be physically recovered and ready for sex again. But readiness is definitely conditioned by the breastfeeding relationship and hormones involved, which tend to repress sexual desire in many women. At six weeks a mother is still totally absorbed with her baby; they are almost inseparable. They are also psychically attuned in such a way that mother will wake seconds before her baby begins fussing, or baby will wake crying when the mother has had a bad dream. What with these powerful rhythms and responses, it's no wonder sex gets disrupted or pushed aside.

The most obvious solution is for the couple to get away together and have a grandmother, another nursing mom or sitter take the baby for the afternoon or evening. Expressed breast milk can be frozen in a glass bottle and then reheated in a pan of warm water, and should be accepted by the baby as long as it has been introduced beforehand. Once in privacy, the parents can take time to relax and talk intimately before diving into sex with overloaded expectations.

It's important for the man to understand how the sexual response of his mate is affected by her overwhelming feelings of dependency. As one new mother expressed it, "I realized when I was pregnant that I really need to depend on this guy, now here I am with a little baby, and I feel so helpless . . . what if he (mate) turns out to be a creep?" A rather graphic statement, but expressive of a typical insecurity felt by most postpartum women when confronted/bombarded by cultural pre-

miums on youth, vitality and sexual expression. No wonder new mothers often feel somewhat dowdy, uninteresting or even invisible in their new role, which naturally affects self confidence and communication. The situation is definitely made worse when the man involved does little to reassure and validate his partner.

Communication with other mothers is part of the answer, as is reading material for both parents on the nature of the postpartum period. There are excellent books available on the art of fathering which acknowledge the emotions commonly experienced. Reading can serve to stimulate conversation, which can provide ground for intimacy and help both parents feel positive about the rate and intensity of change. *Then* sex can take on a magical, transformative power and become relevant in a new way.

Contraception

When sex begins again, the birth control issue must be confronted once more. It is odd to go back to birth control after being without it so long, and depending on the method used can be seen as just one more obstacle to getting together.

The pill is not particularly suitable for breastfeeding mothers and the IUD is no longer available. The fertility awareness method is difficult to follow postpartum, as changes in cervical mucus and fluctuations in basal body temperature are erratic with lactation. This leaves the barrier methods: condom, diaphragm or cervical cap.

One of the sexual conflicts facing a couple after a positive birthing, particularly if conception was conscious and fully experienced, is the desire for that level of intensity again versus the desire not to have any more children (at least for a while). Almost always this conflict is unspoken, and may not be felt for some time. But after a year or so has passed and the family has stabilized, the desire for conception itself can rise up and wreak havoc with all the logical plans and beliefs a couple may be harboring. The woman who has had an unsatisfactory birth experience may also feel overwhelming urges to get pregnant again to bring broken

Don't forget to share the tenderness you feel for the baby with your partner.

threads to completion. Reckoning with these feelings depends on acknowledgement and communication; it's essential. *Contraception only works with the mental and emotional agreement of both partners.* Otherwise conception may be physically prevented but at the cost of intimacy, unless such feelings are expressly cleared.

A couple with good emotional interplay and sexual sophistication can usually handle this complex but rich intensity of feelings. There is a subtle rhythm in sexual communication whereby leisure and urgency each have their place. Not an easy concept to give to parents who don't already have it, but a lesson implicit in giving birth, which can be pointed to as an example.

CHAPTER 7
Becoming a Midwife

If you are considering practicing midwifery yourself someday, this chapter is for you. However, it is one thing to decide to become a midwife and quite another to face the realities of acquiring the necessary training and knowledge. As mentioned in Chapter 1, the passageway into practice is often circuitous and requires considerable motivation and endurance. Besides which, the service and self-sacrifice so basic to midwifery cannot be overestimated. Many aspiring young women see midwifery as a noble or even glamorous occupation; their desire may be more for personal glory than for honest work. But in order to endure one should feel called to this profession as it is so personally demanding and such a tremendous responsibility.

If you decide to go the nursing route, your course of study will be fairly well mapped out for you. See Appendix M for listing of nurse-midwifery programs. There are also direct-entry schools (meaning it is not necessary to be a nurse in order to enter the program) and correspondence and intensive courses, listed in Appendix M.

The main advantage of a formal education program is that it provides a firm theoretical base. And certification as a nurse-midwife allows for legal practice anywhere in the country. Nevertheless, most formal educational programs have too much emphasis on the theoretical aspects of midwifery and not enough attention to the practical application of knowledge. Consequently, the student may suffer an overdevelopment of the analytical faculty at the expense of compassionate and intuitive qualities so necessary to humane caregiving. The challenge to midwifery education today is to create curriculum that develops the student as a *human being*, while concurrently providing clinical experience in settings both supportive and problematic. All too often, a student completes a program without any experience in providing continuity of care; she may do rotations in various clinical settings but may never know the full responsibility for a single client from start to finish. And this is exactly what she needs to master in order to practice "on her own responsibility."

Apprenticeship is a good alternative because the student is one-on-one with her teacher's clients throughout the entire perinatal cycle. She is also one-on-one with the teacher, which creates an intensive situation for developing and refining communication skills, assertiveness and receptivity. Learning takes place in context, as the teacher assigns research based on the day's clinical events, and tests as the appropriate situations arise. This integrated approach stimulates learning that is personalized and pertinent. Nurse-midwifery programs may come and go as funding dictates, but apprenticeship will endure because it is community based, cost effective and perfect for women with small children who require a program with elastic time.

If you are considering the apprenticeship route, check first to see if your state has any provisions for qualifying midwives. Some states require that you attend a formal academic program, others have a coursework requirement that can be met in any setting, as long as you can demonstrate your knowledge by exam. (This is similar to the independent study or external degree programs offered by many universities.) Other components of

Assisting at home births affords the chance to share in a team effort.

certification or licensure include skills assessment, documentation of birth experience, clinical evaluation by a qualified observer, and letters of recommendation. If your state has no mechanism of regulation or has registry only, you may need to create your own framework for learning. The next few sections of the book will focus on the essential components an independent program: book study, labor coaching, study group sessions and apprenticeship.

Book Study

Women who have babies or small children and are not yet free to attend births on a regular basis, and those who have not yet given birth and have no particular access to the birthing community should begin with book study. Interested mothers have usually read most everything on childbirth, breastfeeding and parenting and so can concentrate on texts explaining physiology and medical aspects. But others should read personal accounts to glean the emotional and spiritual side of the birth experience. A woman who has not yet had a child should carefully seek to understand her own heartfelt motivation. Not having given

birth herself, she must strive for intuitive understanding so that scientific facts will inform, but not orient or overwhelm her.

Good resources with which to begin include *Spiritual Midwifery* by Ina May Gaskin. This gives a number of in-depth accounts of the birth experience. Another useful resource is Sheila Kitzinger's *The Experience of Childbirth*, which focuses on prenatal preparation and the emotional changes and adjustments to be made in pregnancy and early parenting. Also excellent is *Birthing Normally* by Gayle Peterson, which explores the psychology of pregnancy from a practitioner's point of view. And for orientation to the homebirth movement, read Suzanne Arms' *Immaculate Deception*, which puts midwifery into historical and international context. These books give the aspiring midwife a base of understanding from which to pursue other studies in childbirth education, breastfeeding, parenting, etc.

When ready to move on to obstetrical studies, *Human Labor and Birth* (Oxorn and Foote) gives basic labor and delivery information in concise outline form. It's perfect for beginners. The format makes it well suited for both studying and reference. The diagrams are very clear and easy to understand; they explain practical subjects like pelvic assessment, fetal positioning and palpation quite thoroughly. Obstetrical emergencies are outlined, and treatments-made-simple are given step-by-step. The main drawback of this reference lies in its obstetrical orientation (long section on forceps, with nothing at all on normal prenatal care). However, most of the suggestions for management of complications are middle-of-the-road and fairly sensitive to mother and baby.

The next reference for study is *Textbook for Midwives* (Margaret Myles), which is the main text for nurse-midwives studying in Britain. Most of the information is detailed and complete, with strong emphasis on caregiving. Older editions (maybe available secondhand) have less hospital orientation, but also less information on contemporary obstetrical protocol. This book bears careful reading section by section. The drawings are realistic and profuse. A brief but thorough section on the care of the newborn, including problems and pathology, is also an attribute of this book.

Also useful is Helen Varney's *Nurse-Midwifery*, which is clear and easy to understand. The strong point of this book is its simple step-by-step instructions for clinical procedures such as venipuncture, Pap smear and IV insertion. The scope of information is not as exhaustive as Myles, but a new edition is due out shortly.

Although these texts were adequate for my apprenticeship period, I found I needed a more comprehensive obstetrical guide when I began giving prenatal care. Questions began to arise concerning the effects of pre-existing pathology, or regarding the etiology (root causes) of abnormal conditions developing in pregnancy. A sophisticated and exhaustive reference is essential for in-depth understanding in these areas.

Williams Obstetrics is notorious for being difficult to understand (largely due to its dry, scientific style) but the most recent edition (1985) seems more accessible. A medical dictionary (such as Tabers) is nevertheless essential, because much of the terminology presupposes previous study in areas relevant to midwifery. *Williams* is undoubtedly the most complete reference available.

Obstetrics and The Newborn (Beischer and MacKay) is a middle ground reference that is not as difficult to understand as *Williams*. It is designed specifically for medical students, complete with incredible color photos and sample questions from examinations. The main drawback of this book is that it is not really complete enough to serve as a total reference (and yet is nearly as expensive as *Williams*). But if you purchase one of the more sophisticated texts and can't get through it, this one will fill in the gaps.

So might Benson's *Handbook of Obstetrics*, which gives obstetrical procedures and complications at-a-glance. This book comes in a handy size that's perfect for keeping in your midwifery bag.

Another wonderful reference is *Maternity and Gynecological Care, The Nurse and The Family* by Jensen and Bobak. This book is most remarkable for its pro-woman voice, its broad base of information (1462 pages!) and its extensive section on women's health. This one is a must!

A remarkable reference, now out of print, but probably accessible in medical libraries, is Ian Donald's *Practical Obstetrical Problems*. This book is unsurpassed in its inclusive scope and well-seasoned wisdom. One reading is enough to convince you of its rare value, and to interest you in securing your own copy. Perhaps it will be reprinted soon.

Another important reference is the newsletter, for its up-to-the-minute information on midwifery subjects and issues. The *MANA News* focuses on the political situation in the US and Canada. The *Journal of Nurse-Midwifery*, published by the American College of Nurse-Midwives (ACNM) presents both research and open forum. *Birth* also publishes scientific research, with an emphasis on humanizing obstetrics. *The Birth Gazette*, edited by Ina May Gaskin, is intended for midwives and their supporters and features human interest articles, practical advice and political updates. And the newsletter published by the Association of Radical Midwives in England gives perspective on the European struggle and is full of management gems.

Check to see if your state midwifery association publishes a newsletter. You might also consider subscribing to newsletters from other states. Write to MANA for a list.

See Appendix A for addresses of all the above publications.

Labor Coaching

Attending births as a coach is usually the first step in midwifery training for the woman who has borne children herself and now has some time and energy available. Particularly if she has experienced a difficult birth in the hospital and a more satisfying one at home, she will be motivated to help others have the best possible birth in any setting, and will be sought out by pregnant women for her confidence and first-hand knowledge.

What is the learning experience of coaching? If the laboring woman's mate is with her, occasional assistance with relaxation or breathing will be appreciated whenever he takes a break. This is a great opportunity for the novice to jump into the intensity of birth energy and get used to working with it. Or if the mother is alone, the coach will learn quickly of the unwavering attention and endurance required in midwifery. And as women in labor usually love to be stroked and massaged, these tasks provide the coach with a chance to develop a good, intuitive sense of touch. Touching may be more effective when combined with verbal cues, and so the coach can experiment with soothing phrases, learning to speak spontaneously. Eventually, an intuitive understanding of how to support and facilitate labor begins to emerge.

Home births have a natural, easy pace with few interventions, and so provide unique opportunities for pure observation. *Observe, observe, observe,* and make notes on what you see and feel. Notice how different types of women respond to labor and which styles of coaching and encouragement are most appropriate for each. Pay attention to which positions work

---

Core Areas of Study

General Subjects

Aseptic Technique
Human Reproduction
Anatomy of Pregnancy, Birth, and Postpartum
Physiology of Pregnancy, Birth, and Postpartum
Embryology/Fetal Growth and Development
Nutrition for Pregnancy/Lactation
Obstetrical Procedures for High Risk Pregnancy and Birth
Well-woman GYN and Family Planning
Childbirth Education, Theory
Childbirth Education, Instruction

Provision of Care: Antepartum Period

Risk Assessment
Comprehensive Prenatal Care
Communication and Counseling Techniques
Management of Common Complaints in Pregnancy
Charting

Interpretation of History, Lab Work and Diagnostic Testing
Complications of Pregnancy
Contraindications for Homebirth

Provision of Care: Intrapartum Period

Management of Normal Labor and Birth
Complications of Labor and Delivery
Emergencies/Appropriate Action
Assessment of Lacerations/Appropriate Action

Provision of Care: Postpartum Period

Immediate Care of Mother and Newborn
Newborn Assessment
Management of Normal Postpartum and Lactation
Newborn Care
Management of Common Postpartum Problems
Newborn Complications/Appropriate Action
Maternal Complications/Appropriate Action

Reprinted by permission of California Association of Midwives.

best in the various stages of labor, which breathing patterns seem most effective and which skills work best for involving and integrating the rest of the family.

One of the subtler aspects of effective coaching is wisely assessing the need for focus. An experienced labor coach has the power to direct both parents and friends into comfortable and meaningful participation. A beginner may be tempted to use her authority to gain glory by placing the focus on her own abilities, but her real task is to empower *the mother and family.* Primary relationships can be strengthened tremendously in labor, and old wounds can be healed. A coach's most important task is to instill enough confidence in parents that they both desire and enjoy intimacy during the birthing, which will heighten the intensity of bonding and ease the postpartum transition.

The first five or six births are usually deeply emotional experiences for the aspiring midwife; she should feel her involvement to the full. Reverence for the power of the experience and willingness to feel it on a visceral level will get the student off to a proper start. But after a while the intensity of birth becomes familiar, and then there is opportunity to observe the particular skills and style of the attending midwife or physician. Student midwives are often quite critical of their seniors, focusing on less-than-perfect communication or seemingly arbitrary procedures. This is fine, as it enables a beginner to identify her own philosophy of practice. But it's essential to temper criticism with careful research so your assessments are accurate and complete. Learn from your seniors, don't merely react to them!

Several of the first births I coached were attended by a midwife quite detached from the women she was assisting. She did no prenatal care and essentially served as a delivery technician. I used her as a negative role-model, and so began to realize that my own orientation was more holistic, with strong emphasis on preventative care and family integration. I then devoted myself to studying in these areas before going on to technical training. *Taking responsibility for your negative reactions to procedures or practitioners is the way to integrate yourself with your learning.*

Sometimes a midwife will need to use a coach's extra pair of hands at a birth and, sensing enthusiasm, will do a bit of teaching. I remember one midwife calling me to attention while she was suturing an episiotomy, telling me to "watch and learn." I had been holding a flashlight for what seemed like forever, my arm was killing me and my interest was wavering. But afterwards I had new resources for interpreting instructions on suturing because of what I had actually seen. Never pass up an opportunity to assist, or to assert what you think you've learned from previous assistance, especially at home births where there is more time to ask questions and receive feedback.

Hospital labor coaching offers wonderful opportunities for working with women of diverse backgrounds while learning about current medical procedures. Coaching at a local hospital is the logical second step in training for women not yet being invited to births due to lack of involvement with expectant parents. I began doing hospital coaching because my home birth attendance was very sporadic and I wanted more experience. I registered as a volunteer coach by calling labor and delivery at the local general hospital, and was well received because they were understaffed and had trouble providing one-on-one care. On-the-spot coaching definitely gives unprepared mothers a chance for a decent birthing, but it really tests the mettle of the aspiring midwife.

One very unappealing aspect of hospital coaching is the environment itself. Working with a woman with little or no preparation, who is receiving the standard package of labor bed, IV and fetal monitor, is constricting and oppressive compared to the freedom at home. Often hospital rooms are overheated and lack adequate ventilation, and the overhead lighting is irritating and debilitating. All of this poses an obstacle to relaxation which the coach must overcome in herself, as well as for the woman she's assisting.

The most important thing to remember when doing hospital coaching is that most women with little or no preparation believe that giving birth is something horrible and painful, a cross to be borne. These women know nothing of the importance and physiological function of relaxation, and labor is not

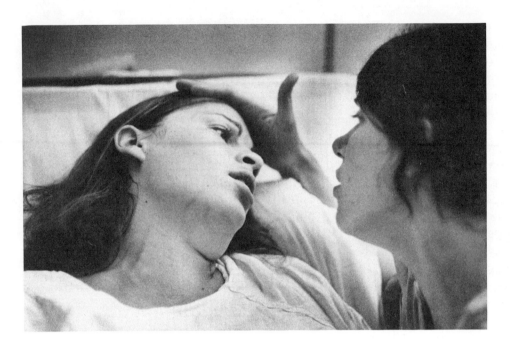

Often you are the mother's only support in hospital situations.

the time for lecturing. It's usually best to begin by establishing a breathing rhythm and solid eye contact, which should foster communication and trust. Here are your lessons in adapting breathing to suit the individual mother; often you just feel or fumble your way into what's workable. Those who are afraid of their sensations often breathe too rapidly. This can be remedied either by keeping the breathing light or by trying to slow it down. Slowing down is best accomplished by having the mother breathe with you as you make each breath a fraction slower and deeper than the one before. Place a hand on her belly and a hand on your own, and as you look into her eyes, show her how to draw her breath down.

Once breathing is established, relaxation can be initiated by using touch, massage and verbal cues. Frightened women will usually tighten up their hips or legs, and a gentle foot massage may be the best way to get the whole lower body loose. Smooth firm strokes on the inner thigh and phrases like "let your legs feel heavy" or "let your bottom melt into the bed" sometimes work. Several times I was called to coach Oriental or Hispanic women who spoke no English, and had to rely entirely on touch and sign. It works!

Mothers without preparation often progress *very* slowly, and more than anything else, hos-

pital coaching will try your patience. A quote from Grantly Dick-Read says it perfectly:

> At the bedside of a woman in labor we have to await the will of intangible forces. The emotional conflicts and physical reactions of women present a constant stream of problems. Initiative, clear thinking and honest exposition must be at hand to control the fearful, encourage the failing and support the tired. No force of mind or body can drive a woman in labor; by patience only can the smooth course of nature be followed.

Basic to the art of cultivating patience is remembering to take care of your own physical and emotional needs. If the laboring woman is alone, perhaps you could bring a coaching partner with you. The two of you can alternate break times and compare notes on what's happening with the labor. Often hospitals have a coffee room for staff, and while one of the nurses is examining the woman, you can slip away for a break. Don't forget to tell your client that you'll be right back.

Be comfortable; wear something light, cool and loose. Coaching is very demanding physically and you'll perspire a lot. You might want to bring an extra change of clothes, in case you're in the way when the woman vomits or her water bag breaks. If you have long hair, bring a tie or clip to put it up and out of your way. Also bring some lip balm (lots of breathing through the mouth will chap you) and something like lozenges to suck on. Some fresh fruit or a bottle of juice is also a good idea.

Labor coaching in the hospital will teach you that assisting at births is not always fun or easy. Often you are on your own and responsible for making important decisions, although no one on the staff will acknowledge this. For example, I once coached a woman who had been involuntarily pushing ever so slightly with each contraction, even though she was only six centimeters dilated. This had caused her cervix to swell, which retarded further dilation. She was lying in bed with an IV and was hooked to a fetal monitor. All that the nurses recommended was "no more pushing!" while discussing the possiblity of an epidural. I reasoned that what she needed was more pressure on her cervix to thin it out, but without the strain of bearing down. I got her breathing evenly in her chest so she couldn't catch and hold down at all with her diaphragm, and had her squat. This necessitated some careful disentangling of the various tubes and wires to which she was connected. Sure enough it worked, and she dilated in another hour to complete.

Volunteer coaching done on-the-spot will also teach you something of the lifestyle and self-sacrifice involved in being perpetually on call. You'll need to give your family your best before you go and as much good energy as you can muster when you return, to compensate for your abrupt and perhaps prolonged absence. You'll also experience the frustration of doing hard work for free, particularly if you are out-of-pocket for gas and a babysitter. This experience will make you aware of the time and energy commitment you'll be making as a midwife, and give you some idea of a reasonable fee to request.

Also, hospital births do not always go well. Sometimes by the time you arrive, the woman has received a mild analgesic and is less responsive to coaching. If she requires something stronger, fetal distress may ensue and the whole thing may end with a Cesarean. Certainly the hospital setting will provide ample

Help your community and learn by teaching.

opportunity to watch pathology orientation in action. Much of what you see and experience will disgust you, but hopefully you'll be inspired to do better when you come into practice yourself.

What are some other possible ways to keep up your birth attendance? For women who have given birth and have specific skills and insights to share, teaching childbirth classes may be the answer. Most cities and towns have women's centers or switchboards where you can register. You might also consider teaching at one of these centers to gain experience and exposure. Childbirth educators are frequently invited to births as support persons, and thus have a chance to observe a variety of practitioners for style and emphasis, at the same time establishing themselves as flexible and reasonable personalities. Teaching is a potent avenue into the birthing community.

Besides birth classes offered in the final months, you might also teach prenatal exercise or yoga classes to women early in pregnancy. Clinics specializing in maternity care might be open to "early bird" sessions for newly pregnant women. These could be quite informal, with basic information on nutrition and health, providing yet another opportunity for you to be asked to births. Certainly there is strategy involved here, but as long as your goal is to assist each woman to get what she wants and needs, it's fine.

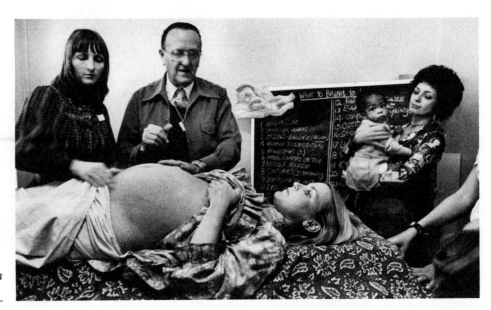

A study group with the late Dr. Ettinghausen; the pregnant volunteer is herself a midwife.

Study Groups

Participating in a study group with other student midwives and experienced instructors is probably the most exciting and integrating form of training. Books have their value, and birthings activate responsibility and understanding, but listening to midwives discuss case histories and management of complications is a practical education that can't be beat. Study groups also provide golden opportunities for students to structure studies in areas on which they feel the need to concentrate.

I participated in a study group for over a year and during that period went from student to primary caregiver. We had a nurse and a physician working along with us and were therefore able to learn and practice skills like giving injections (we practiced by injecting oranges with water) and drawing blood (which we did on each other). We had a few sessions on equipment, several on infant resuscitation and single meetings devoted to studying anemia, neonatal jaundice, hypertension, etc. Often the discussion would rove into related areas as we shared experiences at births. During the time this group met, several of the apprentices formed partnerships which became fairly permanent units. Prior to that, we all had opportunities to trade off working together under the guidance of the senior midwives who were teaching us.

A variation of the study group can be found through a local chapter of a state or nationwide midwifery organization. For example, the California Association of Midwives (CAM) meets every two months in either the northern or southern part of the state. These all day get-togethers usually consist of about 50 people who spend the morning on a specific topic and the afternoon on organizational business. A number of seasoned midwives participate and have much technical information to share. Specialists come and speak. A pediatrician, for example, did a demonstration on the use of oxygen for infant resuscitation.

Starting a study group can be as easy as posting signs in community centers or gathering places announcing a meeting for anyone interested in birth alternatives. Or you could contact women's health centers or referral lines for the names of other childbirth educators and coaches, and organize a meeting yourself.

Apprenticeship

Ideally the connections made in a study group enable the student to find a senior midwife with whom she's comfortable and vice versa, so that apprenticeship is a simple extension of an already established relationship.

How will a student know when she is ready to apprentice? There is a particular feeling of confidence that comes from having attended a wide variety of births and from having mastered basic obstetrical information, which is accompanied by an urge to have "hands-on." Apprenticeship usually begins with participation in prenatal visits and acquisition of simple skills like taking blood pressure, listening to fetal heart tones and palpating the baby. If a senior midwife is training several apprentices at once, she will often rotate their clinic attendance, observe each apprentice's best connections with clients and arrange for those combinations at births.

As a senior midwife, I've sometimes been heavily pressured by students wanting to apprentice with me, and my invariable reaction is to put these women aside. The very nature of the senior-apprentice relationship requires that the apprentice approach with deference to the style and experience of the midwife from whom she is soliciting instruction. A midwife will usually take on an apprentice because she needs assistance *and support* at births; someone to share her work load as well as the joys and responsibilities involved. It follows that the personalities of the two should be compatible. As long as the apprentice remains an apprentice, she should seek to complement, supplement and implement the style and art of the midwife with whom she's working. This requires tact and a certain reserve sometimes, but doesn't preclude asserting new and different ideas in a respectful way. An apprentice can *revitalize* a practice with her enthusiasm. With textbook study fresh in her mind, she can offer appropriate details of information. Most important, her recent coaching perspective can reanimate the emotional aspects of care-giving.

Apprenticeship is traditionally a relationship of exchange wherein a master of a given trade exchanges knowledge for labor. How can an apprentice best serve the needs of the midwife at birthings where the situation is always unique and ever changing? She can provide labor coaching when the midwife is otherwise busy with organization. She can take some responsibility for seeing that fetal heart tones are taken regularly, along with other vitals like blood pressure and pulse. By helping the midwife keep labor notes, she can learn about normal and abnormal labor patterns and the key factors in management decisions. She can assist with delivery; at first just opening up the gauze pads and handing instruments to the midwife, but eventually doing perineal massage and support for cooperative "catching."

She can also help during third stage by keeping an eye on the baby while the midwife delivers the placenta, or vice versa. She can assist with suturing, thus learning sterile, surgical procedure. And after enough supervised experience she might be asked to labor sit and do basic checks on mother and baby until the midwife arrives at the birthing. Eventually she'll be expected to do a delivery on her own.

The apprentice should also be willing to help the midwife meet her personal needs by assisting with childcare, housekeeping and occasional errands. Keeping the clinic room neat and well organized is another appreciated contribution. Sometimes the apprentice will receive a nominal sum to cover transportation and child care, although if the apprenticeship program is more formalized, the student may be expected to pay for her training. It really depends on the nature of the practice; if the midwife eventually intends to rely on the apprentice as a partner she may pay her increasingly over time, but if she already has a partner and the apprentice is there as a student only, she may have to pay for her training.

How will an apprentice know when she is really ready to practice independently? Some women are by nature over-eager and need to be restrained and taught very carefully; others are timid and must be given unexpected responsibilities to let them know that they are competent. If their relationship is good, an apprentice can trust her teacher's judgment concerning her readiness to start working on her own. Often a midwife will simply give the apprentice a few of her own clients to get her going on prenatal care, and will back her up for the birth.

But for women whose training period has been a hodge-podge of birth experiences with no formal or enduring apprenticeship, determining readiness is not so easy. General criteria in midwifery credentialing are *number of births attended* and *number of supervised deliveries.* Minimums of 25 births observed and 25 delivered are fairly standard from state to state. But the real crux of the matter is *level of involvement and responsibility.* A woman who has done 40 deliveries without continuity of care will probably know less than one who has been responsible for 25 mothers throughout every phase

Practical Skills Checklist

_____ 1. Interpret urine dipstick results.
_____ 2. Obtain maternal blood pressure, pulse, temperature.
_____ 3. Perform antepartum pelvic exam; including bimanual, pelvimetry, speculum exam.
_____ 4. Perform Leopold's maneuver; including measurement of fundal height and assessment of fetal weight.
_____ 5. Check for edema.
_____ 6. Check for CVA tenderness.
_____ 7. Check for deep tendon reflexes and clonus.
_____ 8. Perform manual breast exam.
_____ 9. Perform intrapartum pelvic exam; including cervical effacement, dilation, fetal station, presentation, position, status of the membranes.
_____ 10. Obtain intrapartum auscultation of FHT and interpret deceleration and variability patterns.
_____ 11. Time contractions and assess quality.
_____ 12. Maintain aseptic technique.
_____ 13. Give an injection.
_____ 14. Perform amniotomy.
_____ 15. Perform perineal massage and support.
_____ 16. Perform hand maneuvers to assist delivery of baby.
_____ 17. Perform an episiotomy.
_____ 18. Use a DeLee suction.
_____ 19. Perform the screw maneuver for shoulder dystocia.
_____ 20. Obtain an Apgar score.
_____ 21. Perform a newborn exam, including: listening to the heart beat and assessing abnormal rhythm patterns; listening to the lungs and assessing obstructions; observing baby's overall condition and activity level; checking the skin, eyes, head, palate, ears, thorax, abdomen, belly, genitals, anus, testes, spine, hips; checking and observing reflexes; obtaining weight, length, head and chest circumference.
_____ 22. Perform infant and adult CPR.
_____ 23. Use a bulb syringe.
_____ 24. Deliver and inspect placenta, membranes, cord vessels.
_____ 25. Assess blood loss.
_____ 26. Perform bimanual compression.
_____ 27. Manually remove a placenta.
_____ 28. Perform fundal massage.
_____ 29. Assess degree of maternal lacerations and appropriate action.
_____ 30. Suture episiotomy or vaginal/perineal lacerations.
_____ 31. Administer approved eye prophylaxis to newborn.
_____ 32. Assess neonatal jaundice.
_____ 33. Administer oxygen to mother or baby.
_____ 34. Evaluate involution of the uterus postpartum.

Reprinted by permission of the California Association of Midwives.

of the perinatal cycle. Assisting a woman throughout pregnancy gives plenty of opportunity to see cause and effect via suggestions and outcomes. A genuine ability to work with people can only be gained by personal involvement. And this is really 75 percent of a midwife's skill; medical techniques are essential, but supplementary to the care of healthy, low-risk women.

This is not to underrate the importance of medical knowledge; an apprentice about to begin primary care must have perfected certain skills (see opposite page).

A real turning point for an apprentice also attending births in the hospital is the realization that her knowledge puts her in league with the medical professionals. More than once I've had to assist a labor and delivery nurse with the necessary palpation for locating fetal heart tones most clearly. My partner told of a delivery she attended where following the birth of a rather small infant, it was obvious to her by observing the uterine contour that there was still another baby in utero. No one else noticed this, although the second water bag was presenting. In fact, the attending physician was pulling at the cord to deliver the placenta but instead a twin was expelled into the placenta pan! Another apprentice recounted several stories of avoidable postpartum hemorrhage, once caused by excessive cord traction and resulting partial separation, another time by premature episiotomy combined with uncontrolled delivery. The next time this apprentice encountered another "cord pulling" attendant, she firmly suggested waiting while the woman pushed for her placenta, and so it was done!

Many hospital practices are bound to make the natural birth advocate cringe, and adopt a self-righteous attitude. The point, though, is to cultivate an understanding of what constitutes truly responsible care. The main problem with hospital care is that no single practitioner is solely and fully responsible for the treatment of a particular mother and baby. Even the woman who has engaged a private doctor may find herself and her labor being managed by nurses or residents she's never seen before. And when they go off-duty, the responsibility is passed along once again. On the other hand, the midwife takes total responsibility for the entire birth process, combining the roles of nurse, obstetrician and pediatrician. Because she must personally bear the consequences of her actions she must be absolutely certain of her decisions, utilizing every bit of data to formulate a course of management.

To make the most of hospital birth experiences, one must combine a thorough understanding of medical management with an intuitive sense of alternative care. Now and then a beginner will speak or act out from her position and change the course of events. And later, these experiences can be discussed with senior midwives who will often reinforce her judgement and help her gain confidence.

It's so much easier to make a good beginning with communicative medical support. I was lucky to have an obstetrician to consult when I began giving primary care. He was completely willing to answer questions and discuss my diagnoses/remedies for various women with complications. And even in the midst of a difficult birthing, my senior midwife was only a phone call away. *Every beginning midwife must develop a decent, reliable support system.* Midwifery being the humanistic practice that it is, a helping hand is seldom hard to find.

Independent practice requires a tremendous shift in the level of responsibility. You study assiduously, attend births diligently, perfect every skill and then suddenly (it seems) you are asked, chosen; someone wants *you* to assist their birth! As your wisdom ripens and those around you reinforce your skill, you feel a sense of fate, concentration, readiness (and you'll probably feel this repeatedly, before every labor). This ability to focus all your resources is the final touch. Now you are ready to practice midwifery!

CHAPTER 8

The Midwife's Practice

As a midwife's status changes from apprentice to primary caregiver, great changes take place in her personal life as well. The focus shifts from the thrill of involvement to concern with integrating responsibilities and lifestyle. In order to practice successfully, you'll need to combine the demands of your work with the rest of your day-to-day activities. No longer a hobby or part-time involvement as it was in the beginning, midwifery is now your *profession*. In setting up a practice you must consider local politics, availability of backup, finances, the desires of your clientele and the needs of your family. Pulling all this together into a cohesive, comfortable package can be a bit tricky.

Beginning midwives often have problems at this point. Birth attendance is still unpredictable, perhaps not adequate to pay the bills. Philosophical disagreements with other beginners may arise as you seek to distinguish yourselves, and there may be rumors or questions concerning your competence. And then there are numerous practicalities involved in the actual physical setup which must be worked through. The first births seem to take all your energy, as you find yourself studying over and over again in an effort to be fully informed and responsible. Your family life may well begin to show some strain, which of course puts an extra burden on you.

The important thing to remember is to take these things one at a time, and your life, one day at a time. Take time out to reflect on your progress. As in any period of accelerated growth, your aim is to stay open enough not to miss anything, while remaining calm enough to observe congruity and resonance which will enable you to find your own way of doing things, your particular style of practice.

Location: City or Country Practice?

City midwifery has its ease in the availability of emergency medical facilities. Home birth is generally a very safe alternative in the city, considering the top-notch paramedic services and neonatal intensive care units at nearby hospitals. However, close proximity and access to the medical community also means that you need to establish good relations. Difficulties with city practice depend largely on the politics surrounding home birth. If you live in a state where midwifery is legal or if the prevailing attitude is supportive (or at least tolerant), you can practice openly and without anxiety. With good backup, you have the assurance that any emergency will be handled sensitively at the hospital with which you are affiliated. Unfortunately this is the exception; often city midwives are just as isolated as their rural sisters. The city midwife without support is in the untenable position of being obligated to use emergency facilities when necessary, while carefully limiting her *own* use of medical paraphernalia lest her involvement be detected if and when a mother needs to be transferred. Consider the case of a California midwife (a nurse) who attended a home birth which became complicated with retained placenta and postpartum hemorrhage. She administered pitocin before sending the woman to the hospital, and responsibly sent along a note indicating time and dosage. Subsequently she was tracked down and prosecuted for "practicing medicine without a license." Nevertheless, she did the only ethical thing she could have!

The city midwife working under this sort of political and legal pressure must be discreet, keep her practice quiet and gain clear agreements with the couples she assists as to her limited responsibilty and liability. It seems that city midwives suffer more of this oppression than those practicing rurally; often in the country there is greater acceptance of midwifery as a necessary alternative for women so far from hospitals. Economic competition between doctors and midwives is a crucial factor in cities. Consumers are increasingly aware of the padding involved in health care costs and are interested in something of a fair deal. Midwives spend more time, give more personal attention and more of themselves at the birth than just about *any* obstetrician. And often they are adaptable in the fee they require, perhaps working on a sliding scale.

City practice may also be hindered by city lifestyle itself. A common problem is finding adequate time to really get to know your clients, as well as making them aware of their need to slow down, unfold and let the pregnancy be central and determining of pace. The environment itself, with its strong components of artificial speed and stimulation, isn't particularly appropriate for pregnant women. City midwives have the task of modulating the energy at clinic visits to create a feeling of ease and comfort, in order to establish genuine communication.

Sometimes a city will have several competitive midwifery practices, and a sorry state for the art of midwifery is division and factionalism. In that vein, midwifery can be like any other business, with competitive advertising, mutual slander, and poisonous emotions afloat. Such power struggles are self-defeating. Midwives must cooperate by sharing resources and exchanging information in order to generate a broad base of strength to counter the medical establishment.

The real competition for city midwives are the hospital alternative birth center programs. Many people who might otherwise investigate home birth are persuaded by claims of "home-like atmosphere" in the nicely furnished, decorator birth rooms. Although alternative birth centers are more relaxed than traditional labor facilities and allow for greater family participation, the medical orientation remains and transfer to standard facilities is automatic with even the smallest complication. Easy chairs

and flowered sheets cannot substitute for the familiarity and comfort of *one's own home*. Unfortunately, economic considerations weigh heavily here; hospital programs are covered by private insurance or social services, but most midwives require cash payment to support themselves.

So the city midwife has a lot to contend with and yet, with good community relations and supportive backup, the opportunities for learning are tremendous. Training and working in the city can take the midwife across class and cultural boundaries, fostering adaptability in practice while providing the fun and stimulation of getting to know all kinds of people on a very intimate level.

The main advantage to rural practice is the natural environment, which provides some common ground for those who live in proximity. In general life proceeds at a slower pace, the air is cleaner, food is better and exercise more readily available. Country women must face the fact that they are far from emergency facilities and consequently are more likely to maintain a state of health and awareness which will tend to discourage complications. Respect for nature, cultivated by cooperating with natural forces and processes day by day, provides a powerful resource for women birthing in the country. The necessity of relying on one another for exchange of goods and services as well as for friendship and emotional support, creates a tight bond between country women. Most rural birthings are extended family events, in contrast to the nuclear "just us two" city style birth which is a product of city woman's social isolation.

In contrast, problems with rural practice are caused by physical isolation. Although it makes sense to have clinic visits at a central location (ideally your home) and to schedule checkups on certain days at regular intervals, this becomes complicated if a birth comes up, with clients already en route for prenatals and coming a great distance (perhaps an hour's drive). Rural midwives end up doing a lot of home visits unless they have organized a system of backup care to be given by others when necessary. For once the trip has been made to attend a birth you simply cannot come and go as you please, whether you are needed at home, or by another who *might* be in labor, or by a postpartum mom in distress. It's obvious that rural practice necessitates some kind of partnership.

The thing that rural midwives seem to miss the most is contact with others in practice. Midwifery is a *dynamic profession,* not a circumscribed batch of skills. Midwives need opportunities to meet and share experiences, and to participate in continuing education on a regular basis. Medical consultation may also be limited; it can be very difficult to get a second or third opinion on a complication.

For those practicing far from the hospital, extra skills and equipment are essential. The midwife should be able to start an IV to replace fluids in case of hemorrhage. Endotracheal intubation could mean the difference between

An Irish midwife responding to the call of a woman in early labor.

life and death for the baby born severely depressed. Many rural midwives practice without these tools and skills, but should be on the lookout for professionals willing to train them.

Equipment

Most beginning midwives take great pleasure and pride in their growing treasury of equipment. It's usually best to purchase equipment slowly during the apprenticeship period so you can try out various brands and see which suits you best. This bit-by-bit method is also a lot easier on the pocketbook. A complete midwife's kit, including leather bag, can run around $700 and an oxygen system can bring the cost to $1000. Luckily there are now some supply houses, such as Cascade Birthing Supplies and Moonflower Birthing (see Appendix A) which cater to midwives and home birthing couples. Their quantity buying lowers the cost to you considerably.

Take a look at the supply list in Appendix L. Certain basics like urine sticks, exam gloves (non-sterile), Betadine antiseptic, sterile gauze pads, underpads and bulb syringe can be purchased at your local drugstore. Many of the smaller items can be secured from friends who are nurses at nearby hospitals. If you must order from a local medical supply store, try calling them first to see if you can place an order by phone. When they ask who you are, simply cite your affiliation with your backup hospital ("I give prenatal services through St. James Hospital"). This is usually enough to get by. You might want to mail a cashier's check or money order rather than send a personal check, if your area is restrictive.

When it comes to making large purchases certain instruments are fairly standard, such as the Allen type fetascope (the one with black tubing and small forehead piece). Unfortunately, the Allen firm itself no longer makes a fetascope and the Biodynamic model is not as good. But Series Ten makes an amplified version which works fairly well; it's probably your best bet. Other items such as the blood pressure cuff (sphygmomanometer) should be purchased by comparison shopping; your goal being quality without tinsel. There is a well known company that makes a stylish, attractive cuff they call the "nurses model" which

The midwife's office; note birth photos on the wall.

has a totally inferior gauge. Built with an automatic pin stop, this gauge gives no indication of need for adjustment and is virtually irreparable. In other words, it's a cheap, disposable item. Look for a gauge with a warranty and certification; you can see a register number stamped on the face of any decent gauge.

When it comes to your hand tools, be absolutely certain they are 100 percent stainless steel. Chrome plate will rapidly rust and chip. It's especially important that your scissors and curved hemostats be top quality as you'll be using them over and over. The finest instruments are imported from Germany (scissors cost around $20), fairly good quality are produced in the United States ($7 or $8 a pair), and the cheapest come from Pakistan (about $3). This cheaper calibre is probably fine for tools like ring forceps or mosquito forceps which you use so rarely.

A controversial item is the ultrasound doppler, which amplifies the heart beat by ultrasound, and may pose some risk to the fetus due to the effects of sonic waves. Nevertheless, the doppler can pick up heart tones easily with the mother in any position, or late in second stage. Many midwives use it only when necessary, as backup for the fetascope.

Last but not least are the restricted items: oxytocic drugs (pitocin and methergine); anesthetic for suturing (lidocaine) and suture mate-rial; your needles and syringes; DeLee traps and amnihooks. If you have a physician willing to help you, no problem, but otherwise you must rely on assistance from other practicing midwives. Stock up whenever you have the opportunity.

Setup and Administration

In terms of physical setup, you have several choices. You can do clinic visits in your home, using your bedroom for exams and your living room for waiting. Or you might convert a spare room to suit. Another option is to rent an office, which should have separate waiting area and restroom.

The home atmosphere usually appeals to clients and is conducive to intimacy. But an obvious drawback is always having to keep things neat and clean, which can be difficult to pull together if you've just come in from a birth at 3 a.m. and clinic starts at 9. And sometimes there are strenuous objections from the mate who feels the need for privacy or sleep. On the other hand, the cost of renting an office may be prohibitive at first. Consider sharing space with other midwives or health providers in your area before making up your mind.

Whatever you do, your clinic room should be arranged for both comfort and efficiency. Most women prefer to be examined on a bed, so choose a nice firm double mattress with room for midwife and partner to sit on either side of the woman while examining her. Another possibility is a chaise couch; I have an antique "fainting sofa" which is perfect for the purpose. There should be adequate seating available for family and friends. Have some toys on hand for small children who visit, and birth photo albums or pictures on the wall. A bookcase with lending library should be accessible in either the clinic room or waiting area. If space permits, you might consider having an exam table (you don't have to use stirrups) which can be obtained from secondhand medical supply houses or may be donated by sympathetic doctors or clinics. These are unsurpassed for doing accurate pelvic assessment and are practical in that their base consists of drawers and cabinets perfect for storing medical supplies. Designate a corner of the room or a converted walk-in closet for lab work if you will be doing it yourself, and you've got your clinic!

What about supplies? What will you need and how much should you keep in stock? Besides the essential equipment there are various incidentals which you ought to have on hand. Disposable underpads (the kind women purchase for labor) are useful for doing internal exams and can be purchased small sized (23 x 24) and in bulk for economy. For urine testing, be sure to have plenty of paper cups available and lots of toilet paper stocked on your shelves.

Medical supplies that go quickly are exam gloves, lubricating jelly and urine sticks. You need to be aware of your supply; make note of it at least once a week. Also needing constant replacement are your forms: medical history blanks, prenatal care forms, birth records and newborn exam sheets, and postpartum instructions. Don't forget birth supply lists for parents (see Appendix L). Keep these forms in an accordian file (portable and cheap) so you can tell at a glance which ones need replacing. Also keep a good supply of manila folders, paper clips, writing paper and pens available. And if you are living hand-to-mouth and obtaining supplies by the beg or borrow method, post a running list of your needs (highlight priorities. No matter what your level of practice, keep it organized.

How much time should you allow for visits? Again, that depends on your style and volume of practice. I hold clinic two days weekly, and it's been my experience that one hour per visit is optimal time spent. Careful physical examination can take 20 minutes (anything unusual will take longer) and another 40 minutes are needed for discussing personal issues and questions. It seems to take about half an hour for people to relax and get comfortable enough to start speaking freely. Occasionally conversation will elicit some strong emotions and your visit will run overtime. This is why you need a library in the waiting area. A pot of herb tea and healthy snack food is another possibility. If a visit is running late, don't worry but do explain to those who are waiting. If someone has a tight schedule your partner can do the checkup for them in another room, or at least start the discussion.

Women due around the same time can be scheduled so their appointments overlap, thus giving them the opportunity to meet each other or perhaps share in one another's checkups if they are already friendly. This principle of overlap can also be used to bring fathers together. No harm either in introducing a topic designed to stimulate conversation.

Apart from client scheduling, you may also want to schedule weekly business meetings to go over finances with others in your practice and discuss such matters as advertising, PR, special events, etc. The purchasing of books and supplies, or environmental concerns (furnishings, housekeeping, redecorating) might also be on the agenda. There is a tendency for these meetings to rove into case discussion, but it is better to make separate time for this. However, you may wish to divide your weekly meeting into two sections; the first for discussing business and the second for airing interpersonal concerns. The latter is critical to the psychological health of your practice! Occasionally (or perhaps initially) an outside facilitator may be helpful.

Plan also to do an annual (or semi-annual) systematic review of all aspects of your business: facilities, location, image, PR and advertising, competition, community and professional relations. This enables you to create long term goals for your organization, in contrast to the short term, problem-solving focus of your weekly meetings.

Be sure your filing system is orderly. The law may vary from state to state, but in California medical records must be kept for 21 years. A by-year system is probably better than alphabetical, as it allows you to move sections of your files to more permanent storage from time to time.

You may need to hire an accountant, or at least should educate yourself on tax laws relevant to small business owners. A good reference on this subject is *The Business of Midwifery*, by Suellen Miller.

General Presentability and Personal Hygiene

It is important for the midwife in private practice to realize that her clients may have a little trouble adjusting to care in a casual setting. Most appreciate the intimacy, but still expect the midwife to be well organized and professional.

Part of meeting this expectation involves attention to one's personal appearance. Most working women carefully plan their wardrobes for a variety of business occasions; there is no reason the midwife should not do the same. Clothes to wear to births should be readily washable; dark colored pants are most practical. Tops should be layered as frequently one needs extra warmth upon arriving to a cold house in the middle of the night, whereas by birth time the heat is up and something light weight is essential.

Some midwives have special aprons they use for delivery. Apron or no, you *must* have a change of clothes with you at all times. It is not uncommon to be soaked with amniotic fluid or stained with blood; you cannot go out in public like this and expect to debunk the myth of the midwife as "old crone with dirty fingers." In the event of transport, you may need to quickly change before leaving.

One of the reasons there is less infection with home birth is that the mother has a tolerance to microorganisms in her environment. However, she does not necessarily have resistence to what you bring in from outside. This is why your clothes should be completely clean and fresh, and why you should always wash your

Although at work in a rural location, this midwife dresses to suit the clientele she serves.

hands upon arrival and before examining the mother.

When doing prenatals, clean, fresh smelling clothes make a good impression (you know how sensitive pregnant women are to smell!) Wash your hands after each visit and before the next, to prevent transfer of any infected material. This is particularly important in the postpartum period: wash your hands before examining the mother *and again* before handling the baby.

To return to wardrobe, consider several highly presentable outfits for greeting the public. Midwives do have a negative image to live down, be it unkempt ignoramus or bedraggled hippie. Go ahead and buy a suit, heels, the whole bit. And hone your public speaking skills to go along with your appearance (see section on Public Education and Relations).

Do not be offended by the idea of dressing the part. Life is a stage, and it pays to have your costumes in order.

Fees

A midwife's fee should be fair, honest and reasonable. This will probably make it affordable for most parents. Beyond that, the amount should be adaptable via sliding scale for those who are in financial difficulty or temporarily out of work.

Once you've established a fee that you feel is just and acceptable, explain to clients what services are covered and how you would like to be paid. Some midwives prefer to work with a fee schedule and want a certain amount at each visit. This system may provide some protection against rip-offs, but it also eliminates those who have an erratic work-pay pattern or who are new in town, etc. If money is a criterion for accepting a woman for her next appointment she may cancel the visit, or if she comes, the focus on finances may usurp other aspects of caregiving. Most clients respond to a flexible, "bring a little each time" arrangement, without definite amount stipulations. To request full payment several weeks before the due date is not unreasonable.

Midwives who practice rurally report better luck with receiving payment. For one thing, you're all bound to come face to face with each other time and again, and for another, there are less financial draws and diversions in country life than in the glittering city. Rural midwives may also feel comfortable providing services for trade.

A word now about outside work. Beginning midwives often have notions about supplementing their income with some other part-time occupation. Well, never mind that idea, unless the work schedule is very flexible and the work itself easy on the spirit. Midwifery is more time and thought consuming than you might imagine. Part of the problem with a conventional job is that an employer won't tolerate for long a worker who is liable to run off at any moment and then is too tired to work well the next day. Neither is it suitable for a midwife to be preoccupied with extraneous concerns or wound up by tensions which disrupt her concentration on clients about to give birth.

Midwifery requires an even energy level and ongoing sensitivity. Try to take a realistic, long term view of your needs right from the start, then set a fee (and set up your practice) in a way that will keep you financially solvent and anxiety free. No one wants a tense, worried midwife to assist them. It's up to you to create your work situation and set your limits. Then you can devote yourself to the task of giving thorough, personalized care.

Public Relations and Education

The first step in public relations is to become known; list your service with local switchboards and women's agencies. Register your services with every alternative health care facility. Some may even have a feedback system for your former clients so that reports on your care can be made available to the general public.

Midwives occasionally have an opportunity to combine a presentation on birth with an introduction to their services. Consider hosting a slide show and information session for the general public, with business cards or brochures ready for the taking. Even small, informal slide shows with clients and their friends will keep your name circulating and bring you business by word-of-mouth.

Film showings featuring well-known speakers can focus on themes like "freedom to choose," or "alternatives in birthing." These take some work to coordinate and require plenty of advance publicity to assure good attendance. Debate, via panel discussion, is another format which is interesting to the public. Issue-oriented programs can be money-makers, but their main benefit is to expose a large, diverse audience to the benefits of midwifery.

You might also consider renting a booth at the county or city fair. We've done this for several consecutive years in San Francisco with great success. We show birth videos right at the booth to attract the passerby, and have T-shirts, flyers and a directory of local midwives available.

Television and radio appearances can further enhance public awareness of the midwifery option, but adequate preparation is essential. Have your statistics on the tip of your tongue: David Stewart's books are good resources for pro-midwife stats. It helps to understand the media techniques used by professionals, to wit, answer any question you don't like with one of your own, then *answer your own question*. For example, if an interviewer asks you "Is homebirth safe?" you might respond by saying, "Well, who says hospital birth is all that safe?" and then launch a discussion of iatrogenic complications. Particularly with television, it's wise to have several prepared statements that cannot be distorted by being taken out of context, and to present these no

It pays to keep an updated client list, so support can be rallied in time of need.

matter what the line of conversation; again, by asking the appropriate question.

Remember that your appearance and comments reflect on midwifery throughout the nation. Dress for the part, prepare carefully, consult with your colleagues and ask for feedback on your presentations. Promotional packets of information are often available from state midwifery organizations, or contact MANA for information.

Medical Backup and Consultation

As a midwife develops skill, she becomes increasingly aware of the medical limits of safe practice. By grace, faith, or the law of averages, the first births usually go well. Nevertheless, with more experience the reality of the unusual and unexpected begins to manifest, along with the desire for medical consultation and assistance.

The new midwife, especially if she has had an easy time finding a partner and beginning her practice, may be hesitant to search out medical backup. But there is an obvious need for a liaison between home and hospital if she expects to retain the integrity of a birthing experience if and when it must be transferred. Her first priority is to see that the parents' basic rights are preserved. She too must be recognized and respected so that her assessments will be heard and implemented by the attending physician.

My partner and I established backup slowly with an obstetrician and hospital we liked and respected by becoming known and acknowledged first as volunteer labor coaches. Later we came in as apprentices with our senior midwife, and eventually as independent practitioners. We were well received because we were already known as helpful, reasonable women, having kept a low profile at all times. We gained the staff's confidence by being clear headed and articulate regarding our transports and by making complete and well-organized medical records available. After several more drop-ins, the head obstetrician called and asked us if we would like his backup assistance on a continuing basis.

If you must transport a woman to a hospital where you don't have official backup, it is important to maintain an open, adaptable, friendly attitude. The staff may be suspicious at first, but may eventually come to accept you as they discover that you have behaved responsibly and are well-grounded in the technical aspects of the case. Some physicians have an image of midwives as kindly but decidedly naive women, who are dangerous because they are "untrained." On the other hand, most are quite curious to learn just what it is that midwives do and so may provide you with opportunities to demonstrate.

It helps to understand the psychology of labor and delivery personnel. Nurses, for example, are overworked, underpaid and generally unacknowledged. Why not offer your assistance and gain their cooperation? Empty the bedpan, fetch linens and drinking water and change bedding for your client. Don't attempt to take over routine vital assessments, because that is the nurse's job. When the birth is over and you are preparing to leave, be sure to give a personal thank you to each nurse who participated.

If the hospital you're using trains residents, you'll have a challenging but promising situation. Fresh out of school, their heads crammed with information, residents are only too happy to answer questions. In fact, speculative discourse is their forté and your key to establishing communication. If you let them have the authority as per information and you project authority *in action* you will be the perfect complement. Ask permission to do perineal massage and you'll probably find yourself participating in a four-handed delivery.

Residents are also unbelievably overworked and almost always exhausted. A former apprentice of mine would offer lifesavers or gum to break the ice, then give shoulder rubs to all if the hours were long. Again, a personal thank you for a "job well done" will establish you as an appreciative colleague.

The attending obstetrician is often in and out before you have a chance to say anything. Step out in the hall to converse, asking first if he has reviewed the chart or would like to see it. Then ask his opinion on the case. Listen respectfully, chime in agreement wherever you can, but assume a collegial air as you discuss your client in as technical a manner as possible.

If the physician suggests a course of action with which you don't agree, never confront him directly. Gain his confidence, then offer to present his recommendations to the parents and once alone with them, inform them of their options. Naturally you will influence them with your perspective; that's why they hired you. After they choose, present the physician with *their* (not your) decision. Although he may not be interested in your ideas, the physician will generally honor his patients' wishes (to reduce the potential for suits).

In this fashion you may connect with one or several doctors, and if problems arise in the fu-

ture you can muster up the courage to call for an opinion. Often a midwife in these stages of getting backing will need to distribute her clients among various practitioners so as not to overwhelm any one of them. Make your decision according to the situation. If you have a woman with suspected twins, you should have your sonogram done through the obstetrician who will probably take responsibility for the birth itself. On the other hand, if you have an "oblique lie" and want a sonogram to rule out placenta praevia but are not really anticipating hospital birth, you might want to save your OB backup and have a general practitioner do the authorization. You can use the women's health clinics for physical exams and lab work. For minor questions you can call a friendly resident or obstetrical nurse.

In areas where the political climate is very oppressive and the "old boys" are out to get you, your task is especially challenging. Explore any and all inroads to the medical establishment. For example, if you can't find a sympathetic doctor, perhaps you can find a progressive nurse who might lend a hand and put in a good word for you at work. With a change in attitude among the nurses, the attending physicians might begin to be more receptive. This takes time, but you owe it to your clients.

I once attended a birthing which was transferred to the hospital for failure to progress. As the mother curled up contentedly on her hospital bed, it became obvious that she had some deep insecurities about home birth. But after 48 sleepless hours, my partner and I could only feel relieved. Our rapport with the nurses had always been great, and tonight even the head nurse (generally the most conservative) was sympathetic to the birthing team.

Progress with pitocin was much more rapid than anyone expected. Judy and I, braving disapproval, donned sterile gloves to do an exam. Finding the mother completely dilated, we began doing some massage. By the time the head nurse stepped back in, the baby's head was starting to show. She paused and took it all in before going to get the doctor. (Our usual OB backup was not in the hospital, so this was someone new.) As the doctor (a woman) came in and all the nurses gathered 'round, the head was close to crowning, Judy had the heart tones and we were both supporting the perineum. When a nurse brought the instrument tray and asked the doctor where she wanted it, she said, motioning to us, "Ask them, I don't have anything to do with it." It was placed at the end of the bed, and after an awkward moment, someone unwrapped it for us. A good thing, too, for just at that moment the baby girl delivered. The doctor stepped up to help me check for tears; the perineum was intact but there was an internal muscle split. "She may need a few stitches there," said the doctor.

"No," I said, "just press down with some gauze and it will stop bleeding." She did so and watched, waited a moment, and concurred as I told her, "those little tears heal fine if the mother keeps her legs together."

After some time had passed, she motioned me to come outside with her. "Uh oh," I thought, "this is it. I'm busted." Instead, she held up the birth record and timidly asked me, "Do you sign this or should I?"

In my amazement I uttered, "I consider it a privilege to be able to work here, so just do whatever makes it smoothest for you."

"Then I'll sign them," she said. "You know, this is the first time I've ever done this."

Then came the marvelous exchange of warmth and thanks, and great feelings all around.

An entirely different approach to backup is to let your clients negotiate it. This may be particularly useful if you practice in a conservative area. A physician unwilling to back you personally might feel much more comfortable backing your client. An advantage to the client is that she is not automatically funneled into the practice of a physician who may not be her choice. And the liability for the physician, both professionally and politically, is obviously reduced. This approach is in keeping with the MANA Standards and Practice Statement, which says that to require the midwife to have a written or oral physician backup agreement is at odds with the International Definition "conducts a delivery on her own responsibility." Nevertheless, midwives do need medical *consultation* to practice safely. A collaborative relationship often develops spontaneously with the physician assisting your clients.

Whatever the genesis of your consulting relationship, it is essential to maintain good communication. Periodic chart review, with discussion of practice protocol and any changes therein, is critical to developing understanding. Friendly lunch dates are a good idea too. Trust needs to be fostered, and it makes all the difference in a crisis situation.

Medical Records, Charting and Informed Consent

This section will focus on the need for the midwife to document her caregiving. Medical records are the backbone of this process; they are essential for professional practice. The forms in the Appendix are intended not as models but as samples. It is a good idea for the senior apprentice to begin evaluating the forms of various practitioners so she can decide what suits her. The medical history form will vary from midwife to midwife, depending on whether it is a take-home form or intended for oral interview. Don't hesitate to patch together sections or components of various forms until you have

Partners review their records together.

something that is stimulating and easy for you to work with.

The importance of complete and accurate charting cannot be overemphasized! A chart is a *legal document.* In the event of a civil or malpractice suit, your chart may be your only witness to thorough and responsible caregiving. For this reason, write down everything you do and record all significant discussion between you and the parents, you and your backup physician, you and the hospital staff.

When doing prenatal care, make certain that you make notes during or immediately after each visit (and before the next). Sometimes the midwife gets so involved in intuitive, verbal communication with clients that she is reluctant to stop and make concrete notes. This will inevitably lead to forgetting important details.

During labor, there may come a time in late second stage when you are unable to continue charting. This is understandable, but don't neglect to do so immediately after delivery. In particular, write down each and every time you took fetal heart tones.

In the event of transport make absolutely sure you fill in the chart completely before arriving at the hospital (you can do this in the car). Your chart will be carefully scrutinized, possibly photocopied and made part of the woman's permanent record. It also serves as a testament to your professionalism (or lack thereof). To protect your own interests, write down the time you called the hospital, who you spoke to, and what they said. And definitely continue to make notes once you arrive. Again, this is for your protection though it will also be important to the parents, who will want details later.

In addition to noting discussions and interventions, it is also very important to chart *results.* This is how you document the mother as willing participant and demonstrate effects of your caregiving.

Informed consent is a critical part of your documentation whenever a particular test or diagnostic procedure is recommended or refused. Here your charting has to be *extremely thorough.* You must 1) make notes on the discussion of your recommendation; 2) outline all warnings given to parents in the event of refusal and; 3) document any other suggested

alternatives and consequences thereof. For example, if a mother decides not to have a non-stress test you would note her refusal and all that you told her regarding possible consequences for the baby. If you suggest estriols as an alternative you should note that too, along with everything you say regarding pros and cons of that procedure.

Why? You have only to imagine yourself in court, facing the parents of a stillborn, postmature baby who claim, "She told us we needed a non-stress test but didn't tell us what might happen if we said no." Of course none of us want to think this could happen to us but in these lawsuit-happy times, it pays to protect yourself.

Some midwives have parents sign a statement of consent-to-care early in the pregnancy. This contains information on the legal status of the practitioner and outlines responsibilities. Then comes a disclaimer, wherein potential life-threatening complications are cited as inherent risks. Parents sign the form to certify that they are aware of all the above and choose the practitioner and her services regardless.

An extension of this document is a professional disclosure statement which cites the midwife's training, experience, skills and scope of practice. Again, she can have the parents sign to signify their awareness of the above. This is to forestall, "We thought she was trained to handle ___."

Obviously these forms go only so far. Research in the medical community has revealed that the best protection against being sued is a *good relationship with the client.* This is something we midwives have known all along, but it doesn't hurt to enhance this with a bit of legal protection. Remember, the statute of limitations runs a full three years; that means someone could sue you up to three years after you assisted them. People change, so be prepared just in case.

One important way to maintain good relations with clients (not to mention your reputation) is to *maintain client confidentiality at all times.* This is particularly difficult if one client hears that another had a difficult birth and asks you questions about it. The temptation to explain and defend your actions is very strong. But nothing is worse for a woman than having her

Much like a successful marriage, partnership needs nourishing.

birth discussed at large! The best course is to suggest that the curious client speak to the mother directly, and then bring any technical questions back to you.

Midwives with students, or those working in partnership must have a clear understanding within the practice regarding confidentiality and appropriate response to queries. Review sticky situations together as they arise.

Partnership

No matter where you are located, working with a partner is really the best way to practice. Midwives who work alone are very rare. If such is their style, they must instruct the father or other attendant in emergency assistance. I can't imagine why a midwife would choose to work completely alone when she has the option of compatible partnership, unless for purely financial reasons.

Partnership is a safer way of practicing. A normal labor and delivery can be managed by one person, but if complications arise, an extra pair of skilled hands is essential. Long or difficult labors, for example, often produce a tired, mildly depressed baby *and* tired mother (tired uterus) predisposed to hemorrhage. How well can the solitary midwife deal with both of these complications arising simultaneously? How

can she do mouth-to-mouth resuscitation on the baby and bimanual uterine compression on the mother at the same time??

Other benefits of partnership include increased comfort and ease in practicing. Partners can spell one another at births, they can fill in emotionally for each other in times of personal crisis and they can give each other days or weeks off and away once in a while.

But best of all is the sharing of perceptions and information. Midwives work intensely on intuitive levels and will often discuss their feel for a particular woman's situation. Mutually intuiting a course of action in problematic situations is the pleasure and power of partnership. Harmony more than doubles the energy for triggering needed change. To have collaboration and consensus with a partner you know and trust gives you the confidence to advance your opinions with a sense of authority. A unified stand during a difficult labor can make the difference in getting through it.

However, partners do not always agree. Sometimes one midwife will bond intensely and become emotionally involved with a woman that her colleague, taking a more objective, clinical stance, considers at risk for home birthing. Ironing out these disagreements will teach you a lot about your own biases and prejudices, and will keep humility a constant for each of you.

Partners need good humor and sound judgement to make it together. They need to respect one another's intimacies with various clients and take pleasure in both high and low profile roles. A good partnerhsip, one in which the midwives truly enjoy one another's company and respect each other's strong points, sets a friendly example for parents and their family and friends who seek assistance.

Partnership may well be extended to a group practice of three or four women. This allows the midwives to take call for one another, so that time off can be rotated on a regular basis. However, relationship dynamics become more complicated with more people involved. Weekly sessions to air grievances and clear misunderstandings are a good idea!

Taking An Apprentice

Why bother with the added responsibility of training an apprentice? There are several reasons, the obvious being extra help with your practice. The apprentice can save you time and energy by monitoring early labor, assisting at prenatals, running errands, doing bookkeeping and filing, or cleaning the office. Other benefits are less tangible, but include the stimulation of an intensive relationship and the satisfaction of transmitting knowledge. Last but not least, training an apprentice allows you to play your part in preserving this traditional entry route to the profession. As an educational model, apprenticeship has many advantages over conventional schooling. Instruction can be tailored to fit the individual, which makes the learning process more condensed and less time consuming. And the inter-dependency of teacher and student fosters an intimacy that can be a great pleasure.

It can also be a mighty challenge. Training an apprentice requires top-notch communication based on an understanding of the developmental phases of the process. There are several models that are pertinent; let's consider first the stages in the *parent-child relationship:*

1) being one (infancy);
2) being together (childhood);
3) being separate (adolescent challenge and breakaway);
4) being together again (adulthood).

Or for the apprentice, the stages of falling in love are relevant:

1) infatuation (rose-colored phase);
2) disillusionment and struggle;
3) communication and compromise;
4) mature love.

In the beginning, teacher and student are mutually pleased with the excitement and stimulation of the new relationship. But gradually their differences arise; the apprentice may feel disappointed that her senior does not have all the answers, does not wish to experiment or does not give her as much responsibility as she thinks she can handle. The senior midwife may feel that her student lacks humility or genuine motivation, expects too much too soon, and is neglecting basic chores that she did so willingly in the beginning. The subsequent phase of "adolescence" is the most difficult, as struggles may erupt which disrupt the practice or threaten the relationship. The apprentice may openly contradict her senior in the presence of clients, the senior may respond by withdrawing privileges, the apprentice may threaten to leave. But if the two are able to *communicate* their disappointments, expectations and needs, they may arrive at a genuine understanding and begin to develop mutual respect. At this point the relationship matures; the senior and her apprentice are separate but equal, participating in the relationship by choice and maintaining it with honest communication.

The trouble is that many relationships never survive the adolescent/struggle phase and reach resolution. As a mother of two teens, I've been advised repeatedly that no matter how bad it gets or how insulting and critical they become, I *must* keep communication channels open. And it is crucial to help the adolescent find an appropriate outlet for fulminating energies. When your apprentice reaches this phase, consider giving new responsibilities (perhaps just a bit too complex or difficult) to teach her humility and let her know her limits. At the same time, consider taking on another apprentice, a beginner. The senior apprentice can teach the junior; this is a perfect opportunity for her to test her wings while still being supervised. The dynamics of this arrangement work quite well. At first, all three attend births together, with the senior midwife in charge and the senior apprentice directing the junior in basic responsibilities. Then the senior apprentice begins doing deliveries under supervision, while the junior assists. This gives the senior midwife a well-deserved rest!

Since you ultimately want your new apprentice to get accustomed to working with you, don't prolong this phase unnecessarily. You may need to set a graduation date for your senior apprentice, encouraging her to get out on her own. Once she has her business set up, send her a few clients to help her get started.

Of course the growing pains are continuous throughout these relationships. The student has constant need for attention, while the teacher struggles for an appropriate response, i.e., figuring out when to hold firm and when to let go. Much of this emotional confusion can be forestalled by creating a sound academic structure. Give your apprentice required reading, assign reports occasionally so that she learns to do research and have her write up analyses of particularly difficult cases. Test her by written quiz, by practical or oral review. It is very important that the student have a chance to *demonstrate* learning, so both of you can take stock of progress. Some senior midwives prefer to concentrate on practical training and so have their apprentices take formal coursework or follow an external program (like Apprentice Academics, which includes written work and exams). As long as learning assessment occurs concurrently with hands-on, your structure is valid. This is especially critical if your state or midwifery organization has a qualifying examination.

It will help your apprentice tremendously if you and she meet weekly to discuss learning objectives, and to create closure in areas of accomplishment. For example, she may feel she needs more experience doing perineal support, but is totally confident in her ability to take heart tones. Confirm her assessment (if you can) and then adapt your labor routine accordingly. Remember that the apprentice is *there to learn, not to practice!* Her responsibilities should change continuously so she can achieve proficiency in all areas.

What about financial arrangements? These depend largely on the structure of your practice and your expectations of an apprentice. If you are working by yourself and have chosen someone fairly experienced to train up to partnership status, you might pay her expenses initially and increase her wage with her responsibilities. On the other hand, if you already have a partner and your apprentice is there strictly as a student, she might be expected to pay for her education.

Besides having an effect on finances, the structure of a practice also affects the dynamics between participants. There are a variety of possible practice arrangements; here is a sampling, with pros and cons:

1) Senior midwife and single apprentice.
   It is definitely economical for the midwife to practice solo and pay an apprentice a nominal sum to take major responsibility. But it is extremely stressful in the early stages, when the student is new.

2) Senior midwife and two apprentices, one senior and one junior.
   This arrangement has been discussed already as per its usefulness in helping the senior apprentice to consolidate learning, as she teaches the junior. Occasionally there are problems with the apprentices conspiring against the senior. Also training two students at once is ultimately more work and greater responsibility than just training one, even though you receive more assistance.

3) Two midwives and one apprentice.
   This can be a confusing arrangement for the student, particularly if the midwives involved have different styles of practice or management. It can also be hard on the midwives if the student attempts to pit them against each other. A benefit is that the apprentice is strictly in a student role, which prevents the midwives from imposing too much responsibility on her or casting her in a partnership role prematurely.

4) Two midwives and two apprentices.
   This arrangement is optimal in several respects. First, students have an opportunity to observe differing styles of

practice and compare notes. They have an equal voice in the practice. And the midwives can also compare notes on the students, double checking their assessments and opinions of each. The main drawback is that the number of persons involved creates a more complex interpersonal dynamic.

If you do train an apprentice from a solitary practice, you might enhance her learning by asking another midwife who is unencumbered to take your student on for a few births. This is particularly important if you have a small practice, or if your apprentice is pressing for more experience. It is of course wise to discuss your teaching plan and priorities with the other midwife, so she knows what to expect and is better able to complement your efforts.

Training an apprentice is a lot of work but it's worth it. It is both challenging and stimulating to you and your practice. Once you experience the satisfaction of teaching this way, you will probably do it on a continuous basis. And thus you will make an important contribution to the midwifery community, not just locally but internationally, in keeping the tradition of apprenticeship alive.

Peer Review

Peer review provides a mechanism for midwives to get together and review their practices. In a larger sense, peer review promotes quality assurance for consumers by encouraging safe and responsible caregiving. Exposure to the standards and practices of others in the field motivates participants to continually upgrade their knowledge and skills. Participants thus become accountable to one another, and ultimately to the profession at large.

Peer review is also known as chart review because it revolves around the discussion of difficult or challenging cases. In the event of a serious occurrence like fetal death, emergency review can forestall rumors or misunderstandings.

All it takes to start a peer review system is a group of midwives committed to regular attendance. Six to eight participants is ideal; ten is probably maximum. Meetings should take place every six to eight weeks. Each midwife participates as follows:

1. She states the number of normal births attended since the last meeting;
2. She reports fully on any births with complications, including her assessment of what could have been done differently;
3. She mentions all prenatal cases with risk factors, including those referred on to another provider;
4. She takes feedback from the group.

Since quality assurance is a major goal of peer review, it may be necessary to schedule educational workshops as follow up.

Probably the greatest benefit of peer review is self-regulation, i.e., the profession takes care of its own. Many states that have licensing or certification mechanisms either require or recommend peer review on an ongoing basis. This is because discipline through state bureaucratic channels is notoriously slow and encumbered by red tape. Peer review is also being recommended for physician groups, in response to the malpractice crisis. It is one way to weed out incompetent or irresponsible practitioners.

On one occasion recently, we held an emergency review to address a case where the parents complained about their outcome and had threatened to sue the midwife. After hearing details from both sides, we found in favor of the midwife, at the same time giving her suggestions to help prevent a similar occurrence in the future. We then issued a public statement supporting her management of the case, and no further action was taken by parents. This process is particularly appropriate if dissatisfied clients are talking around town.

It takes some courage to participate in peer review at first, especially if you have been isolated in your work. It is common to think that no other midwife thinks or does as you do, when in fact most midwives have a similar base of knowledge and experience. Peer review will improve your practice, and your communication with other midwives.

Student Evaluation: Assessment and Management Abilities

I. **Antepartum Management**

A. Obtains and records all data necessary for evaluation and risk assessment of the client/ couple:
1. Obtains a complete history by asking questions that elicit necessary information in the following areas:
   a. menstrual history
   b. medical, surgical history
   c. family history
   d. obstetrical history
   e. current medications

2. Reviews chart for:
   a. previous findings
   b. laboratory data
   c. treatment and effectiveness of previous management

3. Evaluates the present status of client including:
   a. determination of emotional well-being
   b. laboratory data
   c. recognition of need for genetic counseling
   d. ordering and interpreting appropriate laboratory and diagnostic tests and procedures

B. Assumes direct responsibility for the development of a plan of comprehensive, supportive care for the client and with the client.

C. Implements plan of care:
1. Interprets findings to client accurately, and in a way comprehensible to client.
2. Determines client's reaction to findings.
3. Acquaints client with alternative plans when possible, and determines client's preferences.
4. Encourages client to assume responsibility for her own health.
5. Prepares a defined needs/problems list with participation from client.
6. Evaluates, with corroboration from client, the achievement of health care goals and modifies plan of care appropriately.
7. Consults, collaborates and refers to appropriate members of the health care team.

II. **Management of Labor and Delivery**

A. Obtain interim history completely and accurately.

B. Assesses maternal condition:
1. Differentiates phases of labor by observing client behavior.
2. Shares information with client about care provided:
   a. explanation of examination procedures
   b. preparation for exams
   c. interpretation of clinical findings

3. Provides appropriate support for each stage of labor.
4. Recognizes abnormal progress in labor.
5. Consults with appropriate members of the health care team regarding any abnormalities detected during the process of labor.

C. Recognizes emergency situations and responds effectively:
1. Initiates emergency measures.
2. Reevaluates and modifies emergency treatment as indicated.

III. Immediate Postpartum

A. Assesses maternal condition, including:
1. Emotional status/bonding.
2. Physical stability.
3. Initiation of breastfeeding.

B. Assesses newborn condition, including:
1. Physical adjustment.
2. General appearance and behavior.

C. Develops a plan of comprehensive, supportive care with the client/family during the immediate postpartum period.

D. Implements plan of care:
1. Provides complete postpartum instructions.
2. Supports initial family adjustment.
3. Leaves a stable environment.

E. Recognizes signs of maternal and/or neonatal abnormality and consults or refers to appropriate members of the health care team.

IV. Subsequent Postpartum

A. Facilitates postpartum adjustments and continues to provide supportive, responsible care.
1. Makes followup visits as frequently as indicated.
2. Performs maternal examination at appropriate intervals to insure normalcy and healing.
3. Makes appropriate suggestions for minor postpartum problems.
4. Supports mother and baby in establishing breastfeeding and makes appropriate recommendations.
5. Recognizes problems with breastfeeding and makes appropriate recommendations.
6. Provides support and guidance for postpartum emotional changes and makes appropriate referrals.

B. Helps client/family identity postpartum health care needs and discusses with them the following:
1. Aspects of sexuality during the postpartum period.
2. Available methods of contraception.
3. Newborn care.
4. Community resources available for new families.

C. Demonstrates understanding and supportive skills necessary to help families cope with mal-formed infants, mental retardation, fetal or neonatal death.

V. Recording/Charting

A. Accurate and complete.

B. Concise and easily readable.

C. Clearly communicates plan of management to other appropriate health care providers.

Adapted by the California Association of Midwives from *Method 6,* a midwifery challenge route available through the California Board of Registered Nurses.

CHAPTER 9

The Long Run

This final chapter will focus on the midwife again, this time in terms of the many adaptations involved in continual practice. No doubt about it, midwifery is a *way of life*, both grueling and transformative. The intensive and unpredictable nature of this occupation soon persuades the novice that midwifery is a whole lot more than the joy of catching babies. It works a woman on all levels, either disintegrating her or bringing her to essence.

The dynamic of caregiving is such that intuitive assessments are constantly being made, not just by the midwife but by her clients as well. In order to entrust themselves to her care, parents will scrutinize the midwife most carefully: her appearance, personality and character. At the same time, she works to cultivate an utterly candid atmosphere so that care will be complete. Thus each prenatal visit provides an opportunity to deepen communication and develop mutual trust by sharing impressions, thoughts and feelings. But this doesn't afford the midwife much personal privacy, and so can be draining at times.

On the other hand, the overzealous beginner may be so carried away by the excitement of caregiving that she totally loses perspective. There is a big difference between compulsive caregiving and genuine service, the latter involving a critical sense of appropriate involvement. In order to render service, the midwife must be sensitive enough to pick up her cues and respond without ego.

To take this premise a step further is to see the difference between making assessments and passing judgment. The midwife who cares compulsively is sure to have some heavy expectations in the bargain, often projecting her own needs onto her client. Unchecked, she will draw both the power and dependence of a client and her partner if they allow it. In contrast, the simple ability to make assessments means no strings attached, and it's the key to remaining sane in this powerful profession.

Midwives play some interesting roles in an attempt to sustain unselfish orientation; the nun-role, the super-student role, the big-mama role, etc. A steady diet of spontaneity and discretion demands maturity; it helps if the midwife has faced some of her demons and has developed a sense of humor. Still, many fine midwives struggle with some role-playing in the beginning and most quickly outgrow it through initiatory experience.

The main purpose of this closing chapter is to explore the ways in which practicing midwifery can affect a woman's personal life. What many beginners don't realize is that midwifery will change them so dramatically that all their relationships will be affected. There may be major upheavals in love, particularly if the midwife's mate does not feel ready or willing to open up and share on the levels which she must access in order to practice. Men often feel the midwife's intensity as pressure to communicate, implicit in her character and her way of speaking, touching, nurturing. It's been said that "midwifery is the acid test of a relationship" and there is certainly truth in this.

Sometimes men react with jealousy if their way of making a living seems less principled or exciting. This calls for some mutual exploration of personal and career goals, both long and short term. And it's important that the midwife acknowledge the incredible demands that her work places on her mate, as well as the stresses placed on her family. Running off at inopportune moments can be hard on small children, and really rough on the nursing baby. Not to mention the obvious; more than once I've been interrupted by the phone call in the middle of a lovemaking that was either fantastic or desperately needed. In fact, the phone rings constantly, much to the chagrin of my family. Occasionally I find myself saying as I reach for the receiver, "Don't let this be a heavy one" or even half seriously, "I hope no one's in labor." Usually this is because my children need attention, my partner needs love, I have shopping or cleaning to do or want simply to relax without interruptions. Being on-call means keeping one's self, home, and family in a constant state of readiness. All midwives should consider (and reconsider) limiting their practice to a level that is workable overall. For me, this is four to six births a month, which gives me time to integrate new learning from each birthing, catch up on sleep, get the family back in kilter, and rejuvenate myself before going on.

It's interesting to note how the same principles which apply to smooth labor and birthing also apply to smooth practice. The plateau phenomenon, or stopping to integrate, is basic to midwifery work. And so are the frustrations which come from trying to force labor to fit a preconceived pattern; the continual battle of impatience versus forbearance.

Every midwife needs some way to help herself when she is floundering. She needs to learn how to take as well as give, to humble herself to wise counsel, to be receptive to her mate and to listen well to the experience of other midwives. Mostly though, she needs to be able to heal herself through her own recuperative and psychic powers. An intrinsic part of midwifery practice *is* the development of psychic faculties, as intuitions are validated by events and outcomes. At first the midwife may feel rather uncomfortable with the sharpening of her intuitive perception. But sharpen it should in this line of work, so that management is based on the actual situation, rather than on theory or the general recommendations of others.

Part of the task of nurturing this psychic faculty and protecting the delicacy in oneself

Midwives all, out for some fun!

A pregnant midwife, surrounded by friends and former clients at a celebration in her honor.

when it begins to emerge, is to take time for relaxation and emotional free-flow in one's day to day life. The need for solitude and reflection may be difficult to manage with little children, but older kids can be made to understand that "mom needs to be alone for a while." As for the demanding mate, explain that some privacy is crucial to your ability to love and give to the family. With smaller children you can find childcare, or rotate care with other mothers.

Another essential to maintaining your practice is energy conservation. Sometimes intuition will suggest an appropriate course of action in a tough situation, but you'll find yourself without the strength to carry it out. It's been said repeatedly that power is one of our natural enemies; in midwifery it's power derived from increasing clarity that can lead a woman beyond her capacity. Overextension, even when the calling is clear, is bound to create serious problems. Here is where you must cultivate ability to *delegate responsibility* to students, apprentices, other midwives. Opportunities for involvement will only increase as midwives become high profile politically. Learn to work to your capacity, and then say "no."

Other ways to conserve energy include passing clients along, whenever you find yourself at case load capacity. Learn to recognize signs of burnout such as faulty communication with your clients, general absent-mindedness or distraction, or in progressed cases, hysteria. Midwives need vacations! This means setting up a support system strong enough to allow for your absence. If your partnership is stable and reliable you can get away and truly forget about midwifery for a while.

It is also important for the midwife to develop her professional identity. Join local, state and national midwifery organizations and participate on a regular basis. This can help you overcome feelings of isolation, particularly if you have a rural practice. Or if you work in a highly competitive environment, it will help you to rise above petty concerns or hassles and recall your original dedication to your work. I remember the first time I attended a national midwifery convention; what an incredible awakening of identity and power! And it was also reassuring to find that midwives had the same basic strengths and weaknesses, no matter where they came from!

As many states formalize standards for continuing education, attendance at group events becomes mandatory. This is good because it helps the midwife to stay abreast of the latest information, which can inspire her to try new approaches.

Another possible solution for burnout is to try a new form of practicing. Particularly if you have been working with only an apprentice for assistance, try a partnership or group practice situation. This can alleviate pressure and help you regain perspective and strength once again.

Sometimes midwives forget to use their knowledge of good health in their own lives. For example, nutrition should be optimal on clinic days and in the midst of a long labor watch. Sometimes the mental deliberations regarding a woman's prenatal course or upcoming birthing can take so much energy that extra rest and sleep are required.

Maintaining oneself also means learning to separate the threads of personal problems from those belonging to others. Often this is not a rational process at all, but revelation through contemplative reflection. A relaxed mind can gently sort through thoughts and feelings, without wasting energy pushing for a solution or anxiously awaiting an answer. And this brings us to the crux of the matter, the need for midwives to "bottom out" and get down to essence periodically. Emptying oneself of thoughts and feelings makes room for new insight and direction. This is so important! Although midwifery is ideally a balance of service and self-expression, the on-call routine definitely tends to interfere with basic narcissism. Developing personal interests, new skills, artistry, is essential to keeping one's humanity and humility. A midwife's prime offering to others is her uniqueness, her individuality and independent perspective. And in order to keep this alive it must be nourished. The midwife should find pleasure in many things and in the

Support Your Local Midwife!

Here are some suggestions for keeping midwifery alive in your community:

1. Since the midwife's fee is usually modest to begin with, *consider giving her a bonus if you can possibly afford it*. All told, the average midwife makes about five dollars an hour! Consider the limited services available from a physician and the *astronomical* charges. Particularly if your midwife assisted you above and beyond her usual duties, help her out if you can.

2. If you cannot afford to pay extra, you might *help your midwife with childcare, clerical work or housekeeping*. In the past, midwives were totally supported by their communities; all needs completely taken care of. Midwives have traditionally been grandmothers (past childbearing and with few responsibilities) but today, due to social configura-

tions, midwives are coming from the younger generation. This is why childcare is so important; not necessarily during a birth but afterwards, so the midwife can catch up on sleep or chores. Even if you only volunteer once, it will be greatly appreciated.

3. Understand that in many states, midwives are under-fire politically and may need support for legislative efforts. *Contact local or state midwifery associations to see how you can help*. Perhaps you can make a donation, or send notes to your representatives, write letters to the editor of your newspaper or help with rallies. Let the public know how much having a midwife meant to you!

4. *Tell your friends*. Refer them to appropriate reading material. Answer their questions, and inspire them to investigate alternatives. *With your help, midwifery will not only survive, but flourish!*

resourcefulness to relate broadly. She should be willing to be repeatedly reborn, to be both transformed and transformer.

Take care not to become jaded over the years. Just when you think you've seen it all, some totally new configuration occurs to set you back on your heels. Tune up your sensitivities so that intuitive directives keep coming through, and be grateful for higher intelligence. Also something I've not mentioned directly, but which has been the foundation of this work: the transformative power of love! This is intrinsic to the act of willing, conscious conception and the act of giving birth. Midwives and all birth assistants, don't forget this! Be who you are, and do what you can to keep your love alive.

HEART & HANDS

Our deep appreciation to all of you who have allowed your images to be used in this book. Your contribution to better births for others is of great value, and we thank you!

Elizabeth Davis
Linda Harrison
Suzanne Arms-Wimberley

"SCHOOL OF MIDWIFERY",
East Glamorgan General Hospital,
Church Village,
NR. PONTYPRIDD,
Mid. Glam.

Appendix A

Resource List

American Academy of Husband-Coached
  Childbirth
P.O. Box 5224
Sherman Oaks, CA 91413
(Bradley classes and referrals to educators,
  teacher training)

American College of Home Obstetrics
2821 Rose Street
Franklin Park, IL 60131
(Physicians favoring homebirth practice)

American College of Nurse-Midwives
1522 K Street, Suite 1000
Washington, DC 20005
(Professional organization for nurse-midwives,
  publish newsletter and journal)

American Society for Psychoprophylaxis
  in Childbirth
1840 Wilson Blvd., Suite 204
Arlington, VA 22201
(Lamaze headquarters, referrals to educators)

Association for Childbirth at Home International
  (ACHI)
P.O. Box 430
Glendale, CA 91209
(Homebirth classes, referrals, leader training)

Association of Radical Midwives (ARM)
c/o The Drive
Wimbledon, London
ENGLAND SW20
(Excellent newsletter)

Birth
3 Cambridge Center
Cambridge, MA 02142
(Excellent professional publication,
  $22.50 annually)

Birth and Life Bookstore
P.O. Box 70625
Seattle, WA 98107
(Extensive and complete selection of books)

Birth Gazette
42 The Farm
Summertown, TN 38483
(Midwifery periodical, edited by Ina May Gaskin,
  $25 annually)

Birthworks
42 Tallowood Drive
Medford, NJ 08055
(Childbirth education and teacher training)

Cascade Birthing Supplies
P.O. Box 12203
Salem, OR 97309
(Birthing and midwifery supplies, books)

Casarean Education, Prevention and Concern
  (C/SEC)
22 Forest Road
Framington, MA 01701
(Newsletter, support)

The Complete Mother
P.O. Box 209
Minot, ND 58702
(Magazine of breastfeeding, birth, and mothering,
  $12 annually)

Continental Friends of Midwives
P.O. Box 686
Minot, ND 58702
(Consumer organization, politically active)

Home-Oriented Maternity Experience
511 New York Ave.
Takoma Park, MD 20012
(Meetings, referrals, training)

Informed Birth and Parenting
P.O. Box 3675
Ann Arbor, MI 48106
(Newsletter, referrals, teacher training,
  publications)

International Cesarean Awareness Network
P.O. Box 152
Syracuse, NY 13210
(Newsletter, support)

International Childbirth Educators Association
  (ICEA)
Box 20048
Minneapolis, MN 55420
(Bookstore, conferences)

International Confederation of Midwives (ICM)
10 Barclay Mow Passage
Chiswick, ENGLAND W4 4PH
(International midwives organization)

Journal of Nurse-Midwifery
655 Avenue of the Americas
New York, NY 10010
(Official publication of the American College of
Nurse-Midwives, $40 annually)

La Leche League, International (LLLI)
9616 Minneapolis Ave.
Franklin Park, IL 60131
(Publications, referrals to local representatives)

Maternity Center Association
42 E. 92nd Street
New York, NY 10028
(Teaching aids, Birth Atlas)

Midwifery Today
P.O. Box 2672
Eugene, OR 97402
(An interesting and diverse publication,
$30 annually, published quarterly)

Midwives Alliance of North America (MANA)
P.O. Box 1121
Bristol, VA 24203
(Newsletter, conventions, professional
organization for all midwives)

Moonflower Birthing Supply
P.O. Box 128
Louisville, CO 80027
(Books and supplies of parents and midwives)

Mothering Magazine
P.O. Box 1690
Santa Fe, NM 87504
(Excellent publication for anyone interested in
birth and parenting, $22 annually)

National Association of Childbirth Assistants
205 Copco Lane
San Jose, CA 95123
(Training, referrals)

National Association of Parents and Professionals
for Safe Alternatives in Childbirth (NAPSAC)
Route 1, Box 646
Marble Hill, MO 63764
(Newsletter, conferences, directory of alternative
providers)

Naturopath
1410 NW 13th Street, Suite 2
Gainesville, FL 32601
(Books and supplies for birth and parenting)

FOR CANADA

Alberta Midwifery Task Force
c/o Sandra Botting
507 Pavender Road NW
Calgary, Alberta
CANADA T2K 3M3
(Consumer group, promotes midwifery)

Midwives Association of Canada
2043 Ferndale
Vancouver, BC
CANADA V5L 1YC
(National midwives organization)

Appendix B

Medical & Personal History

Please fill out this medical and personal history very carefully. When you come for your next visit we will go over the history together and discuss any questions that you might have. Just leave blank any technical terms or questions with which you are not familiar.

Name _____   Date of Birth _____ Height _____

Partner _____   Usual Weight (nonpregnant) _____

Address _____   Weight at Birth _____

_____   Baby's Father's Weight at Birth _____

Phones _____

Directions to your home: _____

_____

Names and phone of relatives or friends who can contact you quickly: _____

_____

Drug Allergies and Food Sensitivities: _____

Blood Type _____ Rh _____   VDRL: _____

Baby's Father's Blood Type & Rh _____   Rubella Titer: _____

Date _____ Hct _____   GC Culture: _____

Date _____ Hct _____   HIV Testing: _____

Date _____ Hct _____   Other Lab: _____

PMP _____ LMP _____ EDD _____ Gravida _____ Para _____ Abortions _____

Miscarriages _____ D&C _____ Transfusions _____

Please read the following list and circle any condition which you have experienced. In the space below also record the date, treatment and any follow-up you received. Also feel free to list any other important condition.

Kidney Disease	Allergies/Sensitivities	Emotional Problems	Drug Reactions
Diabetes	Phlebitis/Varicosities	Rh Problems	P.I.D.
Hypertension	Thyroid Problems	Asthma/Hayfever	Hemorrhoids
Epilepsy	TB or TB Medication	Hepatitis	Skin Problems
Heart Disease	Venereal Disease	Anemia	G.I. Problems

_____

_____

_____

_____

Excluding childbirth, have you ever been hospitalized? Please indicate the date, reason and treatment.

_____

_____

Have you ever had any serious accidents, injuries, or fractures? _____

_____

_____

Have you ever had a bleeding problem or a hemorrhage? _____

_____

_____

Is there any hereditary disease or condition in your family such as diabetes, cancer, heart disease, hypertension? (List, and indicate which relative.)

_____

_____

_____

How many days do you menstruate? _____

How far apart are your periods? (Regular or irregular?) _____

Amount of flow: heavy, medium or light? _____

Generally, how do you feel about your period? _____

_____

_____

Please list all methods of contraception you have used and how long you used them. Begin with the last method first.

Method   **Dates**   **Problems**

_____

_____

_____

_____

Please list any infections, abnormalities, surgery or problems you have had concerning your breasts, ovaries, fallopian tubes, uterus, cervix or vagina. Include such things as cysts, biopsies, endometriosis, fibroids, chlamydia infections, pelvic inflammatory disease, venereal warts, etc. Give dates and treatment.

_____

_____

190

What were your mother's labors like? Were they consistently fast or prolonged? Were babies consistently late or early? _____

_____

If there are any twins or triplets in your family or your mate's, please list the relationship and specify how many sets there are.

_____

_____

How many times have you ever been pregnant including now? _____

If you have ever had an abortion, please give the following information: dates; how far along in the pregnancy in weeks; method used; any pain/infection afterwards; emotional trauma.

_____

_____

If you have ever had a miscarriage, please give the following information: dates; at how many weeks did it occur; did you go to a physician or hospital; did you have a D&C; any medication? _____

_____

_____

If you are Rh negative, did you receive RhoGam shots after your abortions or miscarriages? _____

_____

Please list your last *two* menstrual periods and indicate if you are absolutely sure of the dates or estimating.

Last Menstrual Period _____ Previous Menstrual Period _____

Do you know when you ovulated? _____ Do you know when

you may have conceived? _____

Have you felt the baby move? _____ Date _____ Weeks Pregnant? _____

Date fetal heart beat was first detected: _____

Was this baby planned? Please comment if not: _____

_____

_____

Have you had any of the following since you've become pregnant: herpes, rubella (measles), hepatitis, bladder infection. Give dates.

_____

_____

Since you became pregnant, have you had any x-rays of any type? Give dates and type. _____

_____

_____

What prenatal care have you had up to the present? Please list doctors, clinics, and hospitals where you have had care, what was done, and especially if you have had any lab work done or special testing.

_____

_____

_____

_____

Please check any of the following symptoms you have had with this pregnancy. Give dates, severity and any treatment given.

Abdominal Pain _____

Bleeding, Spotting _____

Constipation _____

Dizziness, Fainting _____

Edema, Swelling _____

Fatigue _____

Unusual Weight Gain in Short Time _____

Headaches _____

Gastric Upsets _____

Nausea, Vomiting _____

Sleeping Problems _____

Visual Problems _____

Urinary Disorders _____

Vaginal Infections _____

Other Problems _____

During the three months prior to conception and during this pregnancy, have you undergone any therapy or used drugs to treat a medical or emotional condition? Include use of *any* drug, especially those given just to pregnant women such as sleeping aids, diuretics, tranquilizers, appetite suppressants, anti-nausea pills, antibiotics, etc.

_____

_____

_____

_____

If you use any drug regularly or frequently, whether it is over the counter or prescription, please specify:

_____

If you have used any "illegal" drugs, please specify what you have used, the frequency and the dates of use since your last period. If you smoke marijuana, try to estimate your use during this pregnancy.

_____

_____

To what extent do you drink alcohol? _____

_____

Do you smoke cigarettes? _____ If you ever smoked, indicate when and how much. When did you quit?

_____

Do you work or spend a lot of time around volatile chemicals, paints, pesticides, adhesives, smoke, etc?

_____

Do you have or take care of a cat? _____

_____

Are you employed?_____ If yes, please describe where you work and what you do, and how many hours you work daily. Is work stressful you?

_____

_____

_____

_____

When do you plan to discontinue working? Comment on your present plans for going back to work after your baby is born/childcare arrangements.

_____

_____

_____

_____

Do you go to school? _____ Fulltime? _____

How much time do you usually sleep each night? _____

Do you have an opportunity for rest periods or a nap each day? _____

Do you sleep well? _____

In general, how have you felt with this pregnancy? _____

_____

_____

_____

What do you do to keep in shape physically? Are you doing any special exercises? Do you meditate or do yoga?

_____

_____

Do you feel that your sexual relationship has changed appreciably since becoming pregnant? _____

_____

_____

Have you ever been sexually or physically abused? (You may respond verbally if you like.) _____

_____

_____

Please list the people you plan to invite to your birth: _____

_____

_____

Do you plan to breastfeed this baby? Do you have any idea how long you will nurse this child? _____

_____

Have you faced any opposition to your plans for a home birth? Describe: _____

_____

_____

_____

Do you have any medical insurance? What does it cover re: pregnancy and birth? _____

_____

Please give some thought to the following questions and write your ideas. If you and your partner are together, each of you should answer. Read all questions before answering.

Why do you want to have this baby at home? _____

_____

_____

_____

_____

Partner: _____

_____

_____

_____

_____

What do you see as the duties or responsibilities of your midwife? _____

_____

_____

Partner: _____

_____

_____

There are some things which can go wrong without previous warning during labor and birth and after. If you are a low risk woman, the chances of unpredictable complications are low. However, if such complications should occur, you or your baby might be at greater risk because of being at home. There are risks involved with childbirth just as there are with driving a car, some of which will probably never be eradicated no matter what our state of technology. There is a certain subset of risks involved in having your baby in a hospital as well as in your home (or in an alternative birth center or birthing house). If you opt for the risks involved in birthing at home you need to find out what they are and how they can be dealt with. Please comment on what you know about risks and complications and how you feel about them:

_____

_____

_____

_____

_____

Partner: _____

_____

_____

_____

How do you feel about going to the hospital to deliver if your midwife feels that complications are arising?

_____

_____

Partner: _____

_____

How do you think you might deal with the problem of a baby or mother who suffered permanent injury or died at home?

_____

_____

_____

_____

Appendix B (cont'd)

Partner: _____

_____

_____

What do you think are the benefits of having your baby at home? _____

_____

_____

Partner: _____

_____

_____

Please add any comments or thoughts that you think might be important for your midwife to know about you:

_____

_____

_____

_____

_____

Appendix C

History of Previous Pregnancies

Please comment on your prenatal care with earlier pregnancies: _____
_____
_____

Did you attend any childbirth education classes? _____
_____

If you have ever had a premature birth and lost the baby or if you have had a stillbirth or the death of a young infant, please tell me about your experience. I am sorry to bring up painful memories. Was a diagnosis made?
_____
_____
_____
_____

Please indicate the number of normal births you have had: give the dates of birth, the time and indicate if it was early or late for dates.

Name	Date/Time	Due Date

Where did your other births take place? _____
_____

How much weight did you gain with each pregnancy? _____
_____

How much did each of your babies weigh? _____
_____

If you breastfed, how long did you nurse each one? _____
_____

How long were you in labor for each of your babies? _____

_____

First stage _____ hrs   2nd stage _____   3rd stage _____

First stage _____ hrs   2nd stage _____   3rd stage _____

First stage _____ hrs   2nd stage _____   3rd stage _____

If you were not induced, how did your labor begin? _____

_____

_____

Were you allowed to eat during labor? _____ What did you eat? _____

_____

Were you allowed to drink or eat ice? _____

Did you vomit? _____

Please list all the drugs which were used at your previous births. Try to remember for each child, both before and after the birth. Include sleeping medication, muscle relaxants, analgesics, painkillers, tranquilizers, labor stimulants like Pitocin, anesthetics like caudal block, epidural, pudendal, etc.

_____

_____

_____

_____

Was your labor induced? Do you know why? _____

_____

Was an IV used? Was Pitocin added? _____

_____

If a fetal monitor was used, please specify whether it was internal or external. How long was it used? How do you feel about its use?

_____

_____

_____

Were your membranes (waterbag) ruptured by someone or did they rupture spontaneously? Do you remember how far dilated you were at the time?

_____

_____

Was your baby born head first or breech? _____

A few babies are born facing up or in the posterior position. Have you had a posterior delivery or was it necessary for the doctor to use forceps to rotate your baby?

_____

_____

Did you spend most of your labor in bed? _____

Did you give birth in the lithotomy position (on your back, feet in stirrups)? _____

What positions do you think would be more comfortable? _____

_____

_____

Were you able to help push your baby out? Could you feel contractions and bear down or had you received medication which prevented this?

_____

_____

_____

Did you have an episiotomy? Did you tear? Did you have stitches? _____

_____

_____

Did your stitches bother you much? _____

Were forceps used at previous births? Do you know why? _____

_____

Were you told that your baby was in distress at any time? _____

_____

Do you know if there was meconium staining (the baby had had a bowel movement into the amniotic water during the course of labor which sometimes means danger)?

_____

_____

Did your baby need any special resuscitation at birth? _____

_____

Do you know the baby's apgar scores? _____

When was the cord cut? _____

Did your baby need intensive care of any kind? _____

_____

When was the first time you were allowed to nurse your baby? _____

_____

Did you have rooming-in? _____

Did the baby nurse well? _____

Did you have to follow a schedule? _____

Was the baby separated from you? How soon after birth? _____

_____

Did the baby develop any problems while in the hospital or the first two weeks at home? _____

_____

Did the baby get jaundiced? _____

What treatment was used for the jaundice? Was the baby hospitalized again? _____

_____

Did you yourself have any complications during the labor or after the birth? _____

_____

_____

_____

Were there any problems with the birth of the placenta? Did the doctor do a manual exploration of your uterus or use any equipment at this time?

_____

_____

_____

_____

Did you hemorrhage or bleed heavily after the birth or in the first few weeks after? Was any treatment given?

_____

_____

_____

Did you have any infections associated with the childbirth or breastfeeding? _____

_____

How long did you stay in the hospital? _____

Did you suffer from postpartum depression? What did you do? _____

_____

_____

How would you describe your birth experience? Were things done to you or your baby that you did not like?

_____

_____

_____

_____

Do you have strong feelings about circumcision for male babies? _____

_____

What about eye medications an hour after birth? _____

_____

What are the father's impressions of the birth/s? _____

_____

_____

_____

_____

Other thoughts and comments: _____

_____

_____

_____

_____

_____

_____

_____

_____

Appendix D

Prenatal Care Record NAME _____

LMP _____ EDD _____

PHONE _____

Visit	Date	Weeks Gestation	Urine	Weight	Pulse/BP	FHR	Position	Fundus	
									Pelvis:

Notes:

									Diet/Exercise

Notes:

									Diet/Exercise

Notes:

									Diet/Exercise

Notes:

Appendix E

Labor Record

NAME _____

Date _____ Time labor began _____ Initial events _____

Baby's position _____ Usual FHR _____

Membranes _____ Clear? _____

EDD _____ Concerns: _____

Observations on arrival _____

Time	BP/Pulse	Fetal heart tones	In/out	Contractions	Vaginal exam

Comments

Time	BP/Pulse	Fetal heart tones	In/out	Contractions	Vaginal exam

Comments

Time	BP/Pulse	Fetal heart tones	In/out	Contractions	Vaginal exam

Comments

Time	BP/Pulse	Fetal heart tones	In/out	Contractions	Vaginal exam

Comments

Time	BP/Pulse	Fetal heart tones	In/out	Contractions	Vaginal exam

Comments

Time	BP/Pulse	Fetal heart tones	In/out	Contractions	Vaginal exam

Comments

Time	BP/Pulse	Fetal heart tones	In/out	Contractions	Vaginal exam

Comments

Time	BP/Pulse	Fetal heart tones	In/out	Contractions	Vaginal exam

Comments

Appendix F

Transport Record From Home Delivery

MIDWIFE _____ DATE/TIME _____

MOTHER'S NAME _____ FATHER'S NAME _____

ADDRESS _____

EDD _____ MOTHER'S AGE _____ GRAVIDA _____ PARA _____

PRENATAL HISTORY:

   Gestational age 1st visit _____ Weight gain _____ Usual BP _____

   Urine _____ Edema _____ Pelvimetry _____ Fundus _____

   Hct _____ ABO & Rh _____

COMMENTS:

LABOR HISTORY

   Began labor _____ Initial events _____ Midwife arrived at _____

   General observations: _____ Vaginal exam: _____

COMMENTS:

COURSE OF LABOR:

   Inactive labor _____ Active labor _____ Pushing _____

   Ruptured membranes _____ How? _____ Meconium? _____

   Fetal response to labor: _____

   _____

COMMENTS:

REASONS FOR TRANSPORT:

Appendix G

Birth Record: Mother

Name _____

Phone _____ Age _____

Gravida _____ Para _____ EDD _____ Date of Birth _____ Time _____

Labor Summary

1st stage _____ hrs   2nd stage _____ mins   3rd stage _____ mins

Membranes

Time ruptured _____ Spontaneously or surgically; Waters clear or stained

Placenta	Round	Adherent clot	Cord insertion:	Central
	Irregular	Missing cotyledons		Marginal
	Succenturiate lobe	Calcium deposits		Velamentous

Time cord cut _____ Number of vessels in cord _____

Perineum

Lacerations _____ Repairs _____

Estimated Blood Loss _____ Treatment _____

Delivery Position _____ Baby's Position _____

Comments/Problems _____

_____

_____

Birth Record: Baby

Name _____ Sex _____ Weight _____ Length _____ Chest _____ Head _____

Apgar   1 minute _____   5 minutes _____   Suctioning? _____

Resuscitation? _____

Molding, Caput, Hematoma _____ Eye Medication _____

Nursing _____

Unusual Behavior Problems or Abnormalities _____

_____

_____

If problems develop and you call in, give time of birth, sex, weight, Apgar, respirations per minute, temperature, heart rate and describe symptoms.

Appendix H

Newborn Examination

DATE   APGARS (one minute _____) (five minutes _____)

SEX   WT.

APGAR	0	1	2
Heart rate	Absent	Under 100	Over 100
Respirations	Absent	Slow (Irr.)	Good (cry)
Muscletone	Limp	Some flexion	Active
Color	Blue/white	Blue hands or feet	Pink totally
Response to nasal catheter	None	Grimace	Sneeze or cough

TEMPERATURE

TOTAL LENGTH

HEAD (O.F.)

CHEST

GENERAL APPEARANCE
  (Activity, tone, cry, edema)

SKIN
  (Color, staining, petechiae)

HEAD, NECK
  (Moulding, caput, fontanelles)

EYES
  (Red reflex, medication instilled)

ENT
  (Lips, palate, ear placement)

THORAX
  (Retractions)

LUNGS
  (Rales, grunting, cry)

HEART
  (Femoral pulses)

ABDOMEN
  (Cord, masses)

GENITALS
  (Testes descended, clitoris)

EXTREMITIES
  (Clavicles, hip abduction)

REFLEXES
  (Moro, grasp, sucking, swallowing)

ANUS

COMMENTS

Appendix I

⌂ Examination First Hours

CLINICAL ESTIMATION OF GESTATIONAL AGE
An Approximation Based on Published Data*

WEEKS GESTATION

PHYSICAL FINDINGS		20	21	22	23	24	25	26	27	28	29	30	31	32	33	34	35	36	37	38	39	40	41	42	43	44	45	46	47	48
VERNIX		APPEARS			COVERS BODY, THICK LAYER														ON BACK, SCALP, IN CREASES		SCANT, IN CREASES			NO VERNIX					
BREAST TISSUE AND AREOLA		AREOLA & NIPPLE BARELY VISIBLE / NO PALPABLE BREAST TISSUE													AREOLA RAISED		1-2 MM NODULE	3-5 MM	5-6 MM		7-10 MM		7-12 MM					
EAR	FORM	FLAT, SHAPELESS														BEGINNING INCURVING SUPERIOR		INCURVING UPPER 2/3 PINNAE			WELL-DEFINED INCURVING TO LOBE								
	CARTILAGE	PINNA SOFT, STAYS FOLDED												CARTILAGE SCANT RETURNS SLOWLY FROM FOLDING				THIN CARTILAGE SPRINGS BACK FROM FOLDING				PINNA FIRM, REMAINS ERECT FROM HEAD							
SOLE CREASES		SMOOTH SOLES T CREASES											1-2 ANTERIOR CREASES		2-3 ANTERIOR CREASES		CREASES ANTERIOR 2/3 SOLE		CREASES INVOLVING HEEL			DEEPER CREASES OVER ENTIRE SOLE							
SKIN	THICKNESS & APPEARANCE	THIN, TRANSLUCENT SKIN, PLETHORIC, VENULES OVER ABDOMEN EDEMA										SMOOTH THICKER NO EDEMA						PINK			SOME DES-QUAMATION PALE PINK		THICK, PALE, DESQUAMATION OVER ENTIRE BODY					
NAIL PLATES		AP-PEAR										NAILS TO FINGER TIPS								FEW VESSELS			NAILS EXTEND WELL BEYOND FINGER TIPS					
HAIR		APPEARS ON HEAD			EYE BROWS & LASHES			FINE, WOOLLY, BUNCHES OUT FROM HEAD										SILKY, SINGLE STRANDS LAYS FLAT						PRECEDING HAIRLINE OR LOSS OF BABY HAIR SHORT, FINE UNDERNEATH					
LANUGO		AP-PEARS		COVERS ENTIRE BODY											VANISHES FROM FACE		PRESENT ON SHOULDERS					NO LANUGO					
GENITALIA	TESTES								TESTES PALPABLE IN INGUINAL CANAL								IN UPPER SCROTUM					IN LOWER SCROTUM					
	SCROTUM										FEW RUGAE					RUGAE, ANTERIOR PORTION			RUGAE COVER		PENDULOUS					
	LABIA & CLITORIS								PROMINENT CLITORIS LABIA MAJORA SMALL WIDELY SEPARATED							LABIA MAJORA LARGER NEARLY COVERED CLITORIS			LABIA MINORA & CLITORIS COVERED							
SKULL FIRMNESS		BONES ARE SOFT								SOFT TO 1" FROM ANTERIOR FONTANELLE						SPONGY AT EDGES OF FON-TANELLE CENTER FIRM		BONES HARD SUTURES EASILY DISPLACED			BONES HARD, CANNOT BE DISPLACED					
POSTURE	RESTING	HYPOTONIC LATERAL DECUBITUS					HYPOTONIC				BEGINNING FLEXION THIGH		STRONGER HIP FLEXION		FROG-LIKE		FLEXION ALL LIMBS		HYPERTONIC			VERY HYPERTONIC					
RECOIL - LEG		NO RECOIL							NO RECOIL			PARTIAL RECOIL					PROMPT RECOIL									
ARM		NO RECOIL										BEGIN FLEXION NO RE-COIL			PROMPT RECOIL MAY BE INHIBITED				PROMPT RECOIL AFTER 30" INHIBITION					

207

Appendix J

Postpartum Care

NAME _____

PHONE _____

	Breasts/nipples & Breastfeeding	Perineum sutures	Lochia	Uterus	Baby's cord	Jaundice Baby behavior
1st HOME VISIT DATE						
SUGGESTIONS:						
2nd HOME VISIT DATE						
FIRST PHONE CALL DATE						
SECOND PHONE CALL DATE						

	Breastfeeding	Uterus	Vaginal exam	Lochia	Parenting
3 WEEK CHECKUP DATE			Cervix Muscle tone		
6 WEEK CHECKUP DATE			Cervix Muscle tone		
BIRTH CONTROL?					

Appendix K

Postpartum Instructions

1. Let us know if you soak more than one pad in 20 minutes – massage your uterus firmly to re-contract it, and if bleeding doesn't stop, go into the hospital.

2. Check your uterus for firmness several times a day, for three days at least.

3. Notice if your flow has any bad odor (it should smell like your period) – and report to us.

4. Take your temperature 2 times daily for at least four days.

5. Drink lots of water (about three quarts daily to establish milk flow) and make one quart of that a mixture of shepherd's purse and comfrey tea (for healing and bleeding control).

6. If you've had stitches, soak them in (or use compresses of) comfrey, golden seal and ginger tea – three or four times daily.

7. Clean your baby's cord stump carefully with peroxide every few hours (or at each diaper change). Pay special attention to the folds where cord joins skin.

8. Notice your baby's color while in good light (by the window) – if you notice any yellow tinge to the skin, let us know. If the baby seems suddenly very yellow, not just the face but extremities as well, call your pediatrician – your baby may need a jaundice test.

9. Don't hesitate to call us if anything seems unusual or troublesome with the baby.

10. Get lots of rest, sleep when the baby sleeps, eat lots of good food with plenty of iron to replenish lost blood, and ask visitors for real help – like doing your dishes or laundry. Work into activity slowly, and you won't have any sudden breakdowns later.

11. Try to take the parenting one day at a time – call if you need to.

Appendix L

The Midwife's Kit

fetascope
watch, with second hand
blood pressure cuff
stethoscope
2 curved hemostats
1 pair scissors with blunt points
1 pair scissors with sharp points
1 needleholder
3 mosquito forceps
1 ring forceps
stainless steel cord clamps (Hazeltine)
stainless steel instrument tray with cover
sterile gloves
regular exam gloves
5cc syringes
3cc syringes
1½ inch, 21 gauge needles (injections)
½ inch, 23 gauge needles (suturing)
suture material (3-0 chromic, or 4-0)
lidocaine anesthetic
pitocin
methergine
tetracycline or erythromycin eye drops
nitrazine paper
urine testing sticks
plastic disposable amnihooks
DeLee mucus trap (either glass or plastic disposables)
cord blood tubes
bulb syringe
Betadine solution
alcohol prep pads
4 x 4 sterile gauze pads, or topper sponges
water bottle
heating pad
plasticised or fiberglass tape measure
infant scales (hanging fish-scale type)
oxygen system with infant resuscitation unit (Hope II or Air-Shields)
IV equipment (optional)
herbs: shepherd's purse, comfrey, blue cohosh, liquorice root, hops, scullcap, chamomile
herbal tinctures: shepherd's purse, blue cohosh, angelica

Care and Preparation of Instruments

Most of the instruments require no special care, except for those which must be scrubbed and sterilized repeatedly. Careful cleansing immediately after use is a good idea; dried blood cakes up the hinges and is difficult to remove. Use scouring pads to clean blood from the grooved blades of the forceps and needleholder.

The first method for sterilizing your instruments is by boiling. Boil instruments and instrument tray in a large pot of water for 25 minutes. Be sure to remember to sterilize the tongs that you will use for removing instruments from the water, and be sure to place them in the water with handles up. Once the 25 minutes have passed, let the pot cool off a bit and then remove the tray with your tongs. Open some packets of sterile gauze, put on a sterile glove and line your tray with the gauze. Then use the tongs once again to place the instruments in the tray, and cover (either drip-dry the cover as it's removed or blot with sterile gauze). Place in a doubled paper bag, wrap it up snugly, tape and date it.

A simpler method is the baking method. All you have to do is bake your double wrapped package of tray, liner and tools for one hour in a 250 degree oven. Be sure to add a pan of water so the bag doesn't scorch. Simple remove, cool and store.

Repeat sterilization every two weeks.

Parents Supply List

Betadine solution
olive oil
bulb syringe (rubber ear type, 3 oz.)
4 x 4 sterile gauze pads (two dozen)
cotton balls
hydrogen peroxide
oral thermometer
bendable straws
plastic drop cloth and tape, or plastic sheet
bleach
plastic trash bags
disposable underpads (at least 20)
sanitary napkins (heavy and mini-pads) plus belt
4 sheets, 4 washcloths, 4 towels, 8 receiving blankets — all dried in hot dryer for ten extra minutes and
    bagged in plastic, taped shut
herbs: shepherd's purse, comfrey, ginger root
plastic eye dropper

Appendix M

Midwifery Schools and Training Programs

Direct-Entry Programs

Academy of Midwifery Arts
Jeanie Rosburg
330 A Untah, Suite 133
Colorado Springs, CO 80903

Apprentice Academics
Carla Hartley
P.O. Box 788
Claymore, OK 74108

Artemis
Nan Koehler
P.O. Box 1005
Occidental, CA 95472

Association for Childbirth at Home, International
Tanya Brooks
P.O. Box 430
Glendale, CA 91209

Association of Professional Birth Assistants
P.O. Box 1304
Ashland, OR 97520

Association of Texas Midwives
603 W 13th, Suite A 202
Austin, TX 78701

Birth Resource Center
71 Seabord Lane
Hyannis, MA 02601

Birth Right Educational Center
DeeAnne Dominick
P.O. Box 276
Madisonville, LA 70477

Casa de Nacimento
Linda Arnold
1511 Missouri St.
El Paso, TX 97402

Christian Homesteading School
R.D. 2
Oxford, NY 13830

Family Birth Services
Helen Jolly
814 Dalworth
Grand Prairie, TX 75050

The Farm
Ina May Gaskin
156 Drakes Lane
Summertown, TN 38483

Fellowship of Christian Midwives
Renee Stein
7661 Deertrail Drive
Parker, CO 80134

Frazer Valley School of Midwifery
c/o MTF
P.O. Box 65343, Station S
Vancouver, BC
CANADA V5N 5P3

Heart & Hands Midwifery Intensives
Elizabeth Davis
555 Pistachio Place
Windsor, CA 95492

Hygieia College
Jeanine Pavarti Baker
Box 398
Monroe, UT 84754

Informed Homebirth
Rahima Baldwin
Box 3675
Ann Arbor, MI 48106

Massachusetts Midwifery Study Course
368 Village St.
Millis, MA 02054

Maternidad La Luz
Deb Kaley
1308 Magoffin
El Paso, TX 79901

Midwifery Education Foundation
RFD 1 Box 248-A
Old Town, ME 04468

New Life Birth Service
MariMikel Penn
2311 W. 9th
Austin, TX 78703

Northern Arizona School of Midwifery
Joan Remington
318 W. Birch, Suite 5
Flagstaff, AZ 86001

Northern New Mexico Midwifery Center and
    National College of Midwifery
Elizabeth Gilmore
Drawer SSS
Taos, NM 87571

Resourcing Birth
Terra Palmarini Richardson
P.O. Box 3146
Boulder, CO 80307-3146

Sage Femme Midwifery School
Patty Craig/Karen Erlich
507 Altivo
La Selva Beach, CA 95006

Seattle Midwifery School
J. Myers-Ciecko/T. Stallings
2524 16th Avenue S., Suite 300
Seattle, WA 98144

South Florida School of Midwifery
P.O. Box 557342
Miami, FL 33255

Spiritual & Scientific Non-Medical Midwifery
Mister Midwife
315 Sampson
San Diego, CA 92113

Traditional Midwifery and Womancraft
Sherry Willis
P.O. Box 353
Flint Hill, VA 22627

Utah School of Midwifery
Diane Bjarnson
P.O. Box 793
Pleasant Grove, UT 84062

Via Vita Missions School Midwifery
Vickie Penwell
600 3rd Street
Fairbanks, AK 99701

For updated information regarding schools and training programs, contact the Midwives Alliances of North America (See Appendix A).

Certificate Programs

Baylor College of Medicine
Midwifery Education Program
Dept. of OB/GYN
Smith Towers, 7th Floor
6550 Fannin
Houston, TX 77030

Baystate Medical Center
Nurse-Midwifery Education Program
689 Chestnut Street
Springfield, MA 01199

Charles R. Drew University of Medicine & Science
Nurse-Midwifery Education Program
College of Allied Health Sciences
1621 E. 120th St.
Los Angeles, CA 90059
(MSN option available from University of California)

Frontier School of Midwifery and Family Nursing
Community-Based Nurse-Midwifery
Education Pilot Program
P.O. Box 528
Hyden, KY 41749
(MSN option available from Case Western University

Midwifery Education Program
Education Program Associates
1 W. Campbell Avenue
Campbell, CA 95008

Parkland School of Nurse-Midwifery
Parkland Memorial Hospital
In affiliation with University of Texas
Southwest Medical Center at Dallas
5th Floor, MCH Department
5201 Harry Hines Blvd.
Dallas, TX 75235
(MS option available from Texas Women's University)

State University of New York
Health Sciences Center at Brooklyn
College of Health Related Professions
Nurse-Midwifery Program
Box 93, 450 Clarkson Avenue
Brooklyn, NY 11203

University of California, San Francisco/
San Francisco General Hospital Interdepartmental
Nurse-Midwifery Educational Program
SFGH, Ward 6D, Room 24
1001 Potrero Avenue
San Francisco, CA 94110

University of Medicine and Dentistry of New Jersey
School of Health Related Professionals
Nurse-Midwifery Program
65 Bergen St.
Newark, NJ 07107-3006

University of Southern California
Nurse-Midwifery Program
Women's Hospital, Room 8K5
1240 North Mission Road
Los Angeles, CA 90033

Masters Programs

Boston University
School of Public Health
MPH/CNM Program
80 E. Concord Street
Boston, MA 02118

Case Western Reserve Unversity (MSN)
Frances Payne Bolton School of Nursing
Nurse-Midwifery Program
2121 Abington Road
Cleveland, OH 44106

Columbia University (MS)
School of Nursing
Graduate Program in Nurse-Midwifery
617 W. 168th St.
New York, NY 10032

Emory University (MN or MN/MPH)
Nell Hodgson Woodruff School of Nursing
Atlanta, GA 30322

Georgetown University (MS)
School of Nursing
Graduate Program in Nurse-Midwifery
3700 Reservoir Road NW
Washington, DC 20007

Medical University of South Carolina (MSN)
Nurse-Midwifery Program
College of Nursing
171 Ashley Avenue
Charleston, SC 29425

Oregon Health Sciences University (MS or MN)
School of Nursing
Department of Family Nursing
Nurse-Midwifery Program
3181 SW Sam Jackson Park Road
Portland, OR 97201

University of Alabama School of Nursing (MSN)
Graduate Programs, Nurse-Midwifery Option
University of Alabama at Birmingham
UAB Station
Birmingham, AL 35294

University of California, San Francisco/
   University of California, San Diego
Intercampus Graduate Studies (MSN)
Family Nurse Practice, Nurse-Midwifery
Department of Community and Family
   Medicine, 0809
University of California, San Diego
9500 Gillman Drive
La Jolla, CA 92093-0809

University of Colorado (MS)
Health Sciences Center
School of Nursing Graduate Program
Nurse-Midwifery Program
4200 E. 9th Avenue, Box C 288
Denver, CO 80262

University of Florida (MSN or MN)
Health Sciences Center, Jacksonville
Nurse-Midwifery Program
College of Nursing
653 W. 8th St.
Bldg. 1, 2nd Floor
Jacksonville, FL 32209-6561

University of Illinois at Chicago (MS)
College of Nursing, Nurse-Midwifery Program
Department of Maternal Child Nursing
845 S. Damen Avenue
Chicago, IL 60612

University of Kentucky (MSN)
College of Nursing
760 Rose St.
Lexington, KY 40536-0232

University of Miami (MSN)
School of Nursing
D2-5, Royce Bldg.
P.O. Box 016960
1755 NW 12th Avenue
Miami, FL 33136

University of Michigan
Nurse-Midwifery Program
School of Nursing
400 N. Ingalls, Room 4320
Ann Arbor, MI 48109

University of Minnesota (MS)
School of Nursing, 6-101 Unit F
308 Harvard St. SE
Minneapolis, MN 55455

University of New Mexico
College of Nursing
Nurse-Midwifery Program
Albuquerque, NM 87131

University of Pennsylvania (MSN)
School of Nursing
Nursing Education Bldg.
420 Service Drive
Philadelphia, PA 19104-6096

University of Texas at El Paso/Texas Tech University
Collaborative Nurse-Midwifery Program
Texas Tech University
HSC, Department of OB/GYN
4800 Alberta Avenue
El Paso, TX 79905

University of Utah (MS)
College of Nursing
Graduate Program in Nurse-Midwifery
25 S. Medical Drive
Salt Lake City, UT 84112

Yale University
School of Nursing
Maternal-Newborn Nursing/
   Nurse-Midwifery Program
25 Park St.
New Haven, CT 06536-0740

Pre-Certificate Programs

Frontier School of Midwifery and Family Nursing
Frontier Nursing Service
Hyden, KY 41749

State University of New York
Health Sciences Center at Brooklyn
Nurse-Midwifery Program
450 Clarkson Avenue, Box 93
Brooklyn, NY 11203

For updated information regarding schools and training programs, contact the American College of Nurse-Midwives (see Appendix A).

References

Arms, Suzanne. *Immaculate Deception.* (South Hadley, MA: Bergin & Garvey, 1985).

Baldwin, Rahima. *Special Delivery.* (Berkeley, CA: Celestial Arts, 1986).

Bates, Barbara. *A Guide to Physical Examination, 3rd ed.* (Philadelphia: JB Lippincott, 1983).

Bing, Elizabeth and Colman, Libby. *Making Love During Pregnancy.* (New York: Bantam, 1977).

Brewer, Gail and Brewer, Tom. *What Every Pregnant Woman Should Know: The Truth About Diets and Drugs in Pregnancy.* (New York: Random House, rev. 1985).

Beischer, Norman and Mackay, Eric. *Obstetrics and The Newborn.* (New York: CBS Publications, 1985).

Cohen, Nancy Wainer and Ester, Lois J. *Silent Knife: Caesarian Prevention and Vaginal Birth After Caesarian.* (South Hadley, MA: Bergin & Garvey, 1983).

Dick-Read, Grantly. *Childbirth Without Fear.* (New York: Harper and Row, 1959).

Donald, Ian. *Practical Obstetrical Problems.* (Philadelphia: JB Lippincott, 1979, out of print).

Gaskin, Ina May. *Spiritual Midwifery.* (Summertown, TN: The Book Publishing Co., 1980).

Jensen, Margaret and Bobak, Irene. *Maternity and Gynecological Care: The Nurse and The Family, 3rd ed.* (St. Louis, MO: The C. V. Mosby Company, 1985).

Kitzinger, Sheila. *The Experience of Childbirth, 5th ed.* (New York: Penguin, 1982).

Kitzinger, Sheila. *Giving Birth: The Parents' Emotions in Childbirth.* (New York: Schocken, 1977).

Myles, Margaret. *Textbook for Midwives, 8th ed.* (New York: Churchill Livingstone, 1975).

Oxorn, Harry and Foote, William. *Human Labor and Birth, 3rd ed.* (New York: Appleton-Century-Crofts, 1975).

Peterson, Gayle. *Birthing Normally.* (Berkeley, CA: Mind-body Press, 1981).

Peterson Gayle. *Pregnancy as Healing.* (Berkeley, CA: Mind-body Press, 1984).

Pritchard, Jack, McDonald, Paul and Gant, Norman. *Williams Obstetrics, 17th ed.* (Norwalk, CT: Appleton-Century-Crofts, 1975).

Queenan, John T. and Hobbins, John C. *Protocols for High-Risk Pregnancies.* (Oradell, NJ: Medical Economic Books, 1982).

Varney, Helen. *Nurse-Midwifery.* (Boston, MA: Blackwell Scientific Publications, 1980).

Whitley, Nancy. *Clinical Obstetrics.* (Philadelphia: JB Lippincott, 1985).

INDEX

Hyperreflexia, pre-eclampsia and, 46, 47
Hypertension, 10, 45–46
  as contraindication for home birth, 20
  essential, 45–46
  gestational, 43, 45–46
  maternal, 106
  pre-eclampsia and, 46
Hyperthydroidism, as contraindication for home birth, 10
Hypocalcemia, 18, 44
Hypoglycemia, 44, 52, 135, 139
Hypothermia, 52
Hypoxia, 46

I
Ice, 28
Ice packs
  hemorrhoids and, 144
  after suturing, 125
Immaculate Deception (Arms), 152
In Case of Transport (checklist), 130–132
Incomplete fusion (of spine), 88
Incoordinate contractions, 34, 65, 67
Indigestion, 26, 136
Inevitable abortion, 42
Infant. *See* Baby
Infections
  during early labor, 66
  jaundice and, 141
  neonatal, 140
  pelvic, 144–145
  prolonged rupture of the membranes and, 106–108, 140
  uterine, 135, 136, 144–145
  yeast, 27
Informed consent, 171–173
Informed Homebirth and Parenting, 10
Initial interview, 9–10
Injections, 117, 124
Inlet contractions, 98
Inner labia, 121
Intercourse. *See* Sex/sexuality
Intercranial pressure, during delivery, 82
Internal muscle split, 120
Internal muscle tone, postpartum, 138
International Confederation of Midwives (ICM), 4–5
International Definition of Midwifery, 4–5
International Federation of Gynecologists and Obstetricians (FIGO), 4–5
Interview, initial, 9–10
Intimacy, 96

Intrauterine growth retardation (IUGR), 51–52
Iron, 18
  postpartum, 139
  to fight hemorrhage, 114
Iron deficiency anemia, 39–40
Irregular contractions, 34
Irresponsible attitude, as contraindication for home birth, 20
Irritability, 19
  in baby, 142–143
  pre-eclampsia and, 47
Ischial spines, 15, 16, 34
Ischial tuberosities, 16, 17
Isoimmunization, 21
IUD, 10, 149

J
Jaundice, 52, 135, 136–137, 140–141
Jogging, 19, 45
Journal of Nurse-Midwifery, 153
Juices, 41
  in early labor, 68

K
Kale, 40
Kefir, in early labor, 68
Kernicterus, 141
Ketoacidosis, 95
Ketones, checking for, 71
Kidney disease, as contraindication for home birth, 10
Kidney infection, 26
Kitzinger, Sheila, 152
Koehler, Nan, 100

L
Labia, 121
Labial massage, 76
Labial skin splits, 120, 138
Labor, 65–91
  active, 70–73
  bleeding during, 114–115
  complications in, 92–132
  delivery, 49, 78–83, 100
  early, 65–70
  false, 33–34, 65, 67
  first stage, 93–97
  heavy, 73–74
  plateau phenomenon, 72
  premature, 49
  preterm, 50–51
  second stage, 74–78, 103–104

Also by Elizabeth Davis:

☐ *Energetic Pregnancy* by Elizabeth Davis
"...a wonderful gift of a book...Davis's great knowledge of women's health and her long experience working with childbearing women combine well with her intuition and gentle approach to personal growth."–*The Birth Gazette*
A guide to health and vitality from conception through birth and beyond.
$8.95 paper, 172 pages

☐ *Women's Intuition* by Elizabeth Davis
"Women's Intuition is delight. Davis shows how biological events in women's lives influence intuitive capacities. A Gentle and strengthening companion... (this book) left me feeling confirmed in my own journey as a woman."
–East West
An examination of intuition in women's lives, and how it can be used to help solve problems, make decisions, and deal with personal relationships.
$7.95 paper, 112 pages

More Books on Women's Health and Family Issues

☐ *Special Delivery* by Rahima Baldwin
Midwife, childbirth educator, and internationally-known speaker Rahima Baldwin presents a guide to structuring the birth experience you want for yourself and your baby. Chapters cover choosing hospital or home birth, prenatal care, handling labor, dealing with complications, and more.
$17.95 paper, 192 pages

☐ *Pregnant Feelings* by Rahima Baldwin & Terra Palmarini Richardson
This workbook for pregnant women and their partners helps them to recognize and work with the emotions and energies surrounding pregnancy and birth. Practical exercises lead to a sense of self-confidence and power in new and not-so-new parents.
$14.95 paper, 208 pages

☐ *Women Giving Birth* by Saskiavan Rees, Beatris Smulders, & Astrid Limburg
Profusely illustrated with color photographs, this important new book on natural childbirth covers the latest research into drug-free labor, vertical delivery (an ancient but little-known birthing technique), and water births.
$18.95 paper, 160 pages

☐ *After the Baby's Birth... A Woman's Way to Wellness* by Robin Lim
This complete guide to postpartum care for mother and baby focuses on natural and wholesome practices. Illustrated throughout, this warm, sensitive text has advice on parental nurturing, breast-feeding, nutrition, pelvic health, early education, the role of the father, and the all-importance of love.
$14.95 paper, 320 pages

☐ *Bestfeeding: Getting Breastfeeding Right for You* by Mary Renfrew, Chloe Fisher, and Suzanne Arms
Midwives have known or years that women who breastfeed have healthier, happier children, but few new mothers anticipate problems or realize that breastfeeding is rarely easy or instinctive. This complete and practical guidebook, filled with photos and illustrations, gives mothers support and detailed advice for dealing with common situations.
$12.95 paper, 240 pages

Available from your local bookstore, or order direct from the publisher. Please include $2.50 shipping & handling for the first book, and 50 cents for each additional book. California residents include local sales tax. Write for our free complete catalog of over 400 books and tapes.

Ship to:

Name_____

Address_____

City_____ State ____ Zip _____

Phone _____

Celestial Arts

Box 7327

Berkeley, CA 94707

For VISA or Mastercard orders

call (510) 845-8414